Praise for *Voices from*

Winner of the 1997 Willie Parker Peace History Book Award
— *North Carolina Society of Historians*

Winner of the 1997 Robert Bruce Cooke Family History Book Award
— *North Carolina Society of Historians*

"Not since 1883, when Pulaski Cowper published his Father-in-law's letters and diaries in *Extracts of Letters of Major-General Bryan Grimes to His Wife,* has such a significant group of war-date papers of a North Carolina Confederate officer come to light. The writings of this brave and articulate soldier lay bare the tormented heart of a hard-fighting Confederate who paradoxically hated war and doubted the justice of the cause for which he died. This book is required reading not only for serious students of the Late Unpleasantness in North Carolina, but also for all who would seek to understand the very character of our State."
— Michael W. Taylor, Albemarle, NC,
lawyer and historian,
editor of *The Cry is War, War, War*

"Allen Speer's intriguing account of his family history takes in a lot more territory than one could have imagined. It's an entrancing look at the Civil War from homely perspectives. Valuable as history, it is as readable as fiction."
— Fred Chappell, North Carolina Poet Laureate
and author of
Look Back all the Green Valley

"In his excellent book, *Voices from Cemetery Hill*, Allen Paul Speer allows his soldier ancestor to speak to us in a old American language that is formal, elegant, clear, yet also emotional. . . . I think this book will be important to future generations of readers and scholars willing to listen to the written word."
— Gurney Norman,
writer in residence at the University of Kentucky
and author of *Kinfolks*

"*Voices from Cemetery Hill* is a most valuable book full of detail and insight. It is also impossible to put down. It reads like a novel. I find myself going back again to certain passages in which this young man comes startlingly to life, along with many members of his family."
—Lee Smith, author of
Oral History

Sisters of Providence

The Search for God in the Frontier South (1843-1858)

Edited by
Allen Paul Speer
Janet Barton Speer

The Overmountain Press
JOHNSON CITY, TENNESSEE

For Jennie and Ann,
who are not forgotten.

Book layout and design by Julie Shissler
Cover design by Bill May, Jr.

ISBN: 1-57072-158-0
2 3 4 5 6 7 8 9 0

Table of Contents

I would that I could accomplish something of importance. Would that this was an essay or narrative that might go out into the world and be a blessing to many readers. But oh fated manuscript, thou art doomed on account of the weakness of thy authoress to remain in some hidden corner, unknown, until perhaps some person, after the hand that penned thee shall be motionless in the grave, may turn over thy dusty pages, curious to learn something of the events of former years.

Nancy Jane Speer
29 April 1851

Oh earth, earth, hast thou not a solace for thy dying children? Shall thy cold arms hug me to thy chill bosom, while those whom I love will forget? Oh to be forgotten!

Annis Melissa Speer
10 September 1857

Editor's Note

I do not know if the unseen hand of Providence led me to this story. But I do know that the family papers I inherited from my great-great Aunt Nellie Speer Dobbins are a sacred trust. At some point in her life, Aunt Nell stuffed the family archives into cigar boxes, and I found them at the time of her death in 1980. She was ninety-four. One of the letters I discovered belonged to my great-great-great-great-great grandfather, Aaron Speer Sr., who was born in 1734.

Other papers included the journal of my great-great grandfather, James Speer (Aunt Nell's father), along with the diaries, letters, essays and poems of his brothers, sisters, parents and cousins. James' brother, Civil War Colonel Asbury Speer, was the subject of my first book in this series, *Voices from Cemetery Hill*. *Sisters of Providence* is about James' sisters Nancy Jane Speer (Jennie) and Annis Melissa Speer (Ann). These women did not face the trauma of the Civil War but rather suffered a thoroughly debilitating crisis of the spirit.

The alienation they experienced was at least partially due to the fact that the sisters were far ahead of their time in their thinking. They had the strength of mind to explore philosophical and theological thought, which was a rare quality for daughters of yeoman farmers in that day. Their diaries and letters reveal treatises on God, faith, education, family, nature and ultimately on death. Jennie and Ann desperately wanted to make a difference in the world and contribute to its goodness and well-being. Yet they feared their efforts would fail.

For their sake, may Providence bestow a blessing on all who read their words, and provide hope for those who passionately wrestle with the inscrutable and inexorable will of God.

List of Photographs and Illustrations

Sisters of Providence

*The Search for God
in the Frontier South
(1843-1858)*

Preface

The lives and writings of these two sisters, Jennie and Ann Speer, from the western Piedmont of North Carolina in the mid-nineteenth century provide us a window on a world that for a long time was rarely seen and only recently—through the publications of diaries, letters, and so forth—has been exposed. One finds in the writings of the older sister, Jennie, in particular, a remarkable intellectual curiosity, a questioning imagination, a deep sensitivity to nature, a hope for a life that transcends her own world—at the same time she is very much a part of that world, tending to family and to institutions of her community. She reads widely—*The Life of Horace Greeley, The Life of Margaret Fuller,* Harriet Beecher Stowe's *Sunny Memories of Foreign Lands,* and Dr. Thomas Arnold's articles in *The Eclectic*—and she reflects on social and intellectual currents of the times, finding an attraction to Transcendentalism, becoming, in fact, in may respects, a Transcendentalist in spite of herself. As a teacher at a small women's college in Greensboro, and especially as a scholar at Mount Holyoke in Massachusetts, she has time to contemplate the larger world and her place in it. In Massachusetts as well—as so many southerners before and after her—she comes to see her native South in perspective, and she finds she takes in many ways to the thrifty, industrious habits of Yankees. But she returns to the South.

The life of neither sister is an altogether happy one. The writings of both—Jennie, in particular—are full of a kind of yearning, of sadness, of possibilities not realized. Whether it is the limited opportunities for women in the nineteenth century, the obligations to family that eventually keep them at home, the illnesses that they endured at an early age—in whatever case, one finally feels both a vast sympathy and strong admiration for these sisters who dwelled in obscurity and wanted to be heard. Now, with the publication of their writings, unread for nearly a century and a half past, they are no longer silenced.

Fred Hobson
Lineberger Professor in the Humanities
University of North Carolina

Prologue

Providence is blessed with hills, valleys, abundant springs, and dense forests teeming with deer. The land is adorned with lake, waterfall, orchard and deep creek, which curves through the heart of the farm. Behind the old graveyard on Cemetery Hill, where Providence Methodist Church once stood and generations of the Speer family are buried, the Little Brushy Mountains rise up like camel humps against the horizon. To the northwest, the Blue Ridge is a fitting backdrop for a grand drama, while in the east Mount Nebo and Pilot Mountain grace the landscape on opposite sides of the Yadkin River. The Yadkin, whose headwaters are located in the mountain town of Blowing Rock, snakes its way through the Brushies and Blue Ridge to Wilkesboro, before passing between the bluffs at Jonesville and Elkin and arriving at the old Surry County seat of Rockford. Further east there is a wide turn of the river near the town of East Bend, where the great stream bends against itself before moving southward through the rich and spacious bottomlands of Huntsville and Shallowford, where prominent families of the antebellum period built their plantations.

But life at Providence was far removed from the refined society found among the sprawling plantations along the Yadkin. Its location in the hilly, creek-rich western section of the county, close to the Little Brushies, was tailor-made for mixed farming and making whiskey. Like many farms in the foothills and high country of North Carolina, Providence produced an assortment of crops and livestock, while its patriarch Aquilla Speer worked as a tanner. Along with his wife, Elizabeth Ashby Speer, and a large family (Asbury, Jennie, Aaron, Sylvia, Ann, Vet and James), he did the great bulk of the work himself. He did not own slaves. Aquilla opposed the institution of slavery, and questioned the legality of secession, an issue that would torment his family during the Civil War and claim the life of his oldest son Asbury. Writing in her diary in 1853, Ann said,

> Some speculators came by here—they brought some Negroes. One was handcuffed and his feet were chained together. It looked too bad. A man, one that God created, endowed with rationality, and possessing feelings like us, chained like a brute. [That speculator] must possess a heart of steel that [he] can engage in a traffic so sordid and debasing.

As justice of the peace, Aquilla Speer presided over the Providence area as judge, jury, minister and magistrate. Long before the settlement at Boonville, North Carolina, emerged as a hub of legal, religious, and educational activity, Providence was a gathering place for the community. Mount Nebo was the closest trading center. Aquilla's daughters, Nancy Jane (Jennie) and Annis Melissa (Ann) both taught school at Providence, and the Methodist Church located there was one of the oldest and most active in the area. In 1853 Ann wrote, "This has been a busy week, the estate of Mr. G.P. is being sold—and we have had company nearly every night."

Amidst the whirlwind of activity at Providence—church meetings, legal proceedings, and the chores required for running a farm—Jennie and Ann had ample time to think and reflect. The contemplative nature of the girls seemed to enhance their abilities to appreciate, yet distance themselves from the vibrant energy that enveloped the area. In their minds an aura of enchantment surrounded Providence, and these childhood memories of a magical place and time would never leave them. The land seemed to cast a spell on Ann's exuberant writing style. Her extravagant prose depicts a pastoral world pulsing with life. She loved her mother's flowers, and passionately embraced the wonders of the natural world. "Where is its great author?" wrote Ann, and "all the earth responds, 'the hand that made me is divine.' He is present everywhere and at all times sees all my actions and knows all my thought." And following a winter snowfall she wrote,

It is night—deep, still, awe inspiring night. Above is the sky, spangled with millions of glittering diamonds. On the earth is a mantel so purely white, so delicately wrought, so elegantly grand that nothing but super human fingers could have fashioned it.

And Providence was depicted as the place where Ann found:

...narrow shaded bypaths through the dim old woods that arched so high above us that they filled us with awe—the rippling rills and dashing waterfall...the wild haunts beneath the willow boughs where we watched the fish dart like silver arrows—-where the wild rose and jasmine wreathed their branches so intricately that our infant minds could not divine how they were woven.... The stately old trees, like aged sentinels, guarding the homestead where we flung ourselves and gazed through the waving branches up to the moonbeams and wondered if we might not steal up these golden pathways and meet the angels, whose eyes sparked so brilliantly from their far off home in the sky.

And there was Ann's all-consuming love of flowers "in my papa's meadows or my mother's garden, where I pluck the early Violet that nestled so fondly to the cold, pulseless bosom of the giant rock." Pressed between the pages of Ann's diary are flowers that have been there for 150 years. The flowers, waterfall, and orchard, along with the loving warmth of hearth and home made Providence a mystical place. "A thrill of pleasure vibrates through my heart at the thought of being home," wrote Ann in 1854, but "a spirit of sadness mingles with my feelings, for I fear the pleasure may be alloyed by some evil. Bliss too strongly coveted—too eagerly anticipated—is frequently dashed from our extended hand."

Ann's older sister Jennie, who spent many years away from home, first as a student, then as a teacher and principal, wrote in 1854 that she "dreamed of going home. It did seem so plain. I could scarce believe it was not a reality ... but waking I found it was but a dream." Asbury, older brother of Jennie and Ann, and later a colonel in the Confederate army, wrote in 1853 that he was "compelled to shed the tear of regret that I ever left my father's house." And in 1864, Asbury said Providence was "the next place to heaven." First cousin Joshua Kennerly Speer III looked at Providence from a religious perspective. In 1899 Joshua, who was then an old man, wrote to James Speer, the youngest in the family, that "in the coming age I will see the living of Christ on this very globe; then I shall be at my old home." Joshua was lamenting the fact that his four sons were dead and there was no one to carry on the family name. "We are now closing out the old family—there will soon be no one to speak of us. No One."

Like Joshua and Asbury, Jennie and Ann looked on Providence as a holy place. In Ann's words, not only were there the "sequestered haunts, the old homestead," and the "trees that droop over and guard it like hoary sentinels," but there was also "the faint longings for something deep, holy, and pure, something like God." They believed that Providence was a dim reflection of heaven, where the unbroken family circle was bound with love. The sisters believed the closest we come to heaven on this earth is the sentimental affinity for land and family that we find in our deepest memories of home.

Cemetery Hill, the family churchyard behind the Methodist meeting house, was also a sacred place. "Not one wicked person is buried there," wrote Ann in 1853. For Jennie and Ann, the graveyard was like the entrance to an unseen world where love is indestructible and immortal. It was, in fact, this fascination with the ethereal that is the central theme of their writings. "When I watch the workings of the deathless spirit," wrote Jennie in 1854, "when I feel its strugglings after light and knowledge and immortality I am lost in wonder. And I long to rush into the freedom of the unimprisoned spirit—but may not this be wrong? I will stop—I will pause—I will wait patiently all the days for my appointed time."

Succumbing to the allure of the spirit world was a problem for Jennie and Ann. In 1853 Jennie wrote, "I am weary of all things earthly. But stop, here comes that indefinite longing after the ethereal, the spirit like, the unknown. I must not give way to it. I have a constant proneness to indulge this disposition." And on December 11, 1852, Jennie said,

> I seem to be encaged in this body, and struggle to get free. A two-fold being am I. I reason with myself as with a friend. This body cannot be myself, for I suffer and enjoy independent of it. It is wonderfully made, but more mysterious is my real self, my mind, my spirit self. Shut up in this body, how little access has it to the outer world. Yet how busy is this spirit; as if its very confinement made it more active . . . thoughts are wings to the tireless spirit. More rapidly than lightning's speed, I go from world to world, stand on the most distant verge of creation, and as quickly return to my prison house. But why return? What mysterious chain binds me to this body, and will not let me go?

And Ann writing in 1857 says, "I almost long to go . . . and be free from sin, free from earth, [for] as long as God himself exists, so long as eternity will roll on, then long the souls of men will live."

What was it within the chemistry of the Speer family (the special alchemy of people and place) that nurtured the souls of Jennie and Ann, and filled the daughters of a backcountry tanner with the fire of unshakable faith? Undoubtedly, it was the influence of an extraordinary family. "Although I am blind, I have an eye that pierceth through the upper sky—the eye of faith, by which I see there is a heaven prepared for me," wrote Nancy Speer in a poem she composed in her eighty-fourth year. "Blind Aunt Nancy," as she was called, lived with her brother Aquilla her entire life, and like the blind poet Homer in ancient times, she was the custodian of family traditions, songs, poems and legends.

Her stories and interpretations of the scripture captivated Jennie and Ann. According to the sisters' first cousin Joshua, blind Aunt Nancy was remembered for

> ... her devout prayers, and eloquent exhortations. ... It was no burden for her to quote whole chapters from the Bible, and to repeat with great accuracy, verse after verse, from the hymn books of her time, often dropping into religious poetry, which she would sing with charming sweetness. ... Often have I, when a small boy, wept at her feet on hearing the almost angelic music that seemed to flow without an effort from her devout soul. ... Hanging around her are reminiscences of the revolution, and many a time have we heard from her lips thrilling stories of the early histories of the western counties of North Carolina.

According to Joshua, blind Aunt Nancy would often walk ten miles across the country to attend camp meetings. She attended any and all churches and was famous throughout the Old North State for her recitations and songs. It is little wonder that she was able to exert such a strong influence on Jennie and Ann.

Father Aquilla must also have seemed to Jennie and Ann like a dim reflection of something omnipotent. Ann wrote that in the evenings when the family was gathered around the fire "the large Bible was laid by our father's side. And in a tone so deep and holy that it never ceased to echo in our hearts, he read from that sacred volume and prayed so ardently for us that we might grow up into good and wise men and women." The girls worshipped their father and were greatly influenced by his simplicity and reticence. In a poem to "My Darling Papa," Ann said,

> Earth can give no stronger love than that I have for you
> I know one heart—my father's heart—
> Throbs ever strong and true.

And on Aquilla's 48th birthday Ann wrote,

> The winters of life have slightly sprinkled thy luxuriant locks
> with snow. I love the deep, brown clusters that adorn thy
> noble brow. I love to twine them around my fingers. I love
> to gaze into the clear depths of those eyes expressionate
> beaming. Care, that crushes some hearts, has left thine
> glowing with love. Time, that dims the eye and o'er clouds
> the countenance, has stamped a clear, calm dignity on thy
> brow, [and] has left the piercing glance of those eyes
> unharmed. . . . Oh how I love to gaze upon the beaming
> countenance of my father.

Mother Elizabeth was also revered. She was described by
Ann as "an almost perfect mother," and Jennie often remarked, "was
there ever such a mother," when expressing her need for some
consoling advice. On May 27, 1854, Jennie sent a bouquet of flowers
to her mother in behalf of her brothers and sister Ann. The note
reads as follows:

> We rejoice with our mother on this her fiftieth birthday—
> and tho she stands half a century from the beginning of
> life, yet we pray she may be spared to us for many long,
> happy years. . . . This simple bouquet may fitly represent
> our little number—six buds remain—the seventh the
> great gardener took to wear upon his own bosom. [The
> seventh represented their sister, Sylvia, who died at age
> four.] In the unfolding of these may all the virtues of the
> parent roses be developed.

Elizabeth Ashby Speer was, by anyone's measure, an
extraordinary woman. She would outlive her husband and all
seven of her children but one. (Her youngest child, James, would die
in 1928 at the age of eighty-five.) Elizabeth survived the Civil War,
Reconstruction, and the bone crushing poverty which followed, and
was still able to say, "all is well," a phrase frequently used by blind

Aunt Nancy to finish her songs. Elizabeth Ashby Speer died in 1890 at the age of eighty-six.

Perhaps the most prominent, and arguably the most influential member of the clan was the grandmother of Jennie and Ann, Elizabeth Forbes Jones Speer. Grandmother Elizabeth was twelve years old at the time of the American Revolution, and had lived with her grandmother, Elizabeth Forbes, when she was a child. Grandmother Elizabeth's mother, also named Elizabeth Forbes, had a sister who married Rebecca Boone's brother. (Rebecca was the wife of Daniel Boone.) For Jennie and Ann it must have seemed that the past and present were inhabited by Titans of epic stature like the heroes and heroines their father praised when the family gathered for prayers in the evening. Ann wrote,

> There was no thing that wrought more powerfully upon the mind [than] when all the pleasures and duties of each day had passed and the soft hour of twilight thickened into deeper darkness [that] we all assembled around the cheerful blazing fire and listened to the old legends of other days, or the daring of some gallant patriot in the days of the Revolution, and we thought our dear grandma must be wise to tell us so much.

Abraham Lincoln realized that it was the "mystic chords of memory stretching from every living heart and hearthstone" that defines our identity as a people and solidifies our allegiance to the things we love. For Jennie and Ann memory would become both the blessing and burden of their lives. The mystic chords of memory were anchors in the marrow of their souls. This remembrance evoked great love and passion, yet these very chords of love would became a source of dissonance and despair. In 1844 within a matter of days Grandmother Elizabeth and Sister Sylvia would depart this life. Ann wrote,

> The golden chain that binds us to our homes is composed of links, each of which possesses a history. If one of

these links be lost, there is a blank page in the volume of our lives; if one of them be severed, a tie that binds us to earth is unloosed. These stray links, severed and torn, are strewn all along the pathway of our lives and there are sad sweet memories that linger around each. But they are reunited in the spirit land and form a chain more firmly wrought than any of earth, and binds our hearts to our homes in heaven.

Living with memories of an almost ideal childhood became a burden as Jennie and Ann grew older and was perhaps an impediment to their emotional development and maturity. In any case the sisters were unwilling or unable to let the memories go. They could not escape the spell of the past. In 1854 when Ann was a student at Greensboro Female College she wrote,

Hark! Why do I start? Was that my papa's footstep on the threshold? Did I hear my mother's voice singing among the shrubbery? Was that my brother's silvery laugh? Did my sister call? Oh! Why does this vision fade? Am I not the same careless girl that I may run and fling my arms around my mother's neck? Alas! It is but a dream. I am still in the land of triangles and logarithms . . . . Such is life. Reality is ever folding the scroll that fancy paints with such glowing colors, is ever razing the palace [that] imagination so exquisitely adores.

The poems and essays that Ann wrote at Jonesville Methodist Female Academy and later at Greensboro College bear such titles as "The Pleasures of Home," "The Past," "To My Mother Receiving a Flower," "To My Darling Papa," "The Light of the Past," and "On My Father's Birthday." Jennie, six years older than Ann, spent more time away from home. She taught at Greensboro College, pursued further studies at Mount Holyoke, then became principal of Rockford Female Seminary in 1854. She did not romanticize the past as much as Ann, but neither could she escape its spell. In an 1853 letter to her mother she said,

> I would love to be a little child again, when I had the exclusive right of sitting on my mother's knee, and climbing up in my papa's lap, putting my arms around his neck and my head on his bosom and going to sleep. Then it seemed like a wonderful world to me. Everything seemed new and beautiful. The days were sunny then . . . I was free from care.

There is little question that from an early age Jennie and Ann were precocious children, pampered by adoring parents, a loving grandmother, a blind "all seeing" aunt, and four brothers who allowed them time to read, write, reflect, and speculate on things seen and unseen. Yet one wonders, if the family had curbed their fanciful notions, the sisters might have enjoyed a more normal, if less imaginative life. Instead the girls became frail, dreamy scholars obsessed with the spirit land. Jennie's dreams were too big to yield to the simplicity she dearly loved. She yearned to live in California and Texas and believed that God had a special purpose for her life. "Sometimes I regret that I have an impression of destiny upon me," wrote Jennie. "I am restless—anxiously reaching towards something future—to a wider place, to a greater work." And while studying at Mount Holyoke she said, "I know that I desire to be a perfect Christian, but oh my heart, my deceitful heart!" If Jennie's burden was her desire to become a perfect Christian, then Ann's weakness was an imagination that tended to "run wild." In a letter to her mother, Ann wrote,

> I dreamed a horrible dream about Noah Reece. I dreamed Old Scratch [the devil] came and carried him off alive, and I saw him take a big knife and cut Noah's heart out and chop it up into bits. And he said it was because Noah had been a member of the church, and

had gone to stilling [making whiskey] to ruin the souls of his fellow men. I dreamed it so plain that for some days it seemed so distinct as a reality. I could not think of it without shuddering. May heaven save him!!!

For Ann the dreamer and Jennie the perfectionist, the past and present, as well as the material and spiritual, all seemed to merge. The sisters believed that all things were manifestations of the unseen hand of Providence. And it was their uncanny ability to examine the inscrutable will of God that is truly astonishing. Jennie's quest for perfection is voiced when she says, "I am in a state of probation—in a preparatory school, which is to fit me for that great world of action upon which I am to enter in eternity." And in a March 23, 1853, letter to her mother she wrote,

I have learned to look upon this life as but the beginning of existence, and all things and events here as but the beginnings of a chain of circumstances that will go on through all eternity. This consideration has helped me to reconcile the confusion in which I see men and actions, and accounts for the incompleteness of this apparently unmeaning life.

The despair that Jennie and Ann endured was in many ways similar to the fear and trembling that modern Christian existentialists would wrestle with in their own work. For existentialists, the world is a weighty place. Jennie eloquently expresses this anguish in an essay written in 1852:

What a strange world is this. Mystery is written on all things around me. Whence came this world? He who made it must have wished its inhabitants to be happy. But surely some sad catastrophe has fallen upon it, for it seems the wreck of something grand and beautiful. A master hand must have hung those worlds on high, piled up towering mountains, and spread these valleys abroad . . . . Life is mystery, a scene chaotic. It is made up of plans projected but never completed, of work half finished. Nothing is definite, and things remain not as they were. . . . A curtain hangs before me, I turn to myself, but all is mystery.

Perhaps it was Jennie's presentiment of destiny plus her fear of failure that caused feelings of unworthiness to arise. "I have come to the conclusion," she wrote, "that one of my great deficiencies is a want of faith in myself. But Mother, I do so utterly abhor the idea of being thought self conceited or wise in my own eyes, that I am doubtful whether I shall ever indulge any better opinion of myself than now." Jennie's lack of confidence, along with her incredibly high standards, tormented her throughout life and triggered repeated plunges into the depths of depression. In an 1853 letter to her mother she wrote, "I am not so much weary of the world as of myself. I do not so much wish for friends, as that I may be worthy of those I already have. . . . I tremble lest I fail to meet the expectations of friends."

Ann too suffered from melancholy, but her depression was not as debilitating as Jennie's. Ann, always the exuberant romantic, liked to flirt with depression and, in fact, would fling herself with wild abandon toward whatever struck her fancy. On March 15, 1853, she wrote in her diary,

I feel unaccountably sad this evening. Yet I have no particular cause for such feelings. Yet they haunt me, and I almost willingly abandon myself to their control. I love to indulge in melancholy. I love to wander, in pensive musings, in regions of fancy, and to picture to my mind beings and scenes of imagination.

Ann realized the folly of fanciful speculations, especially with regard to the future, yet she was unwilling or again unable to curb her mind's appetite for pensive musings. In 1854 she wrote,

If we leave the past and present and step into the future, what is that but an unfathomable abyss that no prophetic eye can scan. If fancy exert all her power to trace some enchanting vision of the future, to construct an airy fabrication to feast the mind, these vain imaginings are doomed never to be realized, and the pleasure they afford is as fleeting as the mind. But I am growing, as usual, sentimental, and dealing in things merely like thistledown, things that have no weight.

Time and again, the weighty cares of life would threaten to crush the spirits of Jennie and Ann. Jennie, echoing Ann's melancholy, wrote, "What charms does this life afford to prolong our stay? What joy unmixed with sorrow? What cup replete with sweets, but has a draught of bitterness mingled with its contents!"

In the powerful conclusion of *The Will to Meaning*, existential writer Viktor Frankl, a victim of the Holocaust, quotes the prophet Habakkuk:

Although the fig tree shall not blossom, neither shall fruit be on the vine; the labor of the olive shall fail, and the fields shall yield no meat; the flocks shall be cut off from the fold, and there shall be no herd in the stalls: yet I will rejoice in the Lord, I will joy in the God of my salvation.

For Nancy Jane Speer and Annis Melissa Speer, it took a Kierkegaardian leap of faith to bring meaning to their lives. Yet their eyes were fixed on God. This faith was nurtured by blind Aunt Nancy and her eye of faith "that pierceth the upper sky," and the devout prayers of father Aquilla, and by the love of Grandmother Elizabeth, but most of all it was their longsuffering mother, Elizabeth, who was able to endure the unendurable and still say "all is well."

In 1842 when Jennie was fourteen years old, she had a religious experience that changed her life. It occurred at a Methodist camp meeting she attended with her father. She describes her conversion:

It appeared as though light broke into my soul, and it appeared to me that all things partook of that light; even the trees appeared to be tinged with glory. I felt new and all things looked new. Peace, such as I never felt before, reigned in my bosom. I loved the Lord and I loved all mankind and I felt a desire that all mankind might feel what I felt.

Jennie never lost that love, although her life was a struggle to prove to herself that she was worthy of it.

For Jennie and Ann, Providence Farm was a sanctuary of love, but it was also a stark reminder of all that was lost. For them the voices from Cemetery Hill were, in T.S. Eliot's words, "tongued with fire beyond the language of the living." And it was this spirit embodied in both the living and the dead that filled their souls with a longing for God. When they feared the light of faith might weaken or falter, they prayed and remembered the words of the Lord: "Blessed are those who do not see, yet believe."

"I should indeed despair," wrote doubt-ladened Jennie, "were it not for the hope that when I stand amid the realities, and in the broad sunlight of eternity, I shall know even as also I am known."

And Ann, in a state of great distress, prayed fervently for

The Holy Spirit to hush this anguish in my heart. It is almost unendurable.... Oh Holy Spirit, breathe o'er the troubled deep of my heart and call the wild heaving waves to be still. ... Oh earth, earth, hast thou not a solace for thy dying children, let us not sorrow tho' life's heartstrings wear asunder, and the soul's casket crumble to dust; life, eternal life, is just ahead—Oh blessed Father support me in thy everlasting arms of love.

The words of Nancy Jane Speer and Annis Melissa Speer are an epiphany of faith and a legacy of love for those of us who endure the many deceptions of a feverish world.

Introduction

"It's a feverish world," notes Inman on his Job-like journey to Cold Mountain. Inman's odyssey of hope and despair is an attempt to escape the killing fields of the Civil War, along with the death makers, fire eaters, and bushwhackers of every stripe who tried to destroy his body and soul. Only Cold Mountain "soared in his mind as a place where all his scattered forces might gather." It is in *Cold Mountain*, Charles Frazier's prose masterpiece, that Inman is forced to address a question as pertinent to our time as his own. Will he conform to the world or follow the spirit? Conforming to the world can mean the death of his spirit, while following the spirit might require him to sacrifice the flesh; this is the civil war of the soul that Inman fights. In a feverish world, where does he find a nest for the soul?

Nearly twenty years before the fictional Inman's time, a nonfictional family living at the base of the southern Appalachian mountains embarked upon their own spiritual odyssey. When I remember my great-great grandfather James Speer's family, I am amazed by the diversity I see and deeply moved by the pain they endured. James' sisters Jennie and Ann, as I mentioned in the prologue, were teachers and writers. His brother Aaron was a college professor at the Union Institute which would become Trinity College and later Duke University. James' brother Vet was the Civil War sheriff of Yadkin County, while Asbury, the oldest in the family, became a Whig politician and later a colonel in Robert E. Lee's Army of Northern Virginia. One sister, Sylvia, died at age four. James was a lifelong tobacco farmer and the only one in the family to live to a ripe old age. He died in 1928 at the age of eighty-five.

Yet longevity, I believe, was a burden for James. During the Civil War, he was able to hide out in the Home Guard because of a legal deferment his brother Asbury secured for him. Asbury died near the end of the war while James lived with the guilt of being a draft dodger. Five of James' brothers and sisters died young; only Vet would live to fifty-three. As the youngest in the family (James was born in 1843), he would live through the Civil War, the postwar poverty of a devastated South, the depression of the 1890s, and World War I. And during the 1920s it was farmers like James who suffered the first assaults of the Great Depression. Yet he was able to endure these many trials and still raise a large family on the land that had been farmed by his ancestors. But it was James' grandson (my great uncle of the same name) who helped me better understand his character.

When my great Uncle James Speer was a boy, he nearly died from one of the many diseases that terrorized the country in the early 1900s. But it was a remark his grandfather made to him that shocked me. Uncle James told me that his grandfather was a man hardened by the toils of the postwar South. To a young boy, however, this wasn't clearly understood. On one occasion, when my Uncle James was quite young and quite ill, his grandfather said, "Your family has spent a lot of money on you to keep you alive. You'll have to work hard to pay it back!" After that incident, Uncle James said he never had warm feelings for his grandfather. When I heard this story, I was overwhelmed with sadness for both men. My uncle had suffered his grandfather's anger, and although my great-great grandfather James had probably earned the right to be bitter, only years of shame, guilt, and pain would prompt a grandfather to tell his grandson that the boy would have to work hard to justify his existence on this earth.

The brothers and sisters of my great-great grandfather James Speer were born in Surry (Yadkin) County, North Carolina. Aunt Jennie was born October 8, 1828, the oldest girl in a family of seven; she was two years younger than her older brother Asbury. Her sister Ann was born May 22, 1834. The parents of Jennie and Ann (Aquilla and Elizabeth) were both born during the first administration of Thomas Jefferson in 1804.

Aquilla Speer was a backcountry tanner who lived on the same land as his grandfather, Aaron Speer, Sr. Yet being a tanner and yeoman farmer did not preclude him from participating in politics. He was a staunch supporter of the Whig party, a temperance leader, a devout Methodist, and would later become one of the first Republicans in the county. Southerners in the postwar South (the Solid Democratic South) referred to him as a *scalawag*, which was synonymous with *traitor*. His son Asbury, who was killed in the Confederate army, would not have been surprised to see his father join the Republican Party; this was because of the longstanding consistency of Aquilla's political beliefs, a source of great tension between father and son during the war. Aquilla believed Asbury was wrong to fight for Southern independence, a cause which Aquilla and his wife Elizabeth believed was a sin of rebellion against God and government. For although Uncle Asbury was, like his parents, a supporter of the Whig party, and believed slavery was "a great national sin," and was even opposed to secession, he did not share his parents' depth of commitment to national unity. He thought it was dishonorable to betray the South. And because of this conflict between his beliefs and his sense of duty to his region, he was doomed to suffer great anguish during the Civil War.

As far back as the 1840s and 1850s, family writings are laced with poignant and very powerful reminders of religious conversions at Providence Church and Methodist camp meetings. It was, in fact, evangelical Protestantism and reform movements (i.e. temperance) spawned by revivalism that shaped their view of the world. One clue which reveals the liberal nature of my family's religious and political beliefs was an occasion when Jennie presented her father, Aquilla, with a copy of *The National Temperance Offering, and Sons and Daughters of Temperance Gift*. In the book are illustrations and biographical sketches of such prominent antebellum leaders as northern evangelist Lyman Beecher, father of Harriet Beecher Stowe, and Horace Greeley, abolitionist firebrand and liberal Republican editor of the *New York Tribune*, who was a very important newspaperman during the Civil War.

The Life of Horace Greeley, by J. Parton, was the book in Jennie's personal collection that contained more underlined sentences, marked paragraphs, and hand-written comments than any other book she possessed. Only rarely did Jennie write any comments in her books; most of them contain no marks whatsoever. Yet in the Greeley biography there are twelve separate markings with Jennie's remarks written in the margin. More than likely Aunt Jennie's admiration for Greeley (a temperance leader) was influenced by the two men in her life she loved most, her father, Aquilla, and Dr. Charles Force Deems. Deems, the president of Greensboro Female College, where she taught, was a friend of Greeley and was, no doubt, the person who suggested that Jennie continue her education at Mount Holyoke College in South Hadley, Massachusetts, in 1852.

Another clue to the liberal proclivities of my family— at least liberal within the context of their time and place—was their respect for the value of education. This too had its roots in revivalism. Methodist Bishop Francis Asbury, the namesake of Colonel Asbury Speer, preached in Jonesville, North Carolina, in 1785. And there is little doubt that it was Bishop Asbury's influence which led to the establishment of Providence Methodist Church as well as the Jonesville Male and Female Academies. Aquilla's older brother, Joshua Kennerly Speer II, served as an original trustee of the academies when they were chartered in 1818. And Aunt Jennie's professor at the female academy in 1845 was the Rev. Brantley York, a founder of Union Institute, which was a forerunner of Trinity College and Duke University. (This is also where her brother Aaron taught in 1851.) All of Aquilla and Elizabeth's children who reached school age attended the academies along with two of their nephews, William Sheppard Speer and Joshua Kennerly Speer III. Later in the nineteenth century, Joshua II, Joshua III, and William converted to the Campbellite faith, an evangelical Protestantism that became the largest homegrown religious movement in American history. Revivalism, with its emphasis on the authority of scripture, was changing American history and ushering in an age of reform.

When Alexis de Tocqueville visited America in the first half of the ninteenth century, he was amazed to see how religion served as a catalyst for literacy and moral reform movements. He marveled at the social reticence he saw, even on a frontier that was raw and unrefined. And he was astonished that religion encouraged moral behavior without the need for government mandates. Tocqueville, like the Aquilla Speer family, respected the civilizing influence of religion.

Revivalism would open other doors for the sisters. Though most of the Speers were devout Methodists, Jennie and Ann were attracted to romanticism, transcendentalism, and other spirit-friendly movements, especially Quakerism. Jennie admired Lord Byron's poetry and was an avid reader of William Cullen Bryant. Both sisters brooded over death, struggled with melancholy, overindulged in mystery and fantasy, and desired the distant, unattainable, and ethereal. By nature they were probably transcendentalists, but their Christian beliefs would not allow them to accept the precept that a world spirit was present in all things, though this premise was evident in their writings. Their struggle to understand the spirit world is similar to the present-day conflict between New Age "neo-transcendentalists" and members of the Religious Right. An example of this inner struggle in Jennie was her attempt to attain Christian perfection, which always seemed to collide with her concept of original sin.

It was the perfectionist in Jennie that not only contributed to her social reform mentality (i.e. temperance) but also nurtured her affinity for the Quaker faith. She was powerfully drawn to the Quaker idea of the Inner Light, the notion that God's spirit is present in all people. She was also attracted to the principle of spiritual equality for women practiced by the Society of Friends. "They seem to be the only people who acknowledge the rights of women," wrote fifteen-year-old Jennie in 1844. She often mentioned her admiration of Quakers, a denomination her family had connections with for over a century. She respected their reticence, simplicity, and openhearted inclination to receive the spirit, and she seriously considered becoming a member of their society. Jennie often attended the New Garden Friends meeting in Greensboro, and it is still a mystery to me why she did not convert to the Quaker faith, especially considering the feminist sentiments she harbored. Yet for Jennie, there always seemed to be some deep-seated fear that prevented her from making the final move whenever major decisions of her life confronted her. But ironically, she did not fear death. It seemed to be the only thing in her life that she did not dread. In any case Jennie was—for me—a difficult person to understand. Like her sister Ann and older brother Asbury, she too had an enigmatic side. And also like Shakespeare's Prince Hamlet, she seemed to contradict herself and was cursed with the affliction of excessive thought, a problem that has plagued many of my ancestors.

It was also God-centered revivalism, the desire-to-be-a-perfect-Christian side of Aunt Jennie's personality that encouraged her to support Whig politics, although she rarely mentioned politics in her writing. In *The Life of Horace Greeley* she underlined a passage that, in my opinion, is the foundation of her philosophy. It reads as follows:

> If any pious soul will accurately ascertain what it is in the character of the Man Christ Jesus, the contemplation of which fills his heart with rapture and his eyes with tears, that pious soul will know what is here intended by the expression "supreme interest in

human welfare." The concurrent instinct of mankind, in all ages, in every clime, proclaims, that this, whatever it be named, is the divinest quality known to human nature.

It was this "supreme interest in human welfare" that prompted Jennie's family to pursue Whig politics. For the sisters there was no discrepancy between politics and religion because from first to last they were moralists. "Governments will never be perfect till all distinction between private and public virtue, private and public honor, be done away!" This sentence was underlined in one of Jennie's books, *The Young Lady's Mentor: A Guide to the Formation of Character*, published in 1851.

Jennie's "governments will never be perfect" notation can easily serve as a thesis statement in a position paper on Whig philosophy. The phrase certainly expresses the political philosophy of the Speer family. Whigs believed in working for the common good, government support for education, internal improvements (i.e. roads, canals, infrastructure), social reform, moral edification (i.e. temperance), and Protestant religious unity. Yet as moralists they always ran the risk of intolerance, especially for Catholics, foreigners, and Democrats. Jennie was painfully aware of her pride and prayed ardently for compassion.

The heroes of the Aquilla and Elizabeth Speer family were for the most part not Southerners, but Northern moralists who were leaders in the temperance movement. In her copy of *The Life of Horace Greeley* Jennie wrote the comments "Good Whiggery" and "True" beside a paragraph that praised Greeley:

If every Whig had worked as he [Greeley] worked, how different had been the result [referring to the election of Democrat Polk as President]! How different the subsequent history of the country! How different its future! We had no annexation of Texas, no Mexican war, no tinkering of the tariff to keep the nation provincially dependent on Europe, no Fugitive Slave Law, no Pierce, no Douglas, no Nebraska!

And on page 413 of the Greeley biography, Jennie wrote "good" and "as it should" beside the underlined sentence, "Party, like the heart of a woman, demands all, or refuses any." Yet she was infuriated by the following words written by the author of the biography:

The *Tribune* [Greeley's paper] has stood opposed to the general feeling of the country. Its course on slavery has excluded it from the slave states; and if that had not, its elevated tone of thought would; for the Southern mind is inferior to the Northern.

In response to the preceding sentence, Jennie wrote "an infamous lie!" As insecure as she was, Jennie refused to submit to Northern arrogance.

Jennie's insecurity was probably influenced by her sensitivity. In the Harriet Beecher Stowe book *Sunny Memories of Foreign Lands*, Jennie underlined the sentence "When I think of God my soul is always so full of joy that I want to dance." And in *The Young Lady's Mentor* she marked the phrase "The perception of the beautiful is, next to the love of our fellow creatures, the most unselfish of all our natural emotions. . . ."

Perhaps the most revealing indication of Jennie's sensitivity is shown in a passage from *The Task: A Poem in Six Books* by William Cowper, where she underlined the sentence "I would not enter on my list of friends (though graced with polished manners and fine sense, yet wanting sensibility) the man who needlessly sets foot upon a worm."

The highly developed moral sensibilities of Nancy Jane Speer and her sister Annis Melissa Speer were firmly grounded in a deep-rooted sense of place. And it was this love of place, in conjunction with their love of God, that enabled them to weather the storms that threatened to wreck their lives and destroy their values. Providence Farm and their faith in God were sanctuaries of the spirit that comforted them when the world would not, the calm at the center of the storm.

On their brother Asbury's gravestone is an inscription which is taken from William Shakespeare's tragedy *Macbeth* that reads, "After life's fitful fever, he sleeps well." This quotation well describes the ways of the world in Jennie and Ann's time and in our own. For when the earthly endeavors of the sisters and their family failed, and when their hopes, dreams, and aspirations were scattered to the winds, and when their most cherished beliefs and values were ignored in the postwar South, only their faith in God and their love of Providence Farm remained. Today they lie in rows of graves located on the land where they were raised. Where they sought God in both the church and in the surrounding wonders of nature, the entire family rests together. With such an abundance of love and pain assembled in one place, surely the standing stones of Cemetery Hill speak to us with tongues of fire.

CHAPTER ONE

JENNIE

1843-1849

NOTES TO THE READER:

- In the letters and diaries that follow, some of the words are antiquated and these will be left as they are.

- Words "made up" from Jennie and Ann's extensive knowledge of semantics will be left alone. Jennie and Ann are inconsistent in their use of capitalization, sometimes using capital letters for emphasis.

- There is a light touch of editing for words we could not read or were not spelled correctly, yet we tried to leave the writings as close to the original as possible.

1843

Jennie's diary begins with her memories of a Methodist camp meeting that occurred in September 1842 at Hickory Grove, one of the churches of the Jonesville, N.C., Circuit. Camp meetings were a series of evangelical services of at least one week in duration. Entire families would "tent" on the grounds, affording a time of fellowship as well as worship. One member of the family would frequently return home to do the daily chores. Four services were conducted daily, each announced by a trumpet. Several ministers would lead the service, which was sure to have much rejoicing and shouting. Jennie mentions attending many camp meetings in the Yadkin Valley during the 1840s. Among the services documented are revivals at Mt. Airy, Prospect, Center and Island Ford. Revivalism was an important part of her childhood. The Speer children are very young; Sylvia is age two, Vet age five, and Ann age eight. Aaron, age eleven, is working on the farm, and Asbury, age sixteen, is attending Jonesville Academy. James has not yet been born. Although Jennie writes this very mature treatise describing her religious conversion, she was only thirteen when it happened. This first entry in her diary is a defining moment in her life. She is fourteen years old.

c. 1843 - Jennie's Diary

In the year 1842 there was a camp meting held at Hickory Grove, commencing 2 of September. My father with his family tented. And from that time I have dated the greatest event that ever occurred in my life, for at that camp meeting the Lord convicted and converted my soul.

On Sunday the preachers labored to convince the people of the danger of putting off their return to the Lord until they were old; and gave several cases where individuals had done it and the Holy Spirit had taken its everlasting flight from them. During the day (Sunday) I felt uneasiness that I could not account for, and I tried several ways to relieve my mind but could not. At night I went to preaching but my restlessness became greater. I went back to the tent and there, came to the conclusion that it was my own sins that had so disturbed my mind. But oh! What an awful condition I was in! My heart appeared as hard as stone, and yet not one tear could I shed. I then came to the conclusion that the Holy Spirit had forsaken me and left me in this hardened and awful state. But thanks be to my Heavenly Father I was not left in this awful condition long; for I prayed to my Lord to give me a heart to weep, and to repent of my sins. Soon my eyes were a fountain of tears.

On Monday morning, as soon as the trumpet was sounded for preaching, I hastened to get a seat in the altar (a place I had seldom entered). I was so affected that I could not refrain from weeping, neither do I remember anything of the 8 o'clock sermon, for I was then engaged in the greatest matter that ever had excited my attention. And no wonder I was engaged, when my eternal all was at stake. I then felt the worth of my immortal soul as I had never before felt it and I was determined to secure my soul's salvation, let me sacrifice what I would. Accordingly when mourners were invited I felt a desire to go but my load was so great that it seemed to me almost impossible for me to go. But there was a kind lady (her name I do not know) [who] came and, taking me by the hand, affectionately invited me to go, and with her help I went and never left the mourners bench until I found the Savior precious to my never dying soul. [This] happy change took place after the 11 o'clock sermon.

I [will] now attempt to describe my feelings at the time when my soul was set at perfect liberty; if I should make the attempt I should fall far short of telling it as I felt it. While I was asking for mercy, all at once my load was gone and it appeared as though light broke into my soul, and it appeared to me that all things partook of that light, even the trees appeared to be tinged with glory. I felt new and all things looked new. Peace, such as I never felt before, reigned in my bosom. I loved the Lord and I loved all mankind and I felt a desire that all mankind might feel what I felt. And indeed the least that I can say of what I felt is, that it was "joy unspeakable and full of glory." And I am certain that if sinners would believe half of what Christians tell them about religion, they would not rest until they had tasted for themselves the comforts of religion. And O! That I had it in my power of impressing upon the minds of the young the great necessity and the great advantage of seeking the Lord in early life. I know that it is the opinion of some that religion makes people gloomy but I can testify by blest experience that I never knew what pleasure was until I found it in religion. And I can assure my young friends that religion will make them happy here, will enable them to spend their youthful days in pleasure worth the name. It will crown old age with peace and finally secure unto them a seat around the throne on high.

Holy Father, grant unto me supporting grace while I live, that I may adorn the profession I have made with an upright walk and conversation. Forbid that I should ever stray from thee, or do anything to wound thy cause. Grant that I may be useful while I live and be instrumental in thy hands of turning some of my young friends to thee. Grant me supporting grace in the hour of death, and thine shall be the praise through eternity. Amen.

From this point on, only selected portions of Jennie's diary will be presented because many pages are torn and missing. For the sake of readability and clarity, some repetitive or less pertinent entries will not be included. The 1843 diary has suffered most from the ravages of time, and with the exception of her conversion experience, the entries are short and to-the-point. Later on, her work will become more eloquent. So we pick up in April where she begins to document the events that shaped the family. In two sentences she tells of an important baptism.

April 18 - Sabbath - Jennie's Diary
I heard a sermon preached by the Rev W.J. Chaffin from Romans 11, Ch. 35. Asbury and myself were baptized by pouring.

It will be a pattern for Jennie to write on the Sabbath, praising the day for its expected blessings. Nature is also important to her and she frequently identifies the "look" of the day, connecting it to a larger theme.

June 11 - Sunday Eve - Jennie's Diary
I have spent the day at home. The gentle showers of rain have been descending upon the earth today. [May] peace divine descend into my soul to water the seed of virtue, and may I always remember the Sabbath day to keep it holy.

In light of the fact that the Speer family would be torn apart during the Civil War, it is interesting to note Jennie's fervent patriotic stand for the nation on July fourth.

July 4 - Jennie's Diary
Today is a day of rejoicing to American people. May heaven ever preserve [our nation]. [May the] people ever enjoy the blessing of political and religious liberty.

"May Independence be our boast
Ever mindful what it cost."

With the death of Cousin Rachel Hobson, Jennie begins a long and arduous journey of the soul.

July 15 - Jennie's Diary

Cousin Rachel Hobson died yesterday morning. [She is] with her Savior, whose cause she had espoused while young. How certain is death! This young lady a few days ago was blooming, but now she is cold in the arms of death. How thankful I should be that my life is still spared. How careful then ought I to live, since time is so short. [Lord] help me to live in time, in reverence to vast eternity.

1844

In January Jennie thanks God that she has been spared. She does not believe she will live very long. Her main goal in life becomes a preparation for death and eternity. She is fifteen years old.

Most Likely Jan 1-6 - Jennie's Diary

I have the pleasure of seeing a new year begin. Many during the past year have died, while I have been spared. May I live more to thy honor this year than I ever have, [and may I] be prepared to enter into thy rest.

In 1844 she develops a life-long affinity for the Society of Friends (the Quakers), and at a young age, she concerns herself with women's equality. She becomes an ardent student of theology.

January 7 - Jennie's Diary

Have been to hear a couple of female Friends preach. One preached an excellent sermon. May the Lord bless that denomination for they appear to be the only people who acknowledge the rights of women.

March 28 - Jennie's Diary
An aged gentleman, belonging to the denomination of Friends visited us today. He takes a great delight in conversing about religion; and his conversation is very interesting.

Harriet Newell was a missionary to India.

April 14 - Sabbath - Jennie's Diary
I have been reading some of the writings of Harriet Newell, that great and good woman. I have found great encouragement from her writings: [May I] imitate her in virtue and usefulness.

Jennie begins to indicate an obsession with perfection. Later on this would manifest itself into repeated bouts with melancholy.

May 19 - Jennie's Diary
"O for a heart from sin set free." When I read the Holy Scriptures and see what is required of believers, and then look at my own shortcomings, it causes me almost to despair. But I know his grace is sufficient to enable me to overcome all things.

This state of mind would be enhanced by the deaths of her little sister Sylvia (four years old) and her grandmother, Elizabeth, both of whom died within three weeks' time.

June 18 - Jennie's Diary
My dear little sister Sylvia is at the point of death. How can I bear to give the dear little creature up? Enable me Heavenly Father to give her up unto thee.

June 21 - Jennie's Diary
Have this day followed the lifeless remains of my sweet little sister to the grave. Our loss is great but it is her infinite gain, for she is now at rest. During her sickness she suffered extremely, but she never murmured or complained, but bore her afflictions with patience that would have adorned an experienced Christian. May the Lord enable us all to give her up, and be submissive to his holy will, although it is

a hard trial to part with one so dear. I have thought the Lord only lent her to us to let us know how fair a flower in paradise would bloom.

July 10 - Jennie's Diary

Death has visited our circle again and claimed for its victim our dear grandmother. Thus death has taken two of our family in less than three weeks. What a solemn warning to us, who are left behind, to prepare for death. Our dear grandmother died in peace and is now, no doubt, around the throne of God reaping a rich reward. During the last ten years of her life she suffered great afflictions. But she never murmured or complained; but always manifested a spirit of resignation to the will of the Lord, saying that she did not suffer as much as she deserved. May we all be prepared to meet those who are gone before in the land of pleasure.

August 27 - Jennie's Diary

The rustling wind reminds us that the fall of the year is nigh and the fading flowers tell us the beauty of summer is gone. What a scene for reflections on our own lives.

An avid reader, Jennie concerned herself with issues of the church. The Methodist Church split over the issue of slavery in 1844.

Sept 22 - Jennie's Diary

In reading the Christian Advocate I find that the Methodist Church is likely to be divided. May heaven interpose and preserve the peace of the church.

Jennie's last entry in 1844 reconfirms her doubts about her own self-worth.

November 10 - Jennie's Diary

"O for sanctifying grace
For love's refining fire.
Lord, we beg for Jesus' sake,
A sweet refreshing shower."

O that I had a heart from sin set free then should I serve the Lord as I ought. My best services are mixed with imperfections, and I deeply feel the need of being directed by wisdom superior to my own. Then from this time I will cry unto the Lord, "My Father thou art the guide of my youth."

1845

The diary begins with a poem, then frequently refers to church matters addressed in the Christian Advocate, *particularly the movement to make mandatory the observance of Sundays. She begins to document the spoken theologies presented by various speakers and preachers. Note her attention to her religious conversion, and to her new quest to seek a life in missions.*

1845 - Undated - Jennie's Diary
My Father, thou art the guide of my youth;
Direct my steps aright. Give unto me thy Holy Spirit.

January 12 - Jennie's Diary
While perusing the columns of the *Christian Advocate*, I find that a "National Sabbath Convention" has been held in the city of Baltimore for the purpose of devising means whereby the holy Sabbath may be observed strictly throughout the United States. More than seventeen hundred delegates were present, some from almost every denomination in the United States. May the blessings of heaven attend their efforts, and may the time soon come when the American people will "remember the Sabbath day to keep it holy." Almighty Ruler, hasten the time when our beloved nation shall be a people devoted to thee.

May 17 - Jennie's Diary
I have been solemnly impressed for some time that there is something of vast importance for me to do. And the road marked out by my Heavenly Father for me to walk in, I know will be attended with

many persecutions; yet his grace is sufficient for me, and may he enable me to do the work assigned me on the earth to his name's glory.

July 6 - Jennie's Diary
I have been reading, with deep interest, in the *Christian Advocate* of a meeting of the "Christian Alliance" Society, whose object it is to unite all Protestant Christians in the heavenly work of evangelizing the world. May the Lord omnipotent grant them success in turning over Popery, and establishing true Christianity in this and all other nations of the earth.

August 3 - Jennie's Diary
What should I do if it was not for the blessed Sabbath for on this day I can lay aside all worldly thoughts and care, and meditate on heavenly things? Oh that all people would "remember the Sabbath day to keep it holy," then we would have a heaven on earth begun.

September 5 - Jennie's Diary
This is a day to me never to be forgotten. This day three years ago, I sought the Lord and found him in the forgiveness of my sins. He has been my protector ever since and brought me through many troubles and in him is my trust for years to come.

The Reverend Brantley York was a founder of Union Institute, which later became Trinity College, and then Duke University.

December 2 - Jennie's Diary
I am engaged in the delightful task of improving my mind under the instructions of the Rev. Brantley York. May my Heavenly Father bless my efforts to cultivate my mind, so that I may be useful to my fellow men.

1846

Jennie's 1846 diary expresses her lack of concern for earthly things and her strengthening desire to explore eternity. Each entry is basically a prayer for spiritual development. Notice how, once again, she documents the date when she experienced her religious conversion. Sometime before October she becomes ill and sees the event as an opportunity for closer communion with God. At this time Jennie is at Jonesville Methodist Female Academy studying with the Reverend Brantley York.

March 1 - Jennie's Diary
I have been studying much of late on the subject of heart holiness, and have been led to examine my own heart. I have found that I have lived far beneath my privilege, but by the grace of the Lord I intend to live more holy than I ever have. I see new beauties and greater enjoyments in religion than I ever did before, and I am resolved by grace divine that they shall be mine.

May 10 - Jennie's Diary
I have this day heard an excellent sermon delivered by my dear teacher Rev. Brantley York, from Genesis 3, 17, 18, 19. As the danger of yielding to temptation was clearly shown, may I be watchful, and not yield to temptation. And as I have heard the trial and sentence of Adam, may I live in preparation for the trial and decision of the judgement day. May the sermon be beneficial to all who heard it, and may its effects be seen many days hence.

June 7 - Jennie's Diary
How light and trifling do the things of this world appear when compared to the great realities of eternity. And yet, astonishing to think, the human family appears to devote almost all their time to the things of this world, as though they were to live forever here. What man would spend his fortune in one day's reviling and risk living the remainder of his days in poverty; and yet devoting his time and talents

in perusing earth-born pleasures, and forfeiting those of endless duration?

August 23 - Sabbath - Jennie's Diary

The kind hand of Providence has brought me to see the light of another holy Sabbath morn. Father accept, through the son of thy love, my heart's warmest gratitude for all the mercies of the past week, and help me spend this day in a profitable manner. I feel that time is precious, for our happiness in eternity depends on the proper improvement of time. But alas! How negligent we are; days and weeks pass away, but where is the good account they give? Almighty Father, may the worth and shortness of time suitably impress my mind, so that I may improve its precious moments as they fly. May I live to thy glory, die in thy favor, and spend eternity in thy presence.

September 5 - Jennie's Diary

"The Lord hath done great things for me whereof I am glad." "What shall I render unto the Lord for all his benefits?" This day four years ago, God, for Christ's sake, forgave all my sins and appeared unto me the fairest among ten thousand and altogether lovely. He has delivered me out of many temptations. Blessed be his holy name. And I feel not only willing but anxious to commit my all into his hands. I feel greatly the need of an unerring guide. When I see many youths falling into temptations and snares and remember that evil snares will be set for me, I tremble and greatly fear. For I know that unless I am sustained by a power superior to my own, that I shall fall into the hands of the enemy. My Heavenly Father, thou hast been my protector in years past, O grant me thy protection through future life. Deliver me from the snares of the devil, from the allurements of the world, and from the lusts of the flesh. Guide my youthful steps in the path of piety and intelligence. Help me to acknowledge thee, and direct thou all my ways. Amen.

October 1 - Jennie's Diary

Summer has gone; the beautiful flowers have faded.

"I wish that flowers would always bloom
As fresh as they are made
Then lilies would be white as snow
And roses never fade.
O yes my love but flowers there are
That grow within the breast,
By Heavenly goodness planted there,
The sweetest and the best.
The snow-white lily without stain,
Is not so pure as truth.
It never fades but shall remain,
In everlasting youth.
And sweeter than the sweetest rose,
Is love shed o'er the mind.
The heart is tender where it flows
To every creature kind."

October 8 - Jennie's Diary

Through the kindness of my Heavenly Father, I am permitted to see my birthday return. The scenes have been varied through which I have passed during the year that is gone. In general, I have enjoyed very good health, until lately, I have been afflicted. But my afflictions have been for my benefit; I have been made sensible of the vanity of all earthly things. I have also felt the importance of preparing for sickness in health, and in life, for death. Never did I view the value of religion as great, as when I was sick. I delighted in my studies when I was well, and found great pleasure in them, but I found that they afforded me no solid comfort in afflictions. I desire to return unto the Lord, my heart's warmest gratitude for all the mercies of the past year. I have had the pleasure today of accompanying my teacher (Rev. B. York) to Center [Methodist Church], where the class, under his instructions, was examined. The scholars underwent an honorable examination, and thus clearly proving the value of the systems invented and practiced by him. Heavenly Father grant me thy protection through future life, make me useful while I live and finally receive me to thyself in heaven, for Jesus sake.

1847

In 1847 Jennie begins to doubt the strength of her faith, but she attends every tent meeting, sermon, and church service possible. It is this evangelical Protestantism that is the foundation of her perfectionist proclivities. She continues to see the Quakers as the keepers of a splendid faith. Some deep guilt must have plagued her, however, because she consistently berates herself for it. She believes that she was meant to do something great for mankind, but was unfit for the task. Again, she continues her obsession with her own death. In other areas, family events come to the surface. Her sister, Ann, age thirteen, is converted. Her brother, Asbury, age twenty-one, is embarrassing the family. Her parents are hailed as her strong foundation.

January 17 - Sabbath - Jennie's Diary

It has been a long time since I have written in my diary. I desire this Sabbath morning to write of the goodness of my kind preserver. His arm of protection has been over me, and he has conducted me through many dangers, seen and unseen. I have always found him a faithful friend. Although many have betrayed my confidence, I have ever found my Heavenly Father the same: kind, indulgent, and merciful. I deeply regret that he has found in me so much unfaithfulness and lukewarmness in his service. I feel my inability to do any good of myself. I am dependent on my Father for aid and strength to do his will. Assist thy handmaid, Heavenly Parent, to serve thee more faithfully for time to come. Grant me the enlightening influence of thy Holy Spirit.

February 14 - Jennie's Diary

I find my heart so hard and my affections so cold that I almost despair. But I humbly trust in my Savior for deliverance. I know it is my desire to serve my Lord on earth, but I know without his assistance I shall fail. Holy Father, give me to feel my dependence on thee, and grant me the aid of thy Holy Spirit continually. May it be my guide and comforter through life, and my supporter in death.

March 29 - Jennie's Diary

Last night was the happiest time I ever experienced. Brother York preached an excellent sermon, after which we had a glorious time. The power of the Lord came down, and four professed religion; one was my little sister [Ann]. My soul was filled to o'er flowing of the love of God. Never did I receive such a blessing. Praise the Lord O my soul. Father Almighty keep me by thy power from falling into sin; preserve me from the snares of Satan and guide me by thy counsel through life.

Most likely Asbury was living in Jonesville at this time and working at a tannery. In 1850 we know he married a Miss Kitty Chamberlain and that the marriage didn't last. We do not know if the "strange woman" was Miss Kitty.

April 18 - Jennie's Diary

I have witnessed so much of the follies of youth that I fear and tremble lest I should fall. My dear brother Asbury is pursuing a course which gives us much grief; he will not take the counsel of his parents. Lord pity him and save him from the strange woman. O that I may attend to the counsel of my father, and the instructions of my mother, that I may be a blessing to my parents, and cause their gray hairs to go down in peace to the tomb.

May 6 - Jennie's Diary

O what a beautiful spring. With great pleasure I gaze on the lovely aspect of nature. I have always delighted to study the works of nature, but I do think that it has afforded me more pleasure this spring than in all my life before. In all the works of nature I see the wisdom and goodness of my Heavenly Father richly displayed. This spring has been so very pleasant to me that I have thought possibly it is the last one I ever shall see; but if it is, I have the prospect of going to that "land which is very far off" where youth and spring are perpetual. My only desire to live is that I may do good among my fellow men. To me the idea of annihilation is more tolerable than the thought of living unemployed for the good of others, in a world that presents such a vast field for usefulness. From an early period of my childhood I have felt a strong desire to be employed in something that would be beneficial to mankind; that desire has increased with my years until it has become so strong as almost to render me uneasy. My prayer is that Heaven may direct me aright.

September - Undated - Jennie's Diary
Possibly few persons have spent a pleasanter life than I have. Not that I have been exempted from the troubles of life, but I have ever considered it entirely useless to repine at the common lot of man. There are objects of higher importance, which claim our attention. My kind parents pointed me in early life to the only fountain of pure happiness; they taught me to love and fear my creator when I was young and now I delight to think upon his name. I delight to study upon his works. In the vast volume of nature I see wonderfully displayed his infinite wisdom and almighty power. I love the little flower. The regularity and harmony of its parts show forth his skill. His name and goodness is indelibly stamped on the face of all nature. Who can refuse to love and adore such a good being?!

Oct. 12 - Jennie's Diary
I have just returned from the camp meeting at Prospect. I went there for the express purpose of being benefited, and I write in everlasting praise to my creator that I was not disappointed. My soul feasted on the heavenly manna and I do know that religion gets better every day. It does seem that I never want to engage in anything else but the service of my Heavenly Father.

There is a clear pattern in Jennie's writing of lamenting God's absence and then praising God's mercy. Her thought process resembles that expressed by the author(s) of the Book of Psalms (i.e. Psalms 10:1: "Why standest thou far off, O Lord? Why hidest thou thyself in times of trouble?") According to Biblical writer Phillip Yancey, the reader of the Psalms should look at the text as a journal, revealing the torment of the soul. Jennie's volatile mood swings are not hidden, and her torment in seeking the perfect relationship with God is openly expressed. One might wish she could make up her mind, or find some way to even out her moods, but like the Psalmist, the passionate seeker of God's will is likely to suffer the pain of ambiguity. This next entry in her journal is an example of how she relates to the Book of Psalms in a very personal way.

November - Undated - Jennie's Diary

My soul is exceedingly distressed. What shall I do? Will the Lord forsake me forever? O Lord deliver my soul from the enemy. O my Father there is none able to deliver me but thee. Forsake me not. Though I have been so disobedient, yet I would repent in dust and ashes. I confess my every sin, and pray thee for Jesus' sake to restore unto me the joys of thy great salvation.

December 5 - Jennie's Diary

I have this day been to hear a Friend [Quaker] preach. There were two preachers but only one preached. And O what a sermon he delivered. It was indeed a feast of fat things to me. He preached with artless [simple] eloquence. His language was rich, for it was purely Biblical. His manner of expression was unaffected; and yet it was such as sent light and conviction to every mind. Sure I am that I shall never forget that blessed sermon nor that worthy man who delivered it. He told my own experience, though an entire stranger to me. He told my secret thoughts, though I had never disclosed them to any human being myself—He was from England.

Jennie's teacher, Dr. Brantley York, mentions in his autobiography the devastating social problems brought on by hard liquor. According to Reverend York, in the early 1800s, "Almost everybody around me drank—men, women, and children, even ministers of the Gospel. I found it no easy matter to resist the frequent opportunities to drink . . . for it often leads to drunkenness and ruin; hence total abstinence is the only safe ground that can be occupied."

December 25 - Christmas - Jennie's Diary

Today we have had a very interesting temperance meeting. We had several interesting lectures and six persons gave their names to the temperance pledge.

1848

As in other years, 1848 begins with Jennie's thankfulness that she is still alive. Her doubts and insecurities worsen, yet this is also the year she mentions her desire to write. Her first extant essay is dated June 29 when she is attending school at Jonesville. It is her perspective on the harmony of nature. Close to the end of the year, Jennie is visiting a young woman in prison.

January - Undated - Jennie's Diary

January and I am yet alive! Another year has rolled away; its privileges, its mercies; its cares and toil are all ended. And what am I the better of the past? I believe that I have received benefit during the year that is gone, but I do desire to improve more this year than I did last. But it requires unwearied diligence to keep the mind profitably engaged. When we begin a good work we soon tire, and we suffer the fragments of time to pass away unimproved, waiting for a more convenient season. Thus time passes away and we accomplish nothing.

February 17 - Jennie's Diary

Day by day I am traveling to eternity. Time waits not for us to indulge in the fleeting amusements of this world, yet how much of our precious time is spent in vanity! When shall I learn to improve my time as I ought? I desire to live more holy, and "to grow in grace and in the knowledge of Christ Jesus my Lord." Yet I find my heart so prone to wander from God, my nature so corrupted that I almost despair of obtaining a clear heart. But I am determined to strive for the victory. The blood of Jesus Christ is able to cleanse me from all sin. My hope is in God. I shall certainly gain the victory. Let me put all my trust in God, "for in the Lord Jehovah is everlasting strength."

April 25 - Jennie's Diary

I have to mourn my leanness, my slothfulness, my lethargy. O Father arouse every ransomed power of my soul. Grant to me a spirit of prayer. Take from me everything contrary to thy will. May I be submissive to thee. May I be able to say from the great depth of my heart "thy will be done." O for holiness of heart I want a spirit of watchfulness, a prayer. My Savior help me for without thee I can do nothing. Let me abide in thee.

June 11 - Jennie's Diary

When shall my heart be made perfect? I feel that nothing short of divine grace can purify my nature and make me a fit temple for the indwelling of the Holy Ghost. I would get near the foot of the cross that the healing fountain which flowed so freely might wash my heart entirely clean. If I know my own heart, I know that I desire to be a perfect Christian, but oh my heart, my deceitful heart! But I must go to the strong for help. My Father there is none in heaven or in earth that can accomplish this great work but thee. Now my Lord, I would ask for Jesus sake, and relying on thy premises, that thou wouldst make me every whit whole. Thou hast the power, if thou wilt, thou canst make clean. Create within me a clean heart; renew within me right spirit.

Jennie wrote the following essay at Jonesville Academy. She was continuously enthralled with nature and its wonders. The essay demonstrates the breadth of her knowledge and writing ability.

June 29 - Jennie's Essay

Harmony of Nature

We are naturally so constituted that whatever is harmonious in sound or scenery awakens in our minds the most pleasing sensations.

Hence it is that we experience so high a degree of pleasure, while listening to the melting strains of music, which falls on our ears in sweetly flowing numbers. But nowhere do we find harmony so extensively diffused, and its influence as beneficial, as in the economy of nature. As far as man has been able to penetrate, perfect harmony prevails; there are no extremes but a due proportion is preserved throughout the whole, both in construction and regulation. Ever since the creation the earth has performed with strictest accuracy her daily and annual revolutions, from which we have enjoyed the vicissitudes of day and night, and also the seasons successively; spring with its buds and tender plants, summer with fruits and flowers, winter with snows and ice. The natural scenery, though varied, is harmonious; one part admirably adapted to the other, and contributing to the beauty and perfection of the whole.

The surface rises gradually from a gentle elevation to hills, and finally to the cloud. At the base of these hills and mountains many little rivulets gush out, and as they gently wind their way through the peaceful valleys, they unite. And their currents continue to swell until they become great rivers, and roll their mighty waters into the bosom of the ocean, where they ebb and flow in regular and continued periods.

In the vegetable kingdom the progress is gradual from the smallest moss on the barren rock, to the proudly waving cedars of Lebanon. From the humming bird of tiny wing, to the condor, or Ostrich which roams thoughtlessly over the wilds of Africa. Even the particles of matter obey this harmonizing law of nature. For by chemical experiments it has been clearly demonstrated that the atoms of matter combine with each other in definite proportions. Though the compound be ever so intricate, yet the atoms always adhere to this general law. Were it not for this, in vain insight the physician [would] labor to prepare his medicines. For while he might be preparing, as he believed, a safe and efficient medicine, it would prove to be a fatal poison. We also see that even the particles of matter have not been left to chance.

But the influence of harmony is not confined to this earth, which forms only a small link in the great chain of creation. We will then leave our own little planet, and observe the influence of harmony, which is exhibited with far more sublimity and extensiveness in the regulation of the entire solar system. For six thousand years the planets have performed their revolutions in perfect order around the great fountain of light and heat, never deviating from the path at first assigned to them by the Creator. They also continue to obey those minor laws peculiar to themselves. The sweet influence of Fleiades has never been bound; the lands of Orion have never been loosed. Arcturus with his sons, has ever been guided in his appointed pathway in the Southern heavens. The flaming comet, represented by some as rushing lawlessly through the universe, doubtless obeys the general harmony of nature, for though it requires hundreds of years in performing its journey, yet its return to our system has been readily computed and at the expected time we have seen it passing by.

How far the influence of harmony extends is unknown to us. It may unite to our system other planets circling other suns, of which we are at present entirely ignorant. But from analogy we have every reason to believe that it extends through all the works of creation. It is owing to this general harmony that man has been enabled to calculate events, the future knowledge of which has been beneficial to mankind.

Finally, the consideration of this golden law, clearly convinces us that nothing short of Omnipotent Power could have projected worlds of almost inconceivable magnitude into empty space, and established laws by which their motions have been uniformly regulated for thousands of years. Conscious of the harmony that ever has and still prevails, we have no need to fear that any discord will arise to endanger our happiness or interest. Judging the future by the past, we rest assured that the whole economy of nature will continue to move on, in one harmonious progression, until the same Almighty Power that assigned to each its task, shall bid the whole stand still.

July 15 - Jennie's Diary

Being desirous to do something that will be beneficial to mankind, I have thought about writing a book, but I know that I am not competent to the task. I wish to be profitably employed while I live, and I hope that a wise Providence will guide me aright.

November 5 - Jennie's Diary

I feel truly thankful that I am so highly favored as to see the light of another Sabbath. Though I have been disappointed yet I hope to spend the day profitably. I had intended to visit a poor unfortunate girl in prison but I have been hindered; yet I do sincerely desire and hope that I may have the opportunity before long. Though her crime is of the deepest dye yet I desire to tell her that the Savior died for sinners, even the chief of sinners, and that his blood is able to wash her sins away. May the Lord open and enlighten her dark mind.

November 26 - Jennie's Diary

I have before me the prospect of spending another blessed Sabbath. During the past week I have had the opportunity of visiting that unfortunate girl in prison. It was a heavy cross indeed, but the grace of my Heavenly Father was sufficient for me. She seemed humble and appeared to be glad that I visited her. May the Great Spirit lead her mind to himself, and may she seek to be reconciled to God.

1849

In 1849 Jennie scarcely writes in her diary. This is probably because she was teaching at Greensboro Female College (later Greensboro College) in the Preparatory Department (young girls preparing to attend institutions of higher learning). In the summer she taught at Dowelltown (near Yadkinville). Most entries are fairly typical of her style, but one stands out which illuminates her disdain for T.C. Hauser and John Long, whom she believed needed redemption from sin. Hauser owned a 1600-acre plantation known as Wildwood and ran a store at Dowelltown, which was later moved to Yadkinville. According to to Frances Casstevens, editor of The Heritage of Yadkin County, *John Long lived with the Hausers and worked as a clerk in the store in 1850. We do not know what indiscretions John Long committed. T.C. Hauser was another matter. An article in the August 12, 1999,* Yadkin Ripple *notes that T.C. Hauser fathered,* *several black children by his head housekeeper, Bethania, who was purchased in 1840 in Bethania, N.C., for $850. She became the mother of three sons before she left the household. We have no way of knowing exactly what "sins" Jennie alluded to. Certainly the Aquilla Speer family was opposed to slavery. Whether it was the fathering of illegitimate children or the institution of slavery that Jennie objected to is difficult to say. We do know that Jennie was close to Mrs. Hauser and that Mattie Hauser, daughter of T.C., was Ann's best friend. Since the early 1950s, according to the* Ripple, *the descendants of Hauser, black and white, gather together for family reunions, putting aside the prejudices of the past. Among the descendants are "social workers, educators, nurses, business men and women, policemen, firemen, military personnel, artists, musicians, a dentist, a physician and a state legislator."*

July - Undated - Dowelltown - Jennie's Diary
I have engaged to teach a school at this place, but I tremble lest I shall fail to meet all expectations. My trust is in my Heavenly Father that he will enable me to fully discharge the duties of my station.

August 5 - Jennie's Diary
Today Mr. Hauser and Mr. Long have gone to Mount Maria camp meeting. I am anxious that they may receive some serious impressions that may prove the power of God to their salvation. My Heavenly Father, grant, for the sake of Jesus, that some arrow of conviction but newly dipped in blood divine may reach their inmost soul. May they hear, as they have never heard before. May they reflect, as they have never reflected before, and may they see and feel the exceeding sinfulness of sin.

December 9 - Jennie's Diary
I have today been casting my eye over my diary. I see that I have been very deficient in noting my states of my mind, but I can say it has not been in consequence of coldness in the cause of my Savior.

CHAPTER TWO

JENNIE AND ANN

1850-1853

In 1850 Jennie is teaching at Greensboro Female College. She writes frequently and records in detail the daily life at the college. It is obvious that she takes her teaching seriously, constantly seeking the knowledge of books that might enhance her own mental prowess. Jennie has a deep concern for the spiritual well-being of the girls, and again berates herself for her own idleness (although she wakes up at four or five in the morning). She mentions family letters and a visit from brother Asbury, but it appears that she was not able to return home that year. She continues to explore the possibilities of her career as a writer, and is somewhat envious of her brother Aaron's success in writing. There are also some historical events of interest that she mentions, such as a visit from the governor, and the renowned execution of John White Webster. This is the year we chose to introduce Ann's work. By 1850, at age sixteen, she is attending Jonesville Female Academy and writing numerous essays. Ann is much more flamboyant than her sister, with an exuberance which stands in stark contrast to Jennie's more meticulous style of writing. None of Ann's early essays are dated so they will be wound into the story as they relate to the topic and to the chronology of the sisters' lives. We do know that Ann was a student at Jonesville from 1850 until 1853 and was on the faculty during the 1853-1854 school year. We will begin 1850 with Ann's essay.

1850

c. 1850 - Ann's Essay

The Girl I Would Be

I would be the only daughter of a brave Indian Chief, beloved by my nation, and the pride of my gray-haired father. My rustic home would be a white cottage in a grove of cedars, overrun with wild roses and situated on the margin of a dimpled lake. I would prepare the simple meal for my father and his warriors. I would sing them songs to cheer them on their return from battle. My little canoe I would guide over the lake and as it glided on the sparkling waves, in the rays of the setting sun, I would sing to the chief sitting by my side. I would adorn my jetty tresses with the richest flowers that deck the mountainside. The gray locks of my father I would twine around my tawny fingers.

The foaming cataract, the rugged precipice should be my haunts to enjoy the quiet solitude. The sheets of vapor above my head, the rock at my feet, [and] the birds sing to my pensive heart, and the gentle goats from the mountain cave love me.

I would mount my Arab steed and chase the deer through the forest. My bow and arrow should be my attendants, and my prancing Arab scorn the dangers of the chase. His long flowing mane waves in the breeze. From this I would return to my Indian home and recount to my attentive braves the pleasures of my forest ride.

I would gather around me the daughters of my people and teach them to love virtue, to scorn envy or deceit, to [have] reverence [for] the Great Spirit, and [to] administer to the wants of the poor. I would spend a life of usefulness, and in the innocence and purity of youth, I would lay me down in the quiet springtime, among the tall waving grass, flowers and singing birds, and peacefully and exultingly my soul should depart to the Spirit Land, to wander in the fragrant groves of the "Great Hunting Ground" of my Ancestors.

January 8 - Greensboro Female College - Jennie's Diary

The present finds me in this institution as a teacher. I know that my duties are many and responsible. But may I receive wisdom from above to aid me in discharging them faithfully.

March 15 - Jennie's Diary

How anxious I feel for the salvation of the dear girls around me. There are many here who appear entirely indifferent about religion while others seem to treat with contempt whatever relates to their future.

April 20 - Jennie's Diary

I sometimes feel a rising disposition to complain of my lot in life. When I look upon the young ladies around me, and listen to their excellent performance on the piano, I feel tempted to repine. Yet I would not be guilty of such wickedness, for instead of [complaining] I ought to be continually thanking my Father that it is as well with me as it is.

This is Jennie's first mention of Dr. Deems, the President of Greensboro Female College. He was a man who held her deepest respect and she speaks of him often.

August 9 - Jennie's Diary

President Deems met me in the [?] and asked me if I knew they had faculty meetings. I replied I did. He then invited me to attend. I did so and I was so much pleased that I shall not be absent any more if possible. They are trying to make arrangements so that the town girls may recite during the first two hours in the morning and afternoon and thus give them more time to study at home. Mr. Deems made some very amusing remarks about some of the girls. He said Miss Jane Treadwell was a girl of high animal temperament, entirely above study, but he thought if he could take a game of football with her for about a month she would be brought down so as to make a splendid woman. "If," said he, "she treads well, she treads pounding. I can hear her coming down stairs. If I had her temperament I am sure I would leave a streak upon the world." Many plans were derived to secure the best interest of the girls. The meeting was so interesting that we did not separate until the bell rang for tea.

In this next entry Jennie praises Dr. Deems's preaching. She seems compelled to describe the Sabbath in her diary: everything from her emotions, to the sermons, to the look of nature around her. Note at the end of the day she sits in the parlor with the girls, which she considers great folly.

August 11 - Sunday - Jennie's Diary

Spent the morning reading my Bible. At 10 o'clock went to church. Mr. Deems preached from Heb. 11.27. During his discourse he remarked that God talks about us; he stopped and with a tone of anxious inquiry said, "I wonder what he is saying about you, but I am more anxious to know what he is saying about me." Its effect upon the congregation may be conjectured. At three o'clock the young ladies had prayer meeting in the chapel. At five I walked down in the wood with Miss Hagen [a colleague] The sun was just [setting] and his last golden beams were lingering upon the treetops. A cool breeze sent a low murmuring to me through the thick boughs. There stood the proud oak, whose putting forth I had watched so anxiously only a few months before. It was now in the glory of summer, but I thought how soon the fierce autumn blast would strip it of its rich foliage. We sat upon the brink of the nice rippling streamlet, but now it had sunk from sight on account of the prevailing drought. How dependent upon God is all nature. The bell soon called us to the college for evening prayers. I spent part of the evening in the parlor, which was not right, and I humbly ask my heavenly father to forgive my folly.

Sister Ann had the same devotion to the Sabbath. Note that she, like her sister Jennie, does not believe in idle conversation on the Lord's day. All thoughts should be directed toward God.

This essay serves well as an introduction to Ann, whose writing is more descriptive and flamboyant.
c. 1850 - Ann's Essay

The Light of Sabbath Evening

How soft and calm fades the mellow light of this Sabbath eve in the dim distance. The gentle zephyrs softly float through the wood, and Nature veils herself in a mantle of serenity. Tranquility reels in all surrounding objects. The last ray of the departing Sun lingers about; now piercing the somber forest, then dancing in the turfy graveyard, playing on the dimpled lake, or hiding among the flowers, as if reluctant to say "adieu" to nature on this holy evening. The last lingering Sunbeam has fled to the western hills; the tears of Nature quietly steal o'er the tender grass, and the earth, shrouded in the grey twilight, gently sinks into repose. We come to pay our devotion as the Notaries of high heaven. All is serenity and peace, and yet within, in the heart, a "still small voice" whispers "remember the Sabbath day to keep it holy." God himself "rested on this day and hallowed it." Yes, consecrated it to his own will. One day in seven we are called from our labor to spend one entire day in holiness. Leaving the world and worldly cares in the distance, we are commanded to pray all devotions to God. [We are] to spend one day exclusively in fitting and preparing our hearts for the reception of Christ. [We are to prepare] for the final dissolution of this tenement of clay, and to [make] ready for an entrance to an unseen, but eternal world, preparing the soul for a blessed and eternal home.

"Remember the Sabbath Day to keep it holy." Holy!! How few fulfill this command! Instead of keeping it "holy" it is often set apart for idle chit-chat, meeting of acquaintances and conversing on worldly matters where the name of God is not mentioned. God hallowed this day, he blessed it, and it became a holy day, a day distinguished from all others by its consecration. It is a type of that eternal Sabbath in heaven, where it is not spent in idleness by fallen man, but where the holy Angels join in eternal strains of music and adoration to the great Omnipotent.

This next entry is a good description of what the students and faculty saw in town (Greensboro) in 1850.

August 17 - Jennie's Diary

Rose early; dressed and arranged my room went out in the parlor. The earliest beams of the rising sun were just edging the tops of the tallest trees. The air was unusually refreshing. Alas thought I of how much pleasure do many of my companions deprive themselves of who sleep away such bright mornings. I took my seat near the parlor window and had the history of Abram as contained in the 15th chapter. After reading I went with some of the young ladies shopping. Spent the remainder of the day until six entertaining company. Although I would often greatly prefer going in my recitation room and spend my time some other way, yet I must not be rude. At six o'clock I took tea with Mr. and Mrs. Hopkins in company with the teachers, [the] president and [his] lady. I enjoyed myself very well. The town was very lively, as a great many were coming in from an evening ride to the mineral well. Carriages and buggies were almost continually passing. To see everything so full of life and action was very entertaining to us. We returned about 8 o'clock. Had a most delightful ride from town to [the] college. The moon was shining so very brightly and the evening air was so balmy that we ardently wished we had some five or six miles to ride.

David Steele Reid was governor of North Carolina from 1851 – 1854. He was probably governor-elect at this time.

August 21 - Jennie's Diary

We have had quite a pleasant day. All things have gone smoothly. And now the evening shade invites us to rest. Governor Reid took tea with us. He is quite a gentleman.

On August 23, Jennie justifies her early rising and expresses her disdain for idleness.

August 23 - Jennie's Diary

Rose at 4 o'clock. I was glad that I had waked so early and after arranging my toilet, took my seat in my recitation room. I thought of what a long and pleasant day I had to spend, and after earnestly praying to my Heavenly Father that no crime might pollute the hours of the rising day, I spent the remainder of the morning until school time in study and writing. The day passed away very pleasantly, for I found not only employment but pleasure in instructing my little charge. After school we met in faculty meeting, the reports were generally good—all agreed in saying there was a decided improvement.

The idea Jennie speaks of in this next entry might have been when Dr. Deems suggested that Jennie attend Mount Holyoke College in Massachusetts.

August 24 - Saturday Evening - Jennie's Diary

I now have the pleasure of looking back upon the day as not spent in vain. I keep in my recitation room as much as possible, so I was free from company. I passed the morning in writing, the afternoon in drawing and studying geometry. I am resolved to be more economical of my time hereafter than [I have] formerly [been]. Mr. Deems suggested an idea to me which may afford me some material to think upon.

Jennie's reading must have been uniquely vast, for not only did she know of political, theological, and scientific matters, but also she was aware of the rather scandalous happenings of the day. It would seem her interest in these two murder cases stems mainly from the fact that the murderers were professors, just as she was. John White Webster, a chemistry teacher at Harvard Medical School, murdered Dr. George Parkman, a prominent physician and member of the Boston Brahmin elite. Professor Webster dismembered the doctor and shoved his body parts into a vault under his office. Eugene Aram was a scholar and teacher in England who in 1745 killed Daniel Clark, a man who probably had relieved Aram of his money. The case was unsolved until the skeleton of Clark was found in a cave and Aram's wife testified with evidence that convicted her husband. In prison Aram wrote a paper claiming the right to dispose of his own life and on the day of the execution was found to have so deeply wounded his arms with a razor that the executioner was scarcely required to perform his duties. Eugene Aram was hanged on August 6, 1759, and the following day his body was taken to Knaresborough Forest and hung in chains—a suit of iron bands encompassing the corpse so that it would not drop to pieces in the process of decay.

August 30 - Jennie's Diary

This is a very sorrowful [day]. All our nation has been looking with anxiety, as it is to witness the execution of Professor Webster for the murder of Dr. Parkman. His is said to be a case unparalleled since the trial and execution of Eugene Aram, a man renowned in English Literature. Professor Webster's case adds but another name to the long list of witnesses that bad passions should be checked in early life, and that habits once fixed are seldom overcome, for he attributes all this sad catastrophe to his not being taught while he was young to control his passions. What a warning to hasty youths!

Jennie liked books on most any subject but rejected a popular novel on love.

September 4 - Jennie's Diary

This has been quite a pleasant day to me. My school has moved smoothly on. It affords me pleasure to instruct those little ones. At 3 o'clock in the afternoon the young ladies were called into the chapel to read their compositions before the teachers and each other. Four from each class were called upon to read. Of what may these simple compositions be the buddings! None may tell. After tea I took a volume of Littell's *Living Age* and set me down in the west door of the building and commenced to read. I read for a few moments. As to the piece I was reading, I closed the book and finally concluded I would never read any more of love's tales. I have never read but very few and I am resolved that number shall not be increased.

Jennie speaks again on temperance.

October 8 - Jennie's Diary

My birthday. Never did I spend a birthday more pleasantly. I attended a celebration of the Sons of Temperance held in the new Methodist Church and listened to one of the best speakers our country affords, Mr. Phillip L. White. His speech far exceeded anything I have ever heard on the subject of temperance. The Sons all looked so independent and happy that for once I was glad that I had a brother and father whose names were enrolled among the brave Sons of Temperance. But amid the many pleasures of the day, some sorrowful feelings came over me as I thought how much of my short life was passed and how little improvement I had made. I will try to do better in the future.

At Jonesville Academy, Ann was addressing many of the same issues that Jennie was at Greensboro Female College. This poem was found in her collection of works. We do not know if she wrote it, or if she merely copied it because it was a favorite. Like her sister, Ann was a strong supporter of the temperance movement.

c. 1850-1851 - Ann's Collection

To the Sons of Temperance

Hail noble band, thy cause divine,
Encircles all the human race -

In every land in every clime,
Thy deeds of charity we trace.
Deliver us from a galling chain,
Whose fetters bind - whose iron sway,
Enslaves our friends - to thee we look,
And hail the first grey peep of day.
The mother's sigh by thee is hushed,
The orphan's low and bitter wail,
The widow's tears are stanched that gushed,
On brothers then, we bid thee hail!

November 3 - Sabbath Morning - Jennie's Diary

This is a lovely morning. The sun is just rising in all his beauty, making the earth glad by his genial beams. The forest birds are caroling their earliest and sweetest notes of praise to their great Creator. The bell is ringing for morning prayers, may I engage in them heartily. Sabbath Eve. This has been an interesting day. Mrs. Adams kindly gave us the loan of her carriage to attend the Yearly Meeting of Friends held at New Garden. We arrived there about 11 o'clock. Heard 3 gentlemen and one lady preach. The church was crowded. They preached so simple and affecting that I wished I was of their number. I must confess that I believe they live nearer the standard of the Bible than any other denomination.

November 7 - Jennie's Diary

Received a letter from my dear Mother. All well at home, and sending a strong solicitation for me to return during vacation. Some of my neighbors have been converted. Praise to the good Lord. This evening a spirit of sadness pervades our institution. Our beloved president is going to leave tonight for conference. He will be absent some three weeks. Many tears have been shed at thoughts of parting with him, but may the hand of a merciful Providence protect him and us.

November 10 - Jennie's Diary

I have not attended church this morning but remained in order that Mrs. Deems might have an opportunity of going. Rev. W. Nesbitt is expected to preach. I have this morning [been] looking over my diary which I have kept but imperfectly since my conversion. In looking over it I have occasion to regret that I have been so negligent in keeping a faithful record. While I was in Jonesville at school in 1848, and here in 1849, I find but very few memorandums. I believe that faithfully recording the incidents of the day and the state of one's mind is one of the greatest means of Christian improvement. My roommates have all gone to church and I am all alone. I have been revolving in my mind the anxious inquiry of my present true state. During all the week I am immersed in the duties of my schoolroom and my own private studies, so that I have but very little time for serious reflection. How welcome then, to me, is the holy Sabbath. It is indeed a day of rest. May I improve it.

November 12 - Jennie's Diary
I have just lighted my candle and set me down to my evening studies, but before I engage in them I feel a disposition to make a minute of the day. To me it has been a very pleasant day, especially has this evening been lovely. After my school closed, [I sat] down in my recitation [room] and gave myself up to the luxury of reading. I was so deeply engaged as to be entirely unconscious of what was going on around, until all of a sudden the sun, which had been obscured by clouds during the day, shone out in all his splendor, and threw his golden beams upon the wall of my room. As I gazed upon this bright sun I ardently wished the sun of my life might set this glorious. That however obscured it might be during life, yet in death it might be all brightness and tranquility.

Ann also saw the beauties of nature and wrote of them in one of her essays at Jonesville.

Fall c. 1850 - From Ann's Essay

To Autumn

Welcome lovely Autumn! Welcome to the earth, to our firesides and to our hearts. Where during the long passing year has thou slept? In what grotto or natural palace hast thy home flown? From whence art thou beautiful autumn? Who wove thy golden tinted robe - who thy varied hues embossed? Where did thou find this massive lyre, that lulls so strangely the soul as the winds sweep over it? What Morpheus taught thee to awake such stirring strains, as thou sweepest thy fingers over its cords?

Jennie is ill several times during the year. Her future diary will frequently reveal her "afflictions." She feels guilty that she allows her illness to keep her from church. She also lurches from one thought to another. She talks of the sinful nature of those around her, then condemns her own sin as she speaks of herself. There must have been a young man in her life that she rejected. This entry is the only mention of his existence.

November 17 - Sabbath Morning - Jennie's Diary

Having been much afflicted. My throat [is sore] and the weather very cold this morning. I have not attended church. I have had some doubts as to the propriety of my course. I have thought that if I had so much love for God and his cause as I ought, that the consideration of my health would not have kept me away. Since my roommates have gone to church, I have been all alone, and have been endeavoring to examine my heart to see what my spiritual state is. There seems to be a mist over my spiritual vision, and I cannot discern the things of God as I wish. My spirit is much troubled about the dear girls in college. There is so little piety among them, and they seem as indifferent about salvation. But few attend our Sabbath evening prayer meetings. Many of those who are professors of religion indulge in all the wild amusements of their thoughtless companions. Miss M.C. Turntine [student] has come out of late with earrings in her ears. She is the daughter of a minister, a member of the church, and one who, I had hoped, would be a faithful assistant in prayer meeting. I really fear I do not do my duty. I have tried to persuade them in prayer meetings to seek religion but they are yet careless. I know they will not seek it until they feel the need of it, until they see their lost condition. I need more religion myself. I want more pure, humble and fervent piety. I see my course has been too inconsistent. I have this morning been reading the memoir of Elizabeth Boles. [Elizabeth Boles was a missionary who worked with the Kansas Indians.] Would I were as useful as she was. What a vast difference Christians [make] in their lives and usefulness. **Sabbath evening**. My thoughts this evening have taken a peculiar turn. After supper I came into my schoolroom, and set me down to serious meditation. My mind was very much burdened respecting the young ladies, and also my own sinful heart. I thought how little good I am doing here, and how much I might possibly do in some other situation, and I have almost concluded that this is not the place for me. I have also thought of him whom I once so coolly rejected. If I had accepted his proposal I should perhaps tonight be in quite a different situation, and I have no doubt in one far more pleasant and profitable. Others may do good here, but I fear I cannot. I have some presentiment that Providence has destined me to fill a quite different sphere. It is strange that my thoughts should have taken this turn, for nothing was further from my mind . . . . . He may never be informed of my mind. If my thoughts continue as they are I shall endeavor to make some communication to him, and if another more [deserving] has not accepted that protection and love once professed to me, I may be happy yet. From very early years it has been impressed on my mind that I should take a course quite different from the generality of women. That high vocation can be followed only by uniting with the denomination of Friends. My mind has been peculiarly drawn towards that body. Only a few Sabbaths ago I attended their Yearly Meeting held at New Garden. While I sat and listened to their simple and affectionate exposition of the Gospel my heart rejoiced and I longed to be one of their number. Oh shall I ever see that day? But may be I ought not to indulge in these thoughts. They may have been gendered by the excitement of the movement. One thing I know, I want to do right. At one time I little thought that I should ever have penned the above confession; and even now while I look over it, I think it strange. May God my Heavenly Father guide me aright.

James is now seven years old. Ann is sixteen.

November 18 - Jennie's Diary
This has been a delightful day. This morning I received a box and a letter from home. All well. Mother sent me several little articles, precious tokens of mother's love. Sister sent me a nicely worked collar, little Jamie [James], some flowers. I do esteem these little gifts. My mind is no more satisfied than it was last evening. I will make it a matter of prayer.

November 19 - Jennie's Diary
Nothing particular has occurred today, yet I do not feel satisfied if I let the day pass away without writing. My love for my pen increases. I long to yield that pen of "a ready writer." That is the all-absorbing thought of my mind. It seems to me if I could write fluently, I might accomplish some good. I will not despair, there is nothing like trying; if I fail once I can try, try again.

November 20 - Jennie's Diary
Another day with its toils. I am now seated by a comfortable fire in my recitation room. The cold rain is falling fast without, and my thoughts have often turned to the condition of many poor suffering creatures, who this night are in want of bread and clothing to screen them from hunger and the pinching cold. Here I am in college, free from care, and free from want, and yet how seldom do I think of my highly favored condition?! My mind voluntarily goes back to my earlier life. I remember when I was a little simple hearted girl, daily employed in some useful household labor, and devoting the spare moments to reading or studying. Then it was I sighed for these happy privileges, but at the same time thought it impossible that I should ever enjoy them. What changes come over our life! But I should be cautious. Reverse of fortune may come. I may yet be placed as far below, as I now am placed above my former station. I will at least try to live so that whatever my future lot may be I may look back upon the present period with pleasure.

This next entry is remarkably similar to Puritan diaries written in the seventeenth century.

November 22 - Friday Evening - Jennie's Diary

The duties of another week are over. My school is very little burden to me for the dear little children are generally obedient. I wish I could instruct them better. It is true I apply myself constantly to my studies and reading and writing, but surely it cannot make me feel this tired. When I wake in the morning I feel weary and wish to sleep more. My custom is to rise between 4 + 5 and I do not wish to break upon this habit. If it is mental indolence, I must shake it off. I have no time for idleness. This life is not long. I want to improve it well. O how I regret that I have spent so much of my precious time in idleness. It grieves my heart when I see these young ladies spending their time so foolishly. What an amount of useful knowledge they might now store up if they were disposed. Since I have determined to make efforts to become an authoress I feel like I have some definite object for which to live. I pray the richest blessings of Heaven on my pen. May I be enabled to do some good.

November 23 - Jennie's Diary

Have spent the day in my recitation room reading and writing. Finished [writing] an article on "Novel Reading," and have some thoughts of having it published. I wonder if I shall ever become an authoress! I find my desire to write increases almost every day. My whole heart is fixed, if I may use the expression, in the work. I have determined to write at least one composition every week. If I never make an authoress, writing will improve my mind, and I need not think any labor too great—if I may but accomplish this through the culture of my mind. I enjoy myself greatly by just sitting down here in my study, all alone, and entering into deep thought—thinking what I once was, what I am now, what I ought to be, and what I may be. It does me good; it is like a feast. I am sure I never wasted any time, which I spend in thinking or writing. But oh! The precious time I have wasted this session. Those long sunny summer evenings; if I had them back I certainly would not spend them as I have. It grieves me much, but I cannot recall the past, all I can do is to improve the future. I have been much troubled at the thoughtlessness and misdemeanor of some of the young ladies. I wish they would all do what is right. I shall be under the necessity of reporting some of them and I deeply regret it. How prone human nature is to err.

Aaron is in school, but we are not sure where. He is nineteen.

November 24 - Sabbath Morning - Jennie's Diary

With joy I hail the bright and beautiful sun of this holy Sabbath morning. I rose at half past 4 o'clock, and spent the time from then until daylight in reading my Bible and Mason's *Spiritual Treasure*. I have this morning had renewed occasion to thank God for giving me a mother who taught me to rise early. Breakfast was not ready until between 8 + 9 o'clock and yet many of the young ladies were not dressed. What account will we have to give for wasting our precious Sabbath time in sleep and idleness? It really seems to me that I could spend from morning till night at my desk. This inward aspiration is making me restless. With a perplexed mind I walk my room sometimes thinking what to do. I have heard an article written by my brother, much praised for its excellency; he, younger than I, and yet talking the advance. But just here I fear I am actuated by an ambitious spirit; yet I know if I am not awfully deceived that I want to write to be useful. And then again, I think why is this ardent desire if there is not a corresponding ability to satisfy it by proper exertions? But I am at loss to know about what to write. Every subject seems well nigh exhausted. However, I have one consolation. I can sit down here and write in my diary, and for this privilege I would not take thousands. This day has been spent in my daily avocation very pleasantly. I received a letter from my dear sister, which gave me much joy. She did not give me the wished for satisfaction about the course of life she intends to pursue, but maybe she is too young to decide yet, and it may be Providence has destined her for a different sphere—to that I have thought. I want her to be useful. Her letter was a feast. It bore intelligence, which taught me the necessity of sowing "beside all waters."

Late in the year as the college is coming to a close, Jennie is struggling with melancholy. She begins, again, to question her ability do to something "great" and sees her time spent talking with the girls as frivolous and wasteful. This would lead one to assume that she was standoffish and distant from the girls, yet later documents will illustrate that she was loved by all who knew her. Her loneliness was just that. She felt alone even though she was loved by many.

December 3 - Jennie's Diary

The weather is yet dreary and I feel it has a tendency to make me feel rather melancholy. If outward circumstance so affect the mind I am sure that in examining my heart I should have to respect to my situation. I have been reflecting on the past month, and while reviewing its labors I feel grateful to my Heavenly Father that he has enabled me to make greater improvement than during any month of the session. I saw the very worthless manner in which I had been spending my time, and I resolved at the commencement of last month to spend it more usefully, and I now feel a consciousness that I have in part succeeded. I have spent my time closely in my recitation room, and now I feel much happier than formerly when I passed my evenings in a company of girls, from whom I derived no benefit. I shall ever look back with regret upon the very many precious evenings I have squandered. I have gone through Blair's *Rhetoric* and commenced reviewing. To me there is something fascinating in his writings. I could take his Rhetoric and sit down to read it as an entertainment; I never tire in perusing his works. I have of late had several applications from the girls concerning compositions. If I were to judge from their words I might flatter myself able to write in a more than ordinary manner, but no, I cannot consent to deceive myself as wretchedly. But I will not despair. I have an assurance that I may by industry and perseverance finally succeed. In this as in every thing else I must depend upon God. I know that a good heart is as indispensable for a useful writer as a wise head. It is now late. I will read my Bible and committing myself to a kind Providence, seek repose upon my pillow.

December 4 - Jennie's Diary

Days and weeks roll rapidly away. I am daily reminded that life is but a vapor that quickly vanisheth. Let our diligence be what it may, we scarce commence life's varied duties before we have to leave our work but half-completed. I feel weary this evening, my spirit is drooping. I feel that much study is weariness to the flesh. I am almost ready to despair of ever accomplishing anything good or great. But I must not talk thus; it argues littleness of mind. I have of late been tracing the history of many persons who have been blessings to the human race. I find almost invariably that they had to grapple with difficulties. I cannot be exempt from the common lot of man. I look to God and humbly ask for grace to discharge the duties of life and to answer the end of my being. I will not indulge in sadness any longer for it is doing myself an injury. Weeping may endure for a night but joy cometh in the morning.

Jennie's love of President Deems was deep and abiding, perhaps a type of affection that is not well understood from a modern perspective. She never spoke of a romantic attachment to him but frequently wrote about her feelings toward him. When he took a short trip away from the college, she was distressed. When he came home, she came out of her December depression. Note how she thought he might die while he was away. Again, perhaps it was a sign of the times that travel was dangerous and time on earth was only to be enjoyed for a short while. References to the family are also made in these passages.

December 5 - Jennie's Diary

Our beloved president has returned this evening after an absence of four weeks. How glad we all are to hear his voice once more. So[is] it not striking that the happiness of so many depends upon one? Since his return there seems to be new life and vigor dispersed through our college. We do feel thankful that God has spared his life, and restored him to us. I have this evening received two letters, one from my dear mother, and one from Bro. Asbury. They bore intelligence both joyful and sad. Bro. Asbury is going to pay me a visit in vacation. How glad I will be to see him. From the tenor of Mother's letter I feel great anxiety about my brother Aaron. He is a boy whom I have long considered of no ordinary promise. I little thought he would become wild and thoughtless.

December 8 - Sabbath Morning - Jennie's Diary

This sun has shone out bright and beautiful this morning after having been clouded for a week. Today I may worship God. Oh for the proper spirit. It has been impressed upon my mind sometime that I ought to speak to one of the girls, Laura Durant, upon the subject of religion. I am determined to try to do so today. The cross I feel is heavy, but I must do it. I have thought much about these impressions. Why is it that I should feel more concerned about one than another? But what is that to me; I must follow my Savior. The Lord gave me grace to speak to that dear girl in a way that may effect her salvation. **Sabbath evening**. This holy day is past. Its duties and its privileges are over. It has borne its account to the great tribunal. This morning Mr. Deems preached for us in the chapel. At half past three we had prayer meeting. Altho it was the last and I had requested the young ladies to come; but few were present. Dear children, the Lord have mercy upon them. I took up the cross and spoke to Laura about religion. She seemed serious, and promised to seek religion. May the good Lord impress what was said upon her mind, and may it be instrumental in her conversion. Tonight Mr. Deems preached for us again. What great privilege we enjoy. How shall we escape if we neglect them!

The school year ends with a description of December and a report on the last day of class.

December 9 - Jennie's Diary

The earliest beams of the sun are just falling beautifully upon our earth. There is a fine white frost this morning and the sky clear as crystal, the air cold yet pure and refreshing. Old winter is coming and showing his beauties around, for to me he has many.

How glad, cheerful, and happy I feel. I do thank my kind creator for quiet sleep and now all the blessings of the light. **Evening.** I have spent my day quite pleasantly in my recitation room. This morning I gave my pupils their report for the session and after committing them to the care of kind Providence I dismissed them for the present session. I have spent the remainder of the day in reading. What a luxury it is to me to sit down and read. I anticipate much pleasure and improvement this vacation from reading. I am now reading Howitt's *Homes of the Poets*, and the *History of the Reformation*. As I read I take notes that I may better understand and remember when I read. The bell has rung to go to bed, and I feel very much like obeying its call.

December 14 - Jennie's Diary
This has been a day of pleasure and pain. My dear brother Asbury has paid me a visit. Oh what a treat to have a good brother by my side! He came up to the college in his buggy this morning and took me out to ride. I was very cold yet the ride was greatly enjoyed. But now he has left and I am all alone.

December 31 - Jennie's Diary
We have had snow and hail today. The girls have enjoyed themselves greatly in it. [Some of the girls didn't get to go home between breaks.] I have passed the day as usual in my study reading Hallams' *Middle Ages*, and Prescott's *Ferdinand and Isabella*. I am greatly interested in the story of those two illustrious sovereigns. But amid so much gaiety and so much enjoyment a solemn thought has come over the mind. It is the last day of the year. What! Can it be that I am spared another year? How great is the goodness of God. What an array of mercies, blessings, and advantages is seen as I look back upon the year. They are more than I can number. But there is a reflection yet more sad. How have I neglected my privileges. I have not done the good I might. But if I live to see the new year I will try to improve.

No Date - Untitled - Ann's Collection
It is night, deep, still, awe inspiring night. Above is the sky spangled with millions of glittering diamonds. On the earth is a mantle so purely

white, so delicately wrought, so elegantly grand that none but superhuman fingers could have fashioned it. Around her earth-couch, night has drooped a sable veil, [that] glides serene and majestic through her fairyland. I look above to heaven and it is flashing in starlight. If one of those celestial lights were plucked from its burning pathway, its vacancy would scarcely be realized, so numerous are its companions. I look upon the open fields and deep woodlands, and the same "mantle of purity" is bathed in the light of the night sky. And this mantle, though so elegant in its richness, is formed of snowflakes so light and delicate that in its infancy a fly might cast it aside, but all together go to make up the whole land of whiteness so complete that no mortal eye can detect a deficiency.

1851

In 1851 Jennie was promoted to college professor and was moved out of the Preparatory Department into full college teaching. The diary, in its entirety, will be presented for this year. She begins to write frequently and dwells on her thoughts and concerns in a deeper fashion. She mentions how she values the simplicity of her childhood years and despairs over ever becoming a writer. Revivalism is in full swing at Greensboro Female College. Some very interesting passages are revealing as Jennie prays daily for the salvation of her various students. A dramatic moment when one of the girls is nearly burned to death is only briefly mentioned, demonstrating that she was more interested in salvation than in life on earth. Ann is still at Jonesville Academy, writing work that closely resembles her sister's thinking. Their brother Asbury is superintendent at a tannery in Jonesville and a colonel in the Yadkin Militia. Brother Aaron is a professor of literature and natural science at Union Institute but will leave this position late in the year to become an editor of the Tennessee Patriot. *Vet is attending Jonesville Male Academy. James is eight years old and the only sibling at home.*

January 1 - Jennie's Diary

All hail thou happy New Year! My spirit leaps with joy to see thy blessed light. Thanksgiving and honor to my kind Creator for all the mercies of the past year, and for so auspicious a beginning to the new. This morning the earth is all white with the snow of the past year. I have been reading this morning, and I would feign spend the year reading if I could. I want to commence this morning and see if I can not live a new life. The Lord help me. **Evening.** I have tried to spend this day as I wish to spend the year. I have been reading and writing. I have made the start and prepared two articles for the press. Yes, I have broken the ice this New Year's day. May a propitious Providence favor my beginning. This year, by the grace of God, shall witness greater efforts than I have ever made before. A blessing be on the year.

"Providence" will be a reccurring theme in the sisters' collection of works. They dwelt on its possibilities and took comfort in its promise as they saw it. Ann writes this essay at Jonesville.

c. 1851-1853 - Ann's Essay
The Decrees of Providence

How wise are the ways of Divine Providence. Did we know that at times when we are enjoying ourselves so much, surrounded by many of the pleasures of life, and devoting ourselves so exclusively to the attainment of happiness, that someone, whom we fondly love, is suffering extremely, either bodily or mentally? Our happiness would be useless, for the consciousness that our friends were wretched would displease all our enjoyment, and the contemplation of misfortune that we could not alleviate would render us miserable. I have thought it was one of the greatest gifts of heaven, in rendering us happy for the present, in not bestowing on us the power of knowing what is taking place everywhere at the same time. Did we possess that power, we would doubtless be the most miserable beings ever seen. At one time all our joys would be damped in the consciousness that our nearest and dearest friends were miserable; at another, we would be driven to distraction in comparing our situation with someone to whom fortune and happiness have been more lenient. Could we be witnesses, but for one moment, of the misery, wretchedness, crime and injury that pervade our earth, we would be driven to some desperate act in our haste to leave a place of so much sorrow. Yet God in his infinite wisdom and goodness saw all the great evil that would arise from this knowledge, and mercifully slayed [sic] the evil.

The power of foreknowledge would have been equally destructive to human happiness. In the pursuit of desired object we are stimulated by fear and encouraged by hope. But if we have but little doubt of the loss of that object, our energies relax, we are lost in despondency. But on the contrary if we become almost certain of the accomplishment of the desired end, we are apt to grow careless and indolent and often lose what we might have easily gained. This proves that foreknowledge was wisely withheld from man. If we knew precisely how all our endeavors would end we would not accomplish as much as we do at present. We would not be assisted by that heavenly principle of "hope" which adds so much energy to our actions; the fear of failure would no longer stimulate us to double efforts. We sometime spend much time in trying to divine the future; we would give almost anything we possess if we could know how a certain event would turn out. But at the same time, that knowledge would prove destructive to our happiness, and the contemplation of it would make us more miserable than the experiencing of it. Thus the power of prying into the future is wisely withheld from us.

January 2 - Jennie's Diary

I have often found today a disposition to be impatient and to repine. This I want to overcome. It is the beginning of the year and I wish it to be the commencement of a new life with me. I feel I have much heart [heart is the word she meant to use] work to do. But this I cannot accomplish by myself. I must go to the strong for help. The good Lord help me. My eyes pain me very much tonight. I sometimes fear I employ them too steadily at my reading. I must quit for tonight.

January 18 - Jennie's Diary

It has been many days since I have written in my diary. I have passed through different scenes but this evening finds me well. I have suffered greatly within the last week. I now enjoy ease and comfort and I want to feel very thankful to my Heavenly Father. I have been much perplexed and cast down of late. I feel very much like giving over and never trying to accomplish anything. But my own good sense tells me that will not do; yet what to do I can not tell. I find yet living in my bosom an ardent desire to become a good writer, but of this I have almost despaired. What shall I do? I may as well give it up but how can I? Is this life? Will it always be thus? O for strength of mind and heart to contend successfully with obstacles. This is Saturday night. May the holy Sabbath bring peace and quietude.

January 20 - Jennie's Diary

Our session has commenced under circumstances the most flattering both for mental and moral improvement. Many are the warm hopes which we cultivate for a profitable session. And I am sure if we combine efforts and desires we shall not be disappointed. My whole soul seems drawn out in strong desires for the welfare and full salvation of these dear girls. While all possible pains are taken to instruct the head, I sorrow that so little is done to affect and improve the heart. May the good Lord give me grace to discharge my duties faithfully. And may he send down his blessed spirit in our midst and work wonders. I have made a covenant with Miss Octavia Chander [student] that if she will pray for herself once a day I will pray for her three times. She seems anxious to obtain religion, and I hope God will hear and abundantly answer our prayers.

Jennie presents her father with a copy of The National Temperance Offering *the year it is published.*

January 25 - Jennie's Diary

Two weeks ago I sent my name to become a member of the Daughters of Temperance. Today I have been initiated. I was very much pleased with the ceremony. It was so affecting. I am also highly pleased with the institution. I believe it capable of doing much good. All is love and affection there.

January 28 - Jennie's Diary

I have been busily engaged in my schoolroom today. Miss Leach [teacher] has come to take my place in the Preparatory Department while I take a college class. I am much pleased with this arrangement and hope I may be able to do more good. I am not studying much. My mind has been so disturbed I have felt little like doing anything. I want to do better and improve my time more. I know it is precious. What will become of me?

February 2 - Sabbath - Jennie's Diary

The first Sabbath of the month. It has been a precious day to me. I have learned many useful things upon which I will try to practice during the coming week. I will try to read my Bible more attentively, to attend to my secret devotion better, and examine and watch over my heart more closely. I want to be a more practical Christian. I find much pride in my heart. I want to try to overcome that this week. I do think pride is detestable. I want to live circumspectly before the unconverted girls. The good Lord send his Holy Spirit in our midst to work wonders. A great improvement has been made already but a greater is yet to be made. May the good Lord help us.

February 8 - Saturday Evening - Jennie's Diary

I have passed this bright and beautiful day without accomplishing much. Spent the morning in college. At three attended the meeting of the [Temperance] Union. The meeting was interesting. One of the members read an essay. One name was presented for membership. I am so much pleased with the daughters. Success to their labors. Late this evening Miss Hagan [colleague] and I went to Mr. Adams [?] and spent a few moments very pleasantly. And now the day has closed. "The Holy Sabbath draweth on." May the heart be fully prepared for all its duties.

February 14 - Friday Evening - Jennie's Diary

The duties of another week are ended, and I sit me down to write. 'Tis cold and rainy without, but we have cheerfulness and comfort within. The week has passed away pleasantly. Nothing serious occurred until last night—one of the girls came near being burned to death. I am pleased with the change in my situation, and take great pleasure in instructing my classes. I find some interesting girls, some who study well and appreciate the explanation that may be given. May I have wisdom to instruct them aright. I was invited to a large party given by the Masons of Greensboro tonight but I could not reconcile my notions of right to attend. The other teachers except me are gone, rainy as it is. These things do not agree with the simple notions of my earlier days. There may not be anything improper in them. In looking back over the past week I repent that I have indulged in some unpleasant feelings towards one or two of the teachers. They are ladies whom I highly respect yet I often think they are apt to look down upon me. I know I am their inferior in all points, yet I see not why one teacher should look down upon another. And more than that, I regret that any lady, whom I respect, should treat me indifferently. I will not think of these things any more than I can help. I want to look on the bright side of everything. I have no time to spend in useless repinings. I have much to do.

The "simple notions of earlier days" noted by Jennie in her diary is also expressed by Ann in the following essay:

c. 1851-1853 - Ann's Essay

Lights and Shadows of Life
- Stray links from the chain of memory -

No more refreshing is the early dew to the unfolding rose, than is the memory of other days to the weary soul. It steals up from the buried hopes of the past and blends its sweetness with the soul, melting the feelings of the heart. We live over again the early hours of childhood. The narrow shaded by-paths through the dim old woods that arched so high above us that they filled us with awe - the rippling rills and dashing waterfall - these all sweep over our mind. There are the wild haunts beneath the willow boughs where we watched the fish dart like silver arrows in the clearing wavelets - where the wild rose and jasmine wreathed their branches so intricately that our infant minds could not divine how they were woven. There are the old stately trees, like aged sentinels, guarding the homestead where we flung ourselves and gazed through the waving branches up to the moon beams, and wondered if we might not steal up these golden pathways and meet the Angels, whose eyes sparkled so brilliantly from their far off home in the sky. There is the old field where we went berrying, and the orchard where we gathered the rich luscious fruit.

But much as we love this, there is one other thing that wrought more powerfully upon the mind - it was when all the pleasures and duties of each day had passed and the soft hour of twilight thickened into deeper darkness, that we all assembled around the cheerful blazing fire and listened to the old legends of other days, or the daring of some gallant patriot in the days of the revolution. And we thought our dear Grandma must be wise to tell us so much. Then the large Bible was laid by our father's side and in a tone so deep and holy that it has never ceased to echo in our hearts. He read from that sacred volume and prayed so ardently for us that we might grow up into good and wise men and women. I wonder how far that prayer has been answered.

Years flew by with the speed of lightning, for sunshine and gladness wrought out a beautiful pathway for childish feet - Christmas holidays, Easter, Thanksgivings and New Years all flew by leaving their retinue of gaieties and happiness. Then came school days and first we knew grief when we left the paternal roof with all its hearts overflowing with affection for the coldness of strangers. So life to the present has been varying - each New Year brings some new event. This hour tells the mission of the present year - it is that we may store our minds with knowledge fitting for duties of after life. It is the great connecting link between the hours of childhood, and business and responsibilities of the future. And shall it not be improved? Shall any moment be suffered to pass to Eternity without being stamped with something worth the living, that the world may be the wiser by our having had an existence? "It is not all of life to live, nor all of death to die."

February 16 - Jennie's Diary

This bright and beautiful Sabbath day is fast drawing to a close. The sun has almost set. Just now he is throwing back his last golden rays upon our college walls. Oh how many light and careless hearts are within the walls? This holy blessed Sabbath has been a highly favored day. Yet where is its improvement? Mr. Deems preached for us this morning upon the Sabbath. He is to preach a series of sermons upon the same subject. This evening we had prayer meeting. Before we went in I was tempted to drop them entirely, but I was so much encouraged by the serious looks and the quiet behavior of the girls. The Lord grant it. **Night.** Went to church. Mr. Simpson preached. After sermon mourners were invited, four presented themselves at the altar. I was very much struck with the appearance of a little boy who went up. I feel much interested in him altho I know him not. It must have required an effort for him to have broken away from his companions and approach the altar all alone. May this be the beginning of good times at the church, and may the interest spread to the college. I think indications are favorable for a revival this session. The good Lord send it down now. 'Tis getting very late. I must close my Sabbath duties and retire to rest.

February 24 - Monday Morning - Jennie's Diary

The duties of another week are before me. But I do not feel very much like entering upon its secular duties. Yet I know it is necessary. The good Lord in mercy is visiting us with an outpouring of his good spirit. A revival has been going on in town for the last week. A deep and anxious interest has been manifested by some of the college girls, and some of them have been converted. Others are yet very serious. The great God make this work deep, pure and lasting.

February 26 - Wednesday Morning - Jennie's Diary

Words cannot express my thankfulness to my great Creator for what he has done in our midst. Last night we had prayer meeting and four were converted. Oh what happy children they were: one of the girls whom I love as a sister, Ann Slade, was converted the most clearly of any person I ever saw. The good Lord blesses the dear children. Many are yet very anxious, and I do pray that ere I write again they may be powerfully converted. Many are yet hardening their hearts. The good Lord touch these hard hearts. Let them feel their undone condition. This is all a work of God. It is his Holy Spirit here. He has already done great things for us. He is waiting to do greater.

February 27 - Thursday Morning - Jennie's Diary

Again my pen is employed writing good news. The Great God is yet with us to convict and convert. Last night two or three were converted. Some were deeply concerned who have never been serious before. These things are encouraging. But oh there are some who have been so anxious, that now seem almost ready to give over. One of them, Miss Biggs [student], has been greatly moved upon. She wants religion, yet she has a prejudice against kneeling down as a penitent. She sits upon her seat and weeps and groans. She is miserable. Oh how anxious I am that she should be converted. She is the friend and roommate of Miss Slade's [student] and I fear that if she is not converted, she will be a serious drawback to them. I write it now as a prayer offered up in the name of Jesus, that before I write again she may be happily and powerfully converted. My Heavenly Father, this plea I present to thee in the all prevailing name of Jesus. Oh let it find acceptance in thy sight. Touch and tender that heart and give a willing mind to seek thee in any manner. Oh Father let not that precious one draw back or become discouraged. Display thy mighty power in her behalf. Oh Lord, for Jesus' sake, hear my prayer.

February 28 - Jennie's Diary

"Bless the Lord oh my soul and forget not all his benefits." Last night was more highly favored than any previous night of our meeting. Six were happily converted and very many were deeply convicted. Miss Biggs is not converted yet but she was deeply humbled last night. She kneeled down very humbly and oh may the good Lord carry on the good work in her soul. Miss Barksdale [student] is also very deeply convicted. She was so near the blessing. And once more I write a humble prayer that God would convert these precious souls before I write again. Why is it that I should be more deeply concerned for some than others? One soul is just as valuable as another, and yet it is so. One thing did me much good last night, and that was to see the young converts enjoy themselves so much. Miss Beall [student] and Miss Slade were so happy as they well could be. The old enemy has been tempting them sorely but they have resisted him and gained the victory. But oh my Savior once more I pray for those dear girls who are [not] yet penitent. Before I write again may they be powerfully converted.

March 1 - Jennie's Diary

This is the first day of the month and it is rising oh how bright to many a soul in college. Last night the Lord was very good to us. He converted several among whom was Miss Biggs. Oh how can I be thankful enough. After the girls left she remained, unwilling to go without the blessing. Some of us stayed with her. We all knelt down in prayer and while praying the good Lord spoke peace to her troubled soul, and o what peace! Cornelia Hooker, that dear child that has been seeking Jesus so long was too powerfully converted. Long ago has she wept, but at last her mourning was turned into joy. But yet many weep at the altar. Miss Barksdale I fear became discouraged. The young converts were very happy and amid their rejoicing they too much forgot the penitents. May the great God forbid that Miss Barksdale should despair. And when I made another memorandum in my diary may she and Miss Garris [student] find peace in believing. Oh my Father again hear and answer prayer. Thou hast heard and answered my humble prayers in behalf of others, lend a listening ear this once more. And Father remember the young converts. Oh keep them from falling. Let not the tempter triumph over them. Give them faith, firm, unshaken. **Night.** This day I trust has not been entirely misspent. We went to church. After dinner Miss Harris [student] came to my room very much concerned about her soul. She asked me to pray for her. I went with her into my recitation room where we engaged in prayer. We remained there some time when at last it pleased the good Lord to speak peace to her troubled breast. She was very happy; the lord keep her. Tonight we went to church, four of the girls were penitents, one was converted. So the good Lord is carrying on the work yet. May my heart be prepared for the coming holy Sabbath.

March 2 - Sabbath Evening - Jennie's Diary
This has been a blessed day. We attended church, and heard a sermon from Mr. Jamison. After sermon the sacrament was administered. An invitation was given to all the young converts and I was so much rejoiced to see the college girls partake. This evening we had prayer meeting in the Chapel. One precious soul was converted. Oh how good God has been to us. Others are yet seeking Jesus. May the work go on until all shall be converted. And now the Sabbath closes, and oh how peaceful its close. The Lord make us humble and faithful.

March 10 - Monday Morning - Jennie's Diary
I am now entering upon the duties of another week. The Lord give me strength and wisdom. During the past week more have been converted. We attended church for several successive nights and the ardor of the girls seemed to abate and they have not been in the spirit of devotion since as they were before. We had prayer meeting last evening as usual but none could make up their minds to seek Jesus. At the supper table a thought came into my mind that maybe if I would stay from church and have prayer meeting that some good might be done. I accordingly did so, but before I went into prayer meeting I requested Miss Barksdale to meet me in the chapel. She conversed with me upon the subject of religion, and told me precisely what I had anticipated in regard to her case. She told me ever since a certain night, a night I well remember, that she had not felt as much concerned as before. Her load of guilt seems to be removed, but she

is unwilling to believe. She is falling back into indifference. Oh what shall be done for her! Oh she despairs now her case will be awful. My only hope is in prayer. I will now make a resolution to pray for her three times a day, and may the Great God ever our father hear my humble prayer. I have reason to believe that he has heard my prayers in days gone by. I am sure he is just as willing to hear now. I will try it. And now Heavenly Father, give me faith to pray as I might. Give me the right spirit, a humble, meek, and gentle spirit. I would not depend upon myself or anything that I can do, but on thee and thee alone. And oh! For Jesus' sake in answer to my humble prayer convert that precious soul. Amen.

March 16 - Sabbath Evening - Jennie's Diary

God has been very good to me today. It has been a lovely day. Nature seems to pour a peculiar blessing upon the holy Sabbath. We went to church this morning. Heard a very good sermon by Rev. Simpson from then until half past three. I enjoyed myself very much in reading and meditation. We then had prayer meeting. And it was very good. After the meeting was dismissed, several of the dear girls remained in there, and we spent the time from then until tea singing. Several went to church. I remained and we had prayer meeting again, or rather class meeting. The girls spoke very freely— those that did speak. We had a very interesting time. We had to break up early as Mr. Deems wished to go to the chapel for prayers. While at prayers I felt a sweet peace in my soul. It increased. I could hardly contain myself. After prayers I returned to the schoolroom for that seemed like the best place to me. And there I was abundantly blessed. Several of the girls came in there and we had a happy time. But when we were willing to part, the bell rang and we had to go to our rooms. Bless the good Lord for this holy day. Some time ago I asked Ann Slade to pray in prayer meeting. She refused to do it. She has not been happy since. She told me this evening that she had not felt right about it, and she is now willing to do what she can. Oh can it be possible that that dear child shall be such a devoted child of Jesus? Oh my father keep her by thy mighty power. Let her be useful, let her be holy.

John Motley Morehead was governor of North Carolina from 1841-1845 and is buried in Greensboro. The house Jennie refers to is Blandwood Mansion, one of the state's historical sites.

March 17 - Monday Morning - Jennie's Diary

I rose this morning about 5 o'clock. After prayers Miss Hagen and I took a walk round by Gov. Morehead's and through town. It was very pleasant. Everything wears an appearance of cheerfulness. I feel very glad and joyous this morning. How very thankful should I be that Jesus blessed me so much. To him let endless prayer be made. To him let endless praise be given.

March 19 - Jennie's Diary

This morning is rather cloudy and windy. I have just returned from my arithmetic class. I feel much solicitude about my class. The commencement is approaching and it does appear that my classes are making but little improvement. I know not what to do. I am so constituted as to suffer a great deal of trouble. I have very much care upon my mind and it weighs down my spirits sorely. I care for my pupils; they do not make the advancement I wish. I care for the dear converts, fearing lest they should be discouraged. And then [there are] these precious ones who have sought Jesus but have not been converted, and are not ready to give over. What shall be done for them? And there are some who have passed through this session and are yet unmoved. The Lord have mercy upon them. May he establish the young converts, comfort the penitents, and powerfully convert the sinner. I will try to give up all into the hands of God. He can work and none can hinder him. In him is my trust. Were it not that I can stay my soul, my all upon Jesus, I should be lost. Oh how pleasant to have such an all-powerful friend. Lord Jesus, make me humble and faithful and useful.

March 23 - Sabbath Evening - Jennie's Diary

This has been a busy Sabbath. It was so rainy this morning that we did not go to church, but Mr. Deems preached for us. He explained the plan and principles of conversion plainer than I have ever heard before. It was a profitable service. Anything that Mr. Deems says has more influence upon the girls than what any person else says. After dinner he requested all the members of the church and the young converts to meet him in the Chapel. They did so and he arranged them into two classes for the purpose of having class meeting every Sabbath evening. We had prayer meeting at 4 o'clock. The meeting was of much interest. Miss Troy and Miss Thompson [students] prayed for the first time. Miss Tucker [student] prayed—she has prayed but once before. I called on Miss Beall but she refused. Miss Wade [student] was not in. I cannot tell the reason. I fear it was because she did not want to pray but I do not know why. I wonder why it is that I feel so much solicitude for that dear child. I will try to give her up into the hands of God. He is able to make her stand. Father I trust in thee. Keep all those dear converts from the power of the devil. At night Mr. Deems gave us another exhortation. It was very good. The Sabbath is o'er. May I have grace for the duties of the week.

March 24 - Monday Morning - Jennie's Diary
All nature washed by the "late fallen shower" looks so gay and flourishing. We have had prayers and Miss Hagen and I have taken a walk. Somehow or other I feel cast down; I will try to find the cause. I do not want to be gloomy. I have arduous duties this week; I want to be able to meet them well. I want this to be a more profitable week than any past week. I want humble, simple trust in God. Last week I read the *Fireside Friend* by Mrs. Phelps. It is an excellent work. I caught many valuable ideas from it about teaching. I will try to improve upon what I have learned.

March 26 - Wednesday Morning - Jennie's Diary
Oh what a lovely morning. I do not want any unholy thought, any unkind word or glance to pollute the rising day or destroy the good I might do here. I am trying to throw off my care and anxiety. I will try to do the best I can, and all the good I can and leave the event to God. I cannot save others by my care or tears. I give them up to Jesus. He prayed for them; that prayer will prevail. Let this be

a happy day, a day of good works and of cheerfulness. **Wednesday evening.** This has been a pleasant day. I have been enabled to attend my duties with a cheerful heart. I have cast off my care. The young ladies read compositions in the chapel. Some of them were very good. After the school duties were over, I took the girls to walk. I enjoyed the walk very much. It was good to see them so cheerful and happy. They wandered about in the woods and along the branches to gather wild flowers. I sat down on a stump and let them ramble until they were tired, then we came home and found tea waiting for us. So closes this peaceful day.

April 2 - Wednesday Morning - Jennie's Diary

I see it is just a week since I last wrote. I did not think I should have been so careless. Oh how time flies. Today is very rainy. I am trying to prepare an article for the press. I have not attempted such since New Year's day. I prepared two then; and I thought they had never been printed, but I suppose now they have. I was discouraged and concluded to give it up. Mr. Bumpass is going to publish a paper and wishes me to contribute to it. I am making the attempt. A blessing be on my efforts. **Evening.** This has been a busy day. We have had April showers in abundance. I have been reading English history and learned several interesting items. It is now time for bed. I find that regular hours are best for retiring and rising. Miss Barksdale has seemed very affectionate today. Would I could have a saving influence over her. I pray for her conversion.

April 5 - Jennie's Diary

My mind is very much perplexed. I feel very melancholy. I am displeased with myself and all around me. This is not right. Why is it that I have these strange feelings? I am a wonder to myself. I fear I shall never accomplish anything of importance. I feel weary. Tomorrow is the blessed Sabbath. How glad I am. I hope it will bring rest and peace to my troubled mind.

April 12 - Jennie's Diary

Another week has passed rapidly away. This has been a very busy week to me. But I am thankful that I can close its labors so peacefully. I feel much better than I did last Saturday evening. I have heard from home today. All well. Glad to hear it. None of the children are at home but little Jamie. How soon a family may scatter. But a little while ago we were all small children, now most of us grown, and [far] from home. Tomorrow is the blessed Sabbath. Let it be a day of peace.

April 13 - Sabbath Evening - Jennie's Diary

This has been a pleasant day, and profitably spent. It rained so we did not go to church. Mr. Deems preached for us in the chapel. And oh such a sermon as he did preach. "By thy words thou shalt be justified and by thy words thou shalt be condemned." He placed words in quite a new light, such as I had never thought of before. I think I shall profit by that sermon as long as I live. Mr. Deems met his class at two o'clock. The girls were very backward about speaking. Tonight we have no preaching: the young ladies have prayer meeting. The good Lord be with them and bless them. I have lately been reading Owen on forgiveness. It is most excellent. I have derived much benefit from it. I have had my mind enlightened and my faith very sensibly increased. I see very clearly that the great system of Christianity turns upon one small and simple point, and that is, simple faith in Jesus. I see and understand the plan of redemption now more clearly than ever before. The good Lord grant me an increase of child like faith and confidence.

April 20 - Easter Sunday - Jennie's Diary

This is a pleasant day. We went to church this morning. Mr. Simpson preached upon the resurrection. How thankful should I be that I am spared to see another Easter. The resurrection! The hope of the world. Jesus might have lived and died for us, but had he not risen, vain, vain would have been our hope. O the blessed resurrection! I love to think about it. My faith grows stronger, peace flows, my affections rise. How shall I love him enough who loved me first, and loved me so greatly. Faith, oh simple faith in Jesus. I am glad that the life of a Christian is a life of faith. I never felt and saw it so plainly as now. I feel like a new person, my life is a new life. O, faith in Jesus! This evening had class. As Mr. Deems was not present I had to lead. Most of the girls spoke very freely. They expressed their determination to live the life of the Christian. The good Lord bless them. Ann Slade does not seem to enjoy religion. There is something secretly weighing down her spirit. I have an idea what it is. I believe she feels it is her duty to pray in our prayer meeting but she is unwilling to do it. I fully believe that is why she is so cast down. She would not express her feelings this evening. The majority of the converts have acted consistently so far as I know.

April 24 - Thursday Morning - Jennie's Diary
This is a lovely morning. The young leaves are fast spreading a cool shade over the earth. Our examination is approaching rapidly. I feel much anxiety for my classes. I hope this may be a very successful day. I ask for wisdom that I may instruct these girls aright. What responsibilities rest upon a teacher.

April 26 - Sabbath Night 9 O'clock - Jennie's Diary
Oh what a blessed day this has been. Mr. Deems preached for us from Heb. 12.2. "Looking unto Jesus." He preached at 10 and then tonight from the same text. Words cannot express my feelings while I have listened to the simple, yet all-powerful language of Mr. Deems. The simple story of Jesus and the cross, of simple faith in Jesus, when told so plainly and so forcibly, reaches the inmost soul. There is an untold charm in that blessed name. There hangs an unspeakable glory around that consecrated cross. Oh Jesus and the cross! The hope of the Christian, the hope of the world. Earth would be a dark, dreary waste. Thick gloom would gather around the path of mortal man, and all the future would be a dark and dreaded . . . unknown, without any cheering light. Light of the world, Star of Bethlehem, Lamb of God, help me ever to be looking unto thee. Increase my faith day by day. Blessed be God who giveth us the victory through our Lord Jesus Christ. This

evening we had class meeting. The dear girls spoke . . . . Dear Ann seemed very humble . . . . . she said she had strayed from Jesus, but said she was devoted to him. The Lord bless her, and bless all.

Jennie—who worked hard, lived a pure life, and was far beyond her time in intelligence—was tormented by feelings of unworthiness. Looking at her work, the modern eye can see that she was not only worthy, she was exceptional. This April 29, 1851, notation in her diary gives us permission to tell her story.

April 29 - Thursday Morning - Jennie's Diary

I see that I am near through this manuscript. I commenced it in August 1850. It is almost all I have saved of the past. And if it were all, I should feel that my time had not been entirely misspent. Oh what a variety of thoughts and feelings are herein expressed, thoughts which no human being knows. Many and various have been the scenes thus which I have passed. Events are recorded here that will be memorable through my life, events of which I did not even think when I commenced. I look upon this exercise of daily writing as being of much more importance than formerly. I intend to be more faithful in the future. It does me good in many ways. It serves as a repository for many a random thought while the exercise facilitates my powers of expression, giving me an increasing command of language. There is one improvement which I wish to make in my next, that is, make it more personal and real. I want it to be not only a collection of events but of sentiments, and opinions. I would that I could accomplish something of importance. Would that this was an essay or narrative that might go out into the world and be a blessing to many readers. But oh fated manuscript, thou are doomed on account of the weakness of thy authoress to remain in some hidden corner, unknown, until perhaps some person, after the hand that penned thee shall be motionless in the grave, may turn over thy dusty pages curious to learn something of the events of former years. But whatever be thy future destiny, thou art a friend to me now and never will we part.

After this last entry Jennie either did not write in her diary or the pages are missing until October 1852. For sixteen months we have no diary entries. There are very few threads to pull together the happenings during this time. We know that she taught the 1851-1852 year at Greensboro Female College. One clue to her future intentions is revealed in a letter written to her cousin in October. We see here that she wanted to leave teaching for further study but could not, partly because the college needed her, and partly because she didn't have a traveling companion. One can hear a tone in the letter that suggests a longing for travel. In this letter, Jennie is attending the sick, and feeling a bit envious of her brother Aaron and her cousin by the same name, both of whom had moved west to Tennessee to seek adventure. The language here is slightly affected and was difficult to transcribe, probably because it was important to her to impress her cousin with her words.

October 20 - Monday Evening - Jennie's Letter to her First Cousin, Aaron

Greensboro Female College
Mr. A. B. Patterson, My Dear Cousin,

Your kind letter was received this evening and I hasten to acknowledge its reception. It came unexpectedly but it was all the welcome for that.

Indeed Cousin Aaron, if you had studied to send your letter in the most favorable time you could not have done so more effectually. I sit up all last night waiting on the sick, and had worked hard all day in instructing my classes, so that I felt quite tired, and had just took up [sic] a book to try to forget my labor by giving myself to reading, when a bright eyed little girl came loudly into my room with a letter, her own little heart glad at thoughts of the pleasure which I would receive from its perusal. As I was not expecting a letter from any of my friends, I opened it hastily, when whose name should I see but Cousin Aaron. Very, very many thanks to you for this and I indulge the hope that it is but the harbinger of a pleasant and interesting correspondence.

In a world that promises so much to the young and enterprising aspirant, one can not be so foolish as to think that they can live always in the society of their friends. It is natural for the heart full of young life and high hopes to long to see the world, and despite the pain of parting, the adventure[r] quits his friends and goes out into the world to seek his fortune. [It is] hard to be separated from those whom we love, yet a well-timed correspondence will take away half the pain of separation.

And now Cousin Aaron, since we have been permitted to revive that acquaintance which was commenced in early childhood (for I remember many a play we had when we were very little children) may we not continue it by correspondence? It might be so conducted as to be profitable to us both. This may be asking much of your cousin. You will be engaged in active and absorbing duties of life; the cares of business will be upon you, and the demands of your common county. And it will be much indeed if amid all these (obligations) you stop and sit down to write for the gratification of your cousin Jennie in Carolina.

But before I go farther I will say something of my present situation. I am yet at the college. I have not gone north as I expected when you left N.C. There were two reasons for my not going; one was no one was here to fill my place, the other, I had no company. I regretted it very much, but maybe it was all for the best. I am now trying to content myself with my present situation and doing all I can for the good of the class committed to my care. I have some 35 young ladies in my class, quite a formidable host I think for one poor creature to manage. But I generally manage them with little difficulty. Our College is prospering — we have some 75 [boarders] in the institution. O Cousin Aaron, I wish you could see them as they are all dressed up in uniform, ready for church. Your heart would be taken I am sure. If you would make a visit to Greensboro, with much pleasure would I take you through the College, and make you acquainted with our teachers and pupils. And I imagine you would find Greensboro a pleasant little place, altho it does not boast of anything strange or marvelous. One thing we lack—we have no mighty river upon which to launch the steamboat. But if fortune favor, we hope soon to hear the [sounds] of the great horse with his lungs of iron and breath of fire as he [?] to break away and be off like a flash of lightning. We have some enterprising men among us and maybe we will do something some day.

Night — You will see Cousin Aaron, before you are through [reading this] my letter [is written] in a peculiar manner. I write as I have time. You see where I left off last night. Tonight I am to spend watching with a lady who is sick. It will be a long lonesome night to me as I sit up all alone, and I thought I could not pass away the hours better than by writing to you. At least it will keep me awake, altho I fear what I write in opposition to sleep may not be very interesting.

Cousin, when you see my brother Aaron tell him I am set in Greensboro and expect here to remain. If I knew where he was I would write him. Tell him to be sure to write me immediately and I will answer forthwith. My love to him. You must watch over him and not let him move away. Poor boy, he has not mother or sisters to care for him now. When I think of that I am sorrowful but then I know he is among friends. I appreciate his going. I would never say no to a brother of mine when he wishes to travel. Much as I delight to be with them, I know too well to try to deter them from anything that will give them so much pleasure and profit as traveling. I would travel too if I had the opportunity, and I think I shall someday. If I could, I would go out and make myself acquainted with all the rare and beautiful things of this wide world.

The child whom Jennie was tending did not survive. Her name was Sarah Turner. Shortly before this event, Sarah's sister, Juliet (a graduate of Greensboro Female College) had also died. These deaths so moved Jennie that she wrote to Sarah's parents on the loss of both their daughters. Jennie eloquently describes Sarah's last hours.

c. October 1851 - Jennie's Letter to the Turners

Mr. and Mrs. Turner,

I make the following communication to you for the purpose of committing to you a few lines connected with the sickness and peaceful death of your beloved daughters. Tho a stranger to you I have not been a stranger to those whom you have so tenderly loved, and whose memory you now-hold sacred. It is possible that you may have heard them speak of rooming with me last fall.

I am conscious of the deep grief that must rend the bosoms of such fond parents, and as I was with your precious child more, and had her confidence farther than any other member of the faculty, it may be that I can tell you something that will stay up your hearts in this time of trial. I know yours is a bereavement which is irreparable, and beyond the reach of human consolation, but may not a knowledge of the circumstances of her sickness and death be some comfort to you in coming years?

I then of course became well acquainted with them and they with me. Our acquaintance ripened into a deep and lasting friendship. I knew them, dear children, only to love them. When I parted with Juliet at the last commencement I looked upon her as going out to be (the) pride of her parents and a blessing to the world, for she was anxious to go to work. But the will was enough. God loved her and took her home to live with him. He had higher and holier work for her to do.

When I heard of her death, how much I wished that I had been there to smooth her dying pillow, and receive her parting message. But little thought that I should soon be called to all this for her sister.

When Sarah returned this session, she seemed bound to me by a thousand tenderer ties than before. But I was unconscious of the regard she had for me, until her last illness called me to her bedside. She seemed unwilling that I should leave her, and often when I would get up to leave the room she would ask me so imploringly and so affectionately, "Miss Speer, you are not going, are you?"

I tried to stay with her as much as my complicated duties as a teacher would permit. In the earlier part of her sickness, I was not apprehensive of any danger. Yet there seemed to be some undefinable feeling come over me when I thought of her. I often said to myself, "Shall I ever see Sarah going about the College again?"

The ninth day came, the turning point in her sickness, and she was no better. We then became very anxious, and Mr. Deems wrote you.

The last Sabbath she spent on earth I stayed by her while her cousin went to church. She wished me to read and I did so until she fell into a deep sweet sleep. As she seemed so anxious that I should be with her, and that she might, if possible, be more comfortable and quiet, I had her moved into my own room on Tuesday.

When she got in there she seemed much pleased, and asked me to put back the curtain that she might look upon the beautiful woods - the foliage of which was a fit type of her own precious life. She was now quite satisfied wishing only that she and I might be all alone together. And for her care and comfort I kept my room as free from company as possible, except her cousin who attended her as devotedly as if she was her sister.

On Wednesday we had no recitation on account of fire which had broken out that morning, so I stayed with her all day. She had taken a fancy to lie on my bed, which was quite low and convenient, and Wednesday we moved her on it. During the day she evidently got better, and I became hopeful she would recover. The physician came up that evening and seemed pleased with the manner things had been conducted that day. About dark, however, she became restless and I felt a sad presentiment that things were taking a serious turn. We sent for Mrs. Adams, a lady who had watched her very attentively the night before. She came and Mrs. Doub [wife of William Doub, professor of mathematics] with her. About midnight she grew worse and expressed a wish to see the Dr. He was sent for.

Mrs. Blake [stewardess for the college] was sitting on the side of her bed and she turned to her and said "Aunt Blake, do you think there is any danger of my dying?" Mrs. Blake replied, "My dear, we think you very ill." She then asked Mrs. Blake to pray for her, and turning to me said, "Miss Speer, do not forget to pray for me."

She then remained some time in deep and earnest prayer. A smile would occasionally play over her face, and then she would be deeply engaged.

She continued about the same during the morning. On seeing me making my toilet, she supposed I was going somewhere; she said so sweetly, "Miss Speer, you must not stay long." And when I told her I would not leave her, she became quiet. She called my name again and again during the morning, and in such accents as could fall only from the lips of one so near heaven as she was.

About noon she was resting very peacefully and Mrs. Doub urged me to go lay [sic] down. I went into another room and did so. In a short time someone came and said Sarah was dying. I hastened to her bed when I found her all in an ecstasy of joy. Oh it did not seem like Sarah. Her countenance was all lit up with joy, and she was exhorting her companions to meet her in heaven. I went to her, she reached out her hand, and said, "Oh Miss Speer, meet me in heaven." I once thought I could never die, but now I believe it is the best thing in the world. I said, "Sarah, what shall I tell your father and mother; I want to write
them, what shall I tell them?"

"Tell them," said she, "that I am happy."

I remained with her only a little while, for my feelings so overcame me that I was forced to leave the room. I never saw her move. Yes, that dear child, whom I had watched while sick, I now had to leave. My nervous system became so much excited that it was impossible for me to go where she was. That is the only thing that grieves me now, that I could not be with her in her last moments, and follow her to the grave. They tell me, however, that she died peacefully. Her cousin will be able to tell you what occurred from the time I left her until she died. She died that night . . . if an end so peaceful, so full of joy, can be called death. As the weeping of friends died away upon her ears, she woke to all the melodies of heaven. They tell me that a sweet smile rested upon her in death.

I longed very much to see her as she lay in all the beauty and stillness of death, but I could not. It was too much for me. I then thought I could go and look at her narrow home, but again my wounded feelings came over me like a flood, and I was denied even that. But friends many and kind gathered around her and did all that human aid could do.

And now, my dear Mr. and Mrs. Turner, I freely mingle my tears with yours. I love to weep for I do not grieve, but I weep because I loved her. O it were cruel to wish a being so pure, so gentle, back to this sinful world.

She left the world before its bitter cares came heavily upon her, and she shall know no more trouble.

It was a blessed privilege to be by her dying bed, and since she is gone death seems to me deprived of half its terrors. It seems more like a faithful household servant which a kind parent sends after an absent child than like a king of terrors. If Sarah died, then it were a blessed thing to die. Let me die rather than live.

Surely
— they who saw her look in death
   no more can fear to die.

You ask, why should her death affect me so, I ask in turn, how could it be otherwise than affected? She was dear to me in a threefold sense. She had been my everyday companion, for she had roomed with me. She had been my pupil. And lastly, and most dearly, she was a member of my class. Often have I met her in the classroom. She loved class meetings, for she was never absent. In looking over my class room, I find but one absent [absence] against her until she was sick. When the class meeting bell would ring, I always knew Sarah would be there. O is it possible that I have had the training of one soul for heaven.

While I look over my class roll, against many names I see written "removed." When I come to the names of your two precious daughters, I see the same. But when to heaven. . . .

Although Ann didn't know at the time what her sister was enduring with the loss of Sarah, she penned a beautiful essay on the death of a child.

c. 1850-1853 - Untitled - Ann's Essay

It must be sweet in childhood to give back the spirit to its God; ere sin pollutes the angelic mind of happy infancy, care ruffles the unclouded brow, and tears of grief dim the radiant lustre of the eye. Before the unsuspecting heart of youth is lured from paths of virtue and happiness by the enchanting song of the siren; before tasting of the pleasures of the world; it must be delightful thus to return the immortal soul to its great Giver, to yield it up to heaven untouched by sin; while the innocence and loveliness of the soul are beaming in that eye. The child dreads not the cold damp tomb. It fears not the icy embrace of death. It only sees bright angels waiting to convey its little spirit over the cold Jordan of death and usher it into a blessed eternity. The tear of joy trembles on its eyelid like the gentle dewdrop on the blushing rose.

1852

We have no diary entries from Jennie until the fall of 1852. Our only document from her is the letter which opens the year. In it we can conjecture that she has been sick. The second document, an essay written by Ann, can be loosely dated because we know Jennie departed Greensboro Female College in the fall of 1852 to study at Mount Holyoke Female Seminary in South Hadley, Massachusetts. A letter to her mother also reveals that she was home on July 4, and an essay by Ann reveals that Jennie spent a few weeks at home before she traveled north. Remembering Jennie's last letter to her cousin Aaron, we see that she didn't think that she could travel to Massachusetts alone. She clearly changed her mind. This move must have been a major step for her. She was the only woman from North Carolina to attend

Mount Holyoke College before the Civil War. Only fourteen "tarheels" attended the institution during the nineteenth century; all but two during the 1880s and 1890s. We pick up the story here. Ann is eighteen. Jennie is twenty-four.

March 23 - Tuesday Evening - Jennie's Letter to her Mother, Elizabeth

Greensboro College
My Mother,
    According to promise I take my pen to write you. My letter to my little brothers I fear will make you feel some uneasiness until you hear from me again. I should not have written last week had it not been such a long time since I wrote home.
    I am happy to say that I am fast regaining my former health. I have been able to attend my classes yesterday and today.
    Last evening Mr. Deems took Miss Sherbrooke [colleague] and me to ride. It was quite a treat to get out to breathe fresh air in the open country. It is the second time that I have had the pleasure of riding out since I have been here. I have sometimes almost thought that others should go out and not I. We rode out to the Poor House. We saw some pitiful objects there. Never may a word of complaint escape my lips while I am so highly favored. I think it did me much good to go out there.
    Mrs. Howlett, a lady in town, died last night. She has left several little children. A distressing case. Mr. Deems preaches her funeral tomorrow. Had it been my mother, O what bitterness of soul!
    I will close for the evening. You shall hear from me during the week.

March 24 - Wednesday Evening - Jennie's Letter to her Mother Continues

    Another day, Mother, has gone, with its cares and pleasures. And I am now sitting at my table trying to write. Prayers are over [and] the young ladies are in their rooms quietly at their studies. Miss

Lyman [colleague] has her class in the chapel singing. Miss Sherbrooke is down in the parlor taking a music lesson of Mr. Kern. The other teachers are variously employed. Nothing very uncommon has occurred during the day. I feel, Mother, it would be a great treat to me if I could sit down by your side tonight and spend a few hours in talking. I do not feel in the spirit of writing. But I think I could talk if I were with you.

I would love to be a little child again, when I had the exclusive right of sitting on my mother's knee, and of climbing up in my papa's lap, putting my arms around his neck and my head on his bosom and going to sleep. Then this seemed like a wonderful world to me. Everything was new and beautiful. The days were long and sunny then, but I did not get tired. I was free from care. But as I grew a little older, I recollect that I was much afflicted. Even childhood had its sorrows. Then followed years of youthful aspirations and fancyings [and] a longing after books and the schoolroom and also to be a successful writer. Mother, I love to think of those times but I will not say more about them at present as I so often revert to them.

I am a woman now, and much of the tinsel that was upon the world has worn off. I have learned to be deceived, to be disappointed, to suffer, and occasionally to be glad. I have had friends and foes. But I have learned to look upon this life as but the beginning of existence, and all things and events here as but the beginnings of a chain of circumstances that will go on through all eternity. This consideration has helped me to reconcile the confusion in which I see men and actions, and accounts for the incompleteness of this apparently unmeaning life.

I love that saying of Bishop Butler that our condition hereafter may be as far above our present, as our present is above our condition before our birth. I have been thinking much of late. I have lived within myself more since I was sick than for sometime before. I have come to the conclusion that one of my great deficiencies is a want of faith in myself. But Mother, I do so utterly abhor the idea of being thought self-conceited, or wise in my own eyes, that I am doubtful whether I shall ever indulge any better opinion of myself than now.

I have a notion of making some desperate venture some of these days and see what will be the result. I can but fail as thousands have done before. Yet I believe were I to go at it with a brave heart I could succeed.

March 26 - Thursday Morning - Jennie's Letter to her Mother Continues

Mother, just as I was in the midst of my flourishing last night Miss Sherbrooke came in with three letters for me (one from you, one [from] brother Aaron, and one from Miss Cutherell [?]) and of course there was no more writing to be done. Miss Sherbrooke got one also, and when we read them, the remainder of the evening had to be spent in talking.

Your letter was a blessed treat to me. It was unlooked for, but just the more welcome. Mother, your letter makes me feel anxious about you. I fear your cold will be serious. It was only yesterday that I was thinking of matters and things in general, of my being here, and the thought came into mind that some family affliction might call me home. I will trust in Providence all will be right.

This is a beautiful day, so much so that the young ladies petitioned for holiday and got it. We are to go out in the country and spend the day. I will tell you about it when we return.

Thursday evening. Well Mother, we have had a splendid ramble today. We spent the day in the woods. Got home this evening about 4 o'clock. I am very tired in body but greatly refreshed in spirits. We went out to the railroad [and] saw the hands at work. We purchased some oranges, picnic crackers, and candy, and had quite a little feast. Upon the whole we had a very pleasant time.

The last mail brought me a letter from Brother Aaron. He is giving me a history of his journey out to Tennessee. I want so much to see him. I hope he is doing well.

I am glad to hear from all the neighbors. Good luck to cousin A&C [first cousin, Aquilla Spencer Speer, and Caroline Reece were to be married]. You speak Mother of my coming home. It will be a trial to me to stay away, and yet I think it very doubtful. I shall tell you more definitely on my next [letter]. I shall write again soon. I have some thoughts in my mind which I am revolving, and will be able to tell you in my next [letter]. Will papa please send me another box of pills? Miss Sherbrooke has found relief from them and I let her have one of my boxes. He will keep account of these things and I will settle with him.

How is Mrs. Crummel doing? Remember me to her affectionately. I am glad to hear from the kind neighbors.

July or August - Ann's Essay

On the Departure of My Sister for Mount Holyoke

Adieu my sister, may the richest blessings of divine Providence rest on thee during thy absence. But a few short weeks we felt thy charming presence. All was sunshine and happiness beneath our roof while you remained, but now we no more see thy radiant smile and gloom pervades our hearts.

Thou camest to us free and happy as the morning lark, but departed as suddenly as the meteor, as the visions of night vanish, and left us to mourn in silence. Life assumes its usual monotony and we sit down with each word carefully stored away in our memory. But thou goest to search into the hidden treasures of science, to store thy mind with pure knowledge, mayest thou be successful.

Strangers will receive thy plaintive smile; strangers will administer to thy wants, yet in thy heart will be stamped the image of thy childhood home and early friends.

The cold hearted world may smile at thee, yet in this heart shall thy image be indelibly stamped. Each pensive thought shall flit to thee, and whilst thou art steaming away through crowded cities and silent forests to thy station in the North, one heart in the "Sunny South" shall remain thinking of thee. Thy home shall yet be in our quiet retreat, apart from the vices and snares of the world. Time, renew thy peace. Thy firm and steady steps will soon bring back our lost treasure. How heartily shall be the welcome! How each endearing thought flies to thee, when, reunited to our little family circle, we shall while away the pleasant evenings. But should any evil befall us or thee, then our united prayers shall ascend the hill of Heaven in each other's behalf. Should death steal one away from our already diminished circle, then each silent tear, each pent up sigh, must find a refuge in the bosom of Heaven.

Jennie arrives at Mount Holyoke on September 29. Her first entry is a description of the school, its methods of teaching, the surroundings, and details of women's education in the South Hadley area in the mid-nineteenth century. Only a few years earlier, Emily Dickinson was a student at Mount Holyoke.

c. September - Jennie's Diary
Mount Holyoke Female Seminary

The Seminary is located in South Hadley, Mass. It is easy of access, being near the Connecticut River Railroad. The situation is pleasant, tho very retired, as the town is small. Prospect Hill on the East is a favorite resort of the young ladies in their walks. From different parts of the building, good views may be had of Mount Tom, Holyoke and C [?]. The Seminary is only a few nods from the Church, a great advantage in stormy weather. The grounds around the building are but little improved, yet are quite pleasant for evening walks. Some shrubbery and trees have been planted. The monument to Miss Mary Lyon, the founder of the institution, is east of the Seminary. From the windows of the back room a good view is had of it.

Buildings
The main building is [?] feet long, and [?] feet wide, five stories high. The first or Basement is divided into Dining and Domestic Halls. The Domestic Hall is devoted entirely to culinary purposes. Besides these two Halls, there are several storerooms. Upon the first story are three parlors, a reading and library room, a lecture room, one Cabinet room, and the Seminary Hall. The second story has a chemical room and Hall and several rooms for young ladies to occupy. The third and fourth stories are entirely occupied by the young ladies. There is a double piazza running the whole length of the building in front. There are two wings, one of which is occupied by the pupils, the other is

taken up in wood rooms; that is, rooms containing the [fire]wood to be used by the pupils. The wood room belonging to a room [dorm room] is numbered with the same number as the room, so that no confusion is made in getting wood. The building is covered with slate, and well secured by lightning rods.

Furnishing Rooms

The Seminary furnishes each room with a bedstead, bed, a stove, table, chairs for each occupant, wash stand, bowl and pitcher and a mirror. Each room has a bookcase with five shelves, a case of six drawers, and a closet with some half dozen shelves. The closet is used as a wardrobe. The young ladies furnish window curtains, clothing for their bed, toilets, and many other little conveniences which Yankee ingenuity may invent. The cost to the Seminary of furnishing the rooms is about [?] for each room. The rooms are free from rent. Most of the rooms are lighted by but one window, some have two. The rooms are small, designed for but two occupants. But the crowded state of the Seminary compels them to put three and sometimes more in a room.

Literary Department

The Seminary year is divided into three Terms, the first Term into two series, the other Terms embrace one series each. Such studies are generally taken up as can be completed in one or two series, and then new studies given. At the close of the week, the recitations for the week are reviewed. After the study is finished up, a general review is taken. At the close of the Spring Term about two weeks are spent in reviews of all the studies gone over in the year, and then the classes are examined. At the close of the year the pupils are examined upon the studies pursued during the Summer Term. The whole [process?] is finished up by the anniversary and graduation of the senior class. At the head of the Institution is a Principal (at present Miss Mary W. Chapin) aided by an Assistant Principal and some twelve or fifteen teachers. The Principal and Assistant Principal are chosen by the Trustees; the Teachers are chosen and their salary fixed by the Principal. When first employed they receive $3.00 per week, after about a year's service they receive $4.00 per week. They are generally employed in attending recitations about [?] hours per day; they also have the care of some part of the Domestic affairs. The classes are small, seldom more than fifteen in a class. Some recitations are one half hour long, some an hour. The pupils are required to spend an hour and a half upon such lessons as are recited in half an hour; and two hours or two and a half upon recitations of an hour. Each recitation is marked. The figures, 1, 2,3, and 4 are used, 4 being the highest. A faithful record of these recitations is kept in the Institution, so that the Teachers know at a glance the standing of any young lady. Whenever applications are made for Teachers, the Principal may know whom to select by referring to this record. No reports are given so that a pupil may know how she is marked. Some recitations are conducted by questions, some by Topics. History and Paleontology are studied by topics. In Evidences the arguments are taken up; in Mental Science, the captions at the head of the section. Mathematics is studied as usual. Milton's *Paradise Lost* is read and the Classical and Scriptural allusions given. The pupils do not make any communications in the class by word or sign. If one fails on a question or topic, those prepared to recite raise hands and the teacher calls upon some one. Composition is attended to very strictly. Four hours every Saturday are spent in writing. The compositions are given in over a fortnight, as each pupil is required to spend eight hours on a composition. At the end of every year each pupil is required to rewrite the best composition she has written during the year, and leave [it] at the Seminary. From these, selections made to be read at Anniversary. Considerable attention is given to drawing. Lessons are given without any additional charges. All who can sing are required to attend a singing class one half hour three times a week. Those who have taken lessons on the piano can practice a few hours each week. The whole School is arranged into small classes [which] practice Calisthenics fifteen minutes every day. This is both a healthy and pleasing exercise, giving ease and grace of movement, and cheerfulness of mind. The rules of the institution are strict, yet they are generally observed with much faithfulness.

Domestic Department

The Basement is divided into two large rooms, one Dining, one Domestic Hall. The Dining Room is of sufficient size to accommodate about three hundred. The Domestic Hall is furnished with all conveniences for culinary purposes. The domestic work is done entirely by the pupils, and is so divided out as to be carried on in perfect order, and but few ever think their portion is too hard. The different kinds of work are arranged in Circles - thus there is the breakfast circle, dinner circle, blue crockery circle, white crockery circle, baking circle, glass circle, knife circle, silver circle. Some trusty one is appointed leader, her duty being to see that all things go on right. On most circles the required time for working is one hour and ten minutes. If the work is hard, only an hour, and sometimes 50 minutes. The domestic work is changed twice a year. One going through the whole course of study will generally go thro a whole course of domestic work if her health will permit. On Wednesday there is no study. The house is put in nice order, and wardrobe attended to. At the expiration of the first four weeks, rooms and roommates are changed, and then at the beginning of the Summer Term. The pupils are required to keep their rooms in perfect order, ready for the inspection of a teacher. The pupils do their own washing. The School is divided into two circles - one washes Monday morning, the other Tuesday morning during the winter and spring terms; and Monday evening, and Tuesday evening during the Summer Term. The conveniences for washing are such as to make it more an amusement than labor. Ironing is done on Saturday morning; all the domestic arrangements are such as to make no clashing between work and study. The fare in general is good. The same dish is not served twice in succession. No tea or coffee is used except for the sick, and for visitors. Pure cold water all times. The bread used is all weighed. For flour and butter the Institution pays yearly about $2500.

It is one month later and Jennie is in despair. To the best of our deductions, she took an entrance exam and did not pass. She was also ill and the two of these events combined may have effected a decision on behalf of the seminary to expel her until a resolution was made about her return to the institution. It would seem that now she is staying temporarily in a town called Sunderland with a Mr. and Mrs. Graves awaiting the seminary's decision. (Mrs. Graves was on the faculty.) Jennie believes that she has sinned because pride told her she should try to better herself in a northern school. This diary entry points out her deep sense of insecurity in the midst of the northern education system. She is feeling very much alone.

October 21 - Sunderland - Jennie's Diary

The past few days have been to me days of intense anxiety. My poor brain has been racked with a whirl of thoughts almost to madness. Sleepless nights and anxious days have been appointed me, and all from my own conduct. A kind Providence gently opened the way for my coming north. The 29 Sept I entered Mt. Holyoke Female Seminary. Feebleness of health, and disappointment in examination affected me so powerfully that I nearly decided to leave the Institution. Since then I have been unhappy indeed. A few days ago I wrote for permission to return, as yet I have received no answer. I wait with anxiety and trembling the result. Though I have done so wrong, yet I trust a merciful Providence will still be compassionate and suffer me to return. Oh that one rash act! How many tears, how many heartaches it has caused me. And it was all from pride. I was too proud to acknowledge how ignorant I was. Poor human nature! Did not God know it all and shall I be more afraid for man to know it. Bitter as the cup has been, yet may it be a blessing finally. It places before me, in a clearer light, my proneness to err. Hereafter may I be more distrustful of myself, more trustful in God. And now I remember the thought of leaving the institution employed during the sacred hours of the Sabbath. Should I not have known it was wicked and would end in no good? In this there were three items I wish always to remember . . .I will write them down and may they be engraved upon my heart.

1. I was influenced by pride.
2. I made and matured my plans without consulting my superiors, who were able to advise me
3. And that [I made my decision] upon the Sabbath day.

I know not how the matter may turn, but I pray my Heavenly Father that I may be permitted to return to that Institution [Greensboro Female College]. A strange mysterious something binds me there; my stay there must in some way be connected with the future. Oh if it is not too late. Almighty and most merciful Father I beseech thee, grant [that] the letter I have this morning mailed, may secure, through thy mercy, my return. Favorable disposes the hearts of those teachers that they may grant me permission. Then shall I be more holy, more devoted to thee, and better prepared for doing thy will on earth. And my spirit shall be more perfect and complete, and better fitted for the employments of the Spirit Land. And to God the Father, Son and Holy Spirit shall be all praises now and evermore, amen.

Evening. I have just returned from evening prayer meeting. A pleasant meeting it was. I hope to profit by it. After meeting went to the office hoping to find a letter that would give me information if I could return to the Seminary, but none came. So I am yet in suspense. But I hope maybe tomorrow may bring some intelligence. I fear and yet I hope. I have sinned but may my Heavenly Father forgive. I must commit all to him, though I have erred yet I have none else to whom I can go. Father help. This is a delightful evening. This quiet village is indeed lovely.

Jennie's disposition changes dramatically when she receives a letter that the school will accept her.

October 22 - Friday Afternoon - Jennie's Diary

What changes in our thoughts and feelings a few hours may make! I concluded that it is best for me to return home. I feel that I am able to undergo the duties of a [teacher?]. I want to do right. God does not require us to unfit ourselves for the duties of life. Had I health it would be a lasting blessing to me to spend a year at the Seminary. I feel it is better for me to go home. This morning I felt as if I was almost distracted; I was indeed quite bewildered. This evening I feel better. I have taken two walks which have done me much good. Oh New England is a delightful place. I could live here for life. I do indeed regret to leave it. The beautiful scenery, fertile meadows and neat villages cannot fail to attract and interest the traveler. I have never seen grass grow as in New England. Just now Mr. Graves came in and said he had one apple tree which had borne thirty bushels of apples. Mrs. Graves and I went out to see it, and a fine sight it was. Such beautiful apples! We walked over the orchard and saw much fine fruit, gathered a basket full and returned. Rich autumn is here with all its delights. Of all seasons I think I enjoy it most. Its rich and varied foliage, its abundant harvests of grain and fruit are causes of pleasing and grateful [blessings]. I must say that goodness and mercy have followed me. Last evening I received two letters, one from Miss Chapin [principal of Mount Holyoke] saying I could return to the Seminary and one from Mr. Deems saying what he thought [I could return to Greensboro]. To my Heavenly Father I give praise for his abundant mercy. I now go back [to Greensboro] in a few days, and I hope my return may not be a grief but a comfort to those dear teachers. I would not willingly give them one pain or anxious thought. I do feel thankful for all these mercies. May this experience be of lasting benefit to me. I feel happier now in view of returning than for many long days. Oh the mental anguish I have endured. But I trust I have been enabled to do right. Thanks be unto my kind Creator.

October 23 - Saturday Night - Jennie's Diary

What strange beings we are. I am studying my own self as much as I can, and how little I know of myself. I find I am so ready to repine because I am not as other people are, so gifted, or so favored of fortune. Had it been best, I should have been the daughter of a prince instead of a farmer. All is right. But I feel this complaining spirit rising up most when I look at the educational advantages of very many so far above my own. This is also wrong. If I have improved the advantages I have had to their utmost, then I am blameless. Just now my thoughts were turned to this subject by some passing circumstance. For instance, a letter I received this afternoon was written by Miss Gilbert, a teacher in Mt. Holyoke Female Seminary. A most accomplished young lady. She has the honor of graduating there. She is yet young, not so old as I. And so far my superior.

Thinking of this I have been tempted to repine. But why? Dare I? Did not the same Creator call us both into existence, and could he not have made me her equal had it been best?! Oh that this tormenting disposition might be overcome. I want to be contented to do just as Providence helps me to do. And then, I should remember how many thousands are not even where I am. How many grateful praises would go up to heaven tonight if many young ladies had <u>my</u> advantages? May I never more complain. Oh it is surely wicked. May I have health and strength for the duties before me.

October 24 - Sabbath Morning - Jennie's Diary

A most delightful Sabbath morning is given to us to improve. My mind is more at rest than for several Sabbaths, and I hope to spend it in a more profitable manner. I want to lay aside all thoughts which have so rocked.... weeks, and <u>rest</u> this holy Sabbath. This day how many congregations will assemble to worship God? All over this great land will people meet, and ministers stand up to proclaim theGospel. The same Gospel is preached North and South, the same prayers made to the same God, and why should we not be one people in heart? I have never felt so sensibly that we are one great family as since I came North. When I pray God to help this whole nation and all the world, I know there are others hundreds of miles away who pray for the same thing. This morning I would pray that the blessings of a kind Providence might rest upon those whom I love, who are now separated from me. My little class that I had charge of in college [Greensboro] have met this morning. How often do I think of them. Oh that I may be with them once more. I believe I shall. He in whom I put my trust is able to keep me, and restore me to them again. I do want so much to spend this beautiful Sabbath in such a way that my soul shall be abundantly blessed. Help me, my Heavenly Father. **Sabbath evening.** These sacred hours are fast coming to a close. The sun is hastening to his home in the west. What a blessed Sabbath it has been. A day of rest, a laying aside of cares and anxious thoughts. I know not when I have enjoyed a Sabbath so much as the present. It has been so quiet and so peaceful. A lovelier day in autumn time, nature never gave to man. Not a cloud has been seen. The sky has been that pure transparent hue so peculiar to autumn. But lovely day, thou wilt soon be gone. I attended the Presbyterian Church this morning and this afternoon. The sermons were very good. The sermon this morning was written. This afternoon, extemporaneous. I understand the ministers of New England are preaching more frequently without writing their sermons. I believe more good would be effected if they adapt that course principally, but maybe my opinion is founded on prejudice of education. I have spent a part of this Sabbath in memorizing scripture. It has done me much good, and I regret I have not practiced it before. It so much helps to fix the wandering thoughts, which are so prone to wander to the ends of the earth. I intend recommending it to my sister and brother. As I was studying this afternoon a new idea came up, that this committing of passages of Scripture would be not only beneficial in this world, but a source of much pleasure in the Spirit World. As we live on in that world and one scene after another comes up, and we go on from one degree of knowledge and joy to another, how comforting and strengthening it may be to remember and compare the words of the Bible with the scenes of Eternity. Strange it is that we do not value this Book of Books more. I want to study it more, to love it more. And now that the Sabbath is passing away this week, with its cares and anxieties, is near. I know not what may be, but I will put my trust in my Heavenly Father. He will order all things for the best. It may be a week of trial, may I have faith and patience; it may be a week of prosperity, may I have faith and humility and watchfulness. Whatever befalls me may I have faith in God. If nothing happens I shall go to the Seminary. May my going be a blessing, not a curse. May I be a comfort to those teachers, not a sorrow. I thank my Heavenly Father that I may have the privilege of returning. May I improve it.

Daniel Webster, American statesman and leader in the Whig party, died On October 24 at his home in Marshfield, Mass.

October 25 - Monday Night - Jennie's Diary
Today we have heard the sad intelligence of Honorable Daniel Webster's death. Again is our Nation called to mourn the loss of her

ablest statesman. Only last June we wept for Henry Clay, and now
Mr. Webster has fallen. He died yesterday morning about three
o'clock.

October 26 - Tuesday - Jennie's Diary
Returned to the Seminary. How thankful to be here again. Ungrateful
as I have been, yet the Lord has kept my feet from falling. What shall
I render unto the Lord for all his mercies unto me? May I be more
humble, more faithful.

*Jennie's essays will be wound into plot as they help to tell the
story. Remembering her obsession with death, it is little wonder
that this November essay is on that topic. After returning to the
seminary, this was one of her first works, and is even labeled
"No. 1." In this piece Jennie talks about the deaths of five people:
A young man, who will have to remain anonymous, Sarah Turner,
mentioned earlier in the 1851 documents, her sister Sylvia, her
grandmother Elizabeth, and herself.*

November 9 - Jennie's Essay

No. 1
The Time to Die
N. J. Speer
Mt. Holyoke Female Seminary
Nov. 9, 1852

The Time to Die

"Leaves have their time to fall,
And flowers to wither at the North wind's blast,
And stars to set — but all,
Thou hast all seasons for thine, oh! Death."

Most persons look upon Death as something terrible, as a grim monster, ready to devour them; as a bitter enemy. With Death they connect ideas of fearful gloom and darkness, hence that shrinking back from speaking or thinking of Death; that universal dread of dying.

But not so would I think of it. Spiritual death is terrible. "Oh! What horrors hang around it." But temporal death is not.

It may be thought strange to select this as a subject for school composition. I would think of Death only as a faithful friend and messenger, sent by a kind Father to take home an absent child; as the ending of care and labor, and the beginning of joy and rest. It frees the Spirit, holding only the body in bondage. It closes the visionary, and ushers in the real. But when will Death come? When is the time to die?

Oh Death

> "We know when moons shall wane.
> When summer birds from far shall cross the sea,
> When autumn hues shall tinge the golden grain.
> But who shall tell us when to look for thee?"

I knew a young man, the pride and joy of his friends. He had just entered upon the duties of his professional life. To superior talents and high cultivation, he had early added a pure, firm and ardent piety. His voice was heard in the house of prayer. A disease ravaged the country. He was by the bed of pain day and night. His devotion to those who had called for his aid was unabating. Weary and worn, he still was faithful. But his work was soon done. The disease which had often yielded to his skill now fastened upon him. He sank rapidly. The long tried skill of experienced physicians could not check that raging fever. He died. But,

> "The chamber where the good man meets his fate,
> Is privilege beyond the common walk of life?
> Quite on the verge of heaven."

It was autumn, rich, calm, lovely autumn. The song of the summer songsters was hushed. The hum of insect tribes, busy in preparing their winter stores, was dying away. Forests were clothed in their richest hues. But those fading leaves, most beautiful in decay, were the fit emblems of one at whose bedside I had watched many nights. For ere they were scattered by winter winds, she [Sarah Turner] rested in the grave, and her spirit dwelt with "the pure in heart," in the "land that no mortal may know." She was far from home and parents. Disease came. She laid aside her studies. Teachers and classmates gathered around her bed. She gave us a message to her distant parents, and then went to rest so calmly,

> "Sure they who saw her look in death,
> No more will fear to die."

But Death hath been still nearer and there was nothing to make me dread him. I had a little sister [Sylvia] whom I loved as only a sister can. But she was too frail, too spirit-like, to stay long in this world of pain. From gathering the flowers of her fifth summer she came in, and lay down upon her little couch and quietly fell asleep. And now I like to think of her as a bright little angel, with him who said, "suffer the little children to come unto me." Death came the second time, and took an aged grandmother [Elizabeth] to the home of the good. But in all this he did his work so gently she was not fearful.

A trying time is yet to come. I too must die. Could I choose for myself I would do my work quickly and go home. Not that I am tired of this world. It is a beautiful world, were it not for the sad work that sin hath made. I love its canopy of blue, its carpet of green — its mountains and quiet valleys — its forests, fruits and flowers — its merry sunshine, and deep, still night. They speak to me of a Father who loves me. I can bear its pain — it will make me better. But I would die early that I may be with God.

At the close of a quiet day in autumn, I would come from the schoolroom, in which I had been engaged in the instructions of loved pupils. I would have these instructions be such as should live and do good when I was not. With a few friends I would spend the hours of closing day talking of God, eternal life and the Spirit Land, and then lay me down and die. I would have those whom I loved, in whose instruction I spent the last hours of my life go with me to the quiet grave.

The only monument I would ask, the simple white rose planted by the hands of affectionate pupils. My only requiem, the song of summer birds.

Miles away, Ann is a student at Jonesville Female Academy. She, too, is writing about death. While Jennie is twenty-four and is refining her writing and thinking skills, Ann is just beginning to explore the mysteries of life and death. She, like her sister, seems to see death as a welcome relief from earth's troubles. Her work reflects deep thinking on the subject, but it is not yet refined in its skill. The "child" in the middle of the essay is probably lying in his mother's arms as she dies.

c. 1851-1853 - Ann's Essay

The Light of the Past, the Bliss of the Present, and Hopes of the Future

There is but one grand certainty and one grand uncertainty on earth - the uncertainty of life and the certainty of death. It is solemn to quietly put aside the veil of mortality and life down in the tomb. It is solemn to watch the last fleeting breath of the beloved; to see the child folded by the icy arms of the mother to the cold motionless bosom and receive the last farewell kiss; to receive the last blessing of the father as he departs to the Spirit Land. But when the grave receives its sorrow, [it] alone rends the bosom of the desolated. But death cannot be so gloomy. There is not always a cold piercing frown on his brow. Sometimes he is an Angel of mercy. Life without death would be insupportable in this cold-hearted world. It must be sweet to leave this life and go to our beautiful home in the Spirit Land.

It is obvious that both girls were devoted to their families. Countless diary entries, essays and poems illuminate an unfailing love for their mother and father. This essay was written by Ann upon the arrival of her father's forty-eighth birthday; his birthday was on November 11.

c. November 11 - Ann's Essay

On My Father's Birth Day

The day dawns and we hail the first glimmer of light that gently flickers in the east. The refreshing air slightly disturbs the green trees, and the glittering dewdrop sleeping on the blushing rose sparkles in the sunbeams. We bless this day, Papa, for it is thy natal day. Forty-eight years have rolled away and left thy step buoyant. The winters of life have slightly sprinkled thy luxuriant locks with snow. I love the deep brown clusters that adorn thy noble brow. I love to twine them around my fingers. I love to gaze into the clear depths of those eyes expressively beaming. Care, that crushes some hearts, has left thine glowing with love. Time, that dims the eye, o'er clouds the countenance, has stamped a clear, calm dignity on thy brow, has left the piercing gaze of those eyes unharmed. Disease has not bowed thy manly figure. O how I love to gaze upon the beaming countenance of my father. May many long years, replete with the richest blessings of heaven, ever be thine, dearest Papa.

In December Jennie writes her third essay, describing a crisis of the spirit that would, by modern standards, resemble Christian existentialism. This work reflects a significant improvement in her writing and critical thinking.

December 11 - Jennie's Essay

No. 3.
A Soliloquy
Mt. Holyoke Seminary
Dec. 11, 1852

A Soliloquy

"Silence how dead, and darkness how profound,
Nor eye, nor listening ear an object finds -
Creation sleeps, 'tis as the general pulse
Of life stood still, and nature made a pause,
An awful pause, prophetic of her end."

- Young

Night has thrown her sable mantle over all the earth, and the hum of a busy world is hushed in the stillness of darkness. The winds, low moaning, stir the aspen leaf, and muffled is the sound of the waterfall. Man, beast and bird are gone to rest. Mountains, rearing their hoary heads as of old, stand the undaunted sentinels of the solemn night. There is no sound, the moon is gone, and a thousand stars their vigils keep. And I am alone, alone. Fit hour this for meditation, for night doth give no inspiration to the spirit that fair would leave these scenes of sorrow, and find a resting-place in some far off happy land.

What a strange world is this? Mystery is written on all things around me. Whence came this world? He who made it must have wished its inhabitants to be happy. But surely some sad catastrophe has fallen upon it, for it seems the wreck of something grand and beautiful. A master hand must have hung those worlds on high, piled up towering mountains, and spread these valleys abroad.

Life is a mystery, a scene chaotic. It is made up of plans projected but never completed, of work half-finished. Nothing is definite, and things remain not as they were. The days are no more long and sunny and I have learned that earth hath many sorrows. Friends in whom I fondly confided yesterday, today pass me all unnoticed. The playmates of my childhood hours are not. They died, but whither went they? Live they not in some far off land in a brighter and purer world?

A curtain hangs before me, I turn to myself, but all is mystery. I live, but what is it to live? I seem to be encased in this body, and struggle to get free. A twofold being am I. I reason with myself as with a friend. This body cannot be myself, for I suffer and enjoy independent of it. It is wonderfully made, but more mysterious is my real self, my mind, my Spirit-self. Shut up in this body, how little access has it to the outer world? Yet how busy is this Spirit, as if its very confinement made it more active. Who shall tell of the Spirit's mysteries, or solve the problem of life!

I think, and thinking is living. Thoughts are wings to the tireless Spirit. More rapidly than lightning's speed, I go from world to world, stand on the most distance verge of Creation, and so quickly return to my prison house. But why return? O happy one! Who could thus go on exploring the deep, the hidden and unknown? What mysterious chain binds me to this body, and will not let me go?

Thoughts are never weary: restless wanderers that cannot be tamed. Busy all the day long, the coming of night but quickens their speed. As if to take advantage of this body when deep sleep falleth upon it, the Spirit lives whole days and years in a few moments. The Spirit sleeps not and is not weary.

But why

—"Thus longing, thus forever sighing

For the far off unattained and dim?"

There is naught that satisfies it. The greatest attainments fill not the void within. I long for something purer and holier than is found on earth. Is there not a world to which the Spirit may go and find fullness; a land in which, free from this body, it shall drink in knowledge by a thousand ways now unknown? A Book has told me of a world in which "life is unmeasured by the flight of years," where shadows flee away, and all is real. No death is there, and nothing that offends. The Maker of the Universe has his temple there, and there are beings all untouched by the sins of earth. May not that be the Spirit's home? May it not there live a life infinitely higher than the present, and "know as even also it is known?"

December 20 - Monday Morning - Jennie's Diary
It has now been almost two months since I returned to the Seminary, and all that time I have kept no record. I regret it much. Time and

again I thought I would, but I have suffered my other duties to interfere. I commence today and I will try to be faithful.

December 21 - Tuesday Morning - Jennie's Diary

Just returned from our history recitation. It was almost an entire failure. But Miss Walker [teacher] was very kind. She did not say a word about our not having the lesson, but simply gave us the same for the next day, and said we might be excused. Yet there was something cutting in all this. We felt worse than if Miss Walker had spoken to us in rebuke. From this I will learn a lesson for future days. There is art in teaching. This day is cold, dreary and sleeting. What may its close be? I must now write to my dear mother. I had a letter from her last week. What a blessing to have a dear mother to write to me. May I be a comfort to her.

December 22 - Wednesday - Recreation Day - Jennie's Diary

Busy in putting my room in order. Several of the young ladies called on us. My section teacher, Miss Titcomb [teacher] called on me. She is very kind. At 3 o'clock the Reverend Mr. Grey, agent and Missionary of the American Bethel Society, gave us a short lecture in the Hall, setting forth the claims of that society upon our benevolent sympathies. He related several interesting incidents which came under his own observation. The object of the society is the spiritual good of the boatman on our rivers, canals, and lakes. I was deeply interested, and I would gladly do something for them.

Again, Jennie longs for the possibility of travel.

December 23 - Thursday Morning - Jennie's Diary

Cold and cloudy. Signs of more snow. At devotion we had the pleasure of listing [listening] to the Rev. [?] of Oregon. He is engaged in erecting a Seminary in that country, and is anxious to get teachers, not only for the Seminary, but also to take private schools. My heart burned within me as he spoke, and I longed to go. I do wish the way might open for me to go. I would tell the teachers that I want to go, but I fear they would think me unqualified. O that I could go. But all will be right.

1853

Early in 1853 Ann is teaching school at Providence, and Jennie is still a student at Mount Holyoke. Jennie laments the fact that she cannot stay and graduate from the institution. She also mourns her inability to develop a close friendship with anyone, especially her roommate Ellen. Jennie and Ann fight repeated bouts with melancholy and in an uncanny way seem to suffer from headaches and depression on the same days. Ann describes the death of her uncle, James Jones Speer, when he is thrown from a horse, and she also gives a harsh indictment of the institution of slavery. Jennie falls in love with the North and develops an appreciation of the work ethic there, which stands in stark contrast to the more relaxed way of doing things in the South. Ann falls in love with an unknown man who, more than likely, is a potential fiancé.

January 1 - Jennie's Diary
A new year! Yes a New Year is opening. Can it be that 1852 is gone forever? It is gone, never, never to return. Its work is done. Its records sealed up. What account has it borne to the Spirit World of me? Another chapter in the history of my life has been written. But what a chapter it is! A New Year is before me. Varied have been the scenes through which I have passed in 1852. It has been an event-filled period in my life. It has doubtless done much to determine the future of my life. My character in time and eternity will be much influenced by the events of the past year. My life has been spared. Many of my friends have been taken to the Spirit World. Why was not I? Surely they were better than I, and could do more good. For no small consideration has my life been spared. Divine Providence had a wise purpose in all this. O may I not defeat the design of my Heavenly Father. If I am spared this year also, when I come to review its history may it be full of improvements, so that the review shall be

one of joy and gladness. Help me, O my Heavenly Father. Farewell old year. Thou art gone. I feel as if parting with an old friend. Henceforth thou shalt be numbered with the years beyond the flood. Thou art gone, old year, but I shall meet thee again. When the "books are opened," thou wilt come up to bear witness of all thou borne to the Great Recorder. Farewell old year. Almighty Father, in thy infinite goodness thou has given me another year. To thy name be everlasting praise for all the blessings of the past. And now Father, I desire to dedicate this new year to thee. May it witness me more faithful to thee than any of the past years of my life have been.

Same Day - January 1 - Ann's Diary
New Year's Day has been ushered in most delightfully. A few gorgeous clouds float through the heavens, forming a beautiful contrast with the clear blue sky. The northern winds come howling through the glen, and morning through the leafless forests. Yet this is a beautiful winter's day. The brilliancy of the sun, when it appears from a bright cloud, dazzles our eyes, and enraptures our senses. The old year is numbered with things of the past and the New Year, full of gaiety, comes skipping in the fullness of his delight. Leap year is gone too, and the girls must set in for a four-year heat at home. Joy floats on every breeze, but many sad changes may come before the bell tolls or the requiem is sung for the departing year of 1853.

January 2 - Ann's Diary
The first Sabbath in 1853 steals quietly and devoutly upon us. How serenely nature reclines under the care of her great Creator. A calm holy spell envelops all, and binds earth in suspense of reverence to the Ruler. Her inhabitants quit their daily occupations, for a peaceful retreat around their domestic hearth, to indulge in those vocations so elevating, so refining and purifying to the heart. I will spend the day in reading some good book, writing or [in] useful conversation.

January 3 - Monday - Jennie's Diary
This has been Fast Day in the Seminary. A day for fasting and

prayer for the conversion of the world. A solemn day has it been. I have never spent such a day before. All school duties were suspended, and the whole day given to prayer and meditation. We met several times for social prayer. In the afternoon we attended church. The exercises were interesting. Rev. Mr. Bliss, missionary from Turkey, was present. He gave us many interesting items of the missionary work among the Armenians. He represents them as earnestly seeking for the truth, and calling loudly for more missionaries. The fields are white already to the harvest, but the laborers are few. May the Lord of the harvest raise up, qualify and send forth more faithful laborers into the fields. And now the day is done. A solemn time has it been. A time of heart searching of penitence. May the influence of this day be felt in all coming time. I thank my Heavenly Father for this day. It has been a time of serious thought on my part, and I trust of much good. I hope to be stronger, more faithful than ever before. My Heavenly Father, help me.

Madam Roland was an important figure in the French Revolution. She is remembered chiefly for her outcry as she was being led to the guillotine, "Oh Liberty, what crimes are committed in thy name!" Her memoirs, written in prison, were published in 1795. Her husband committed suicide after hearing of his wife's execution.

January 3 - Ann's Diary

After engaging in the various avocations of the morning, I resume my seat to write a small bit in my memorandum. The day is cold and cheerless, but I have a bit of sunshine in my heart, and that is ever pleasant. This is mail day, but owing to Christmas Times we shall receive no paper - how bad! But I will spend the time I usually take for reading the news in sewing, reading or conversation with my mother. I am reading the *History of Madam Roland*. I have read it twice before, but it is as interesting as when I first read it. I think her a most excellent lady, a heroine. She possessed exalted talents, and cultivated these carefully. Her example is worthy of emulation.

Ann (left) and Jennie

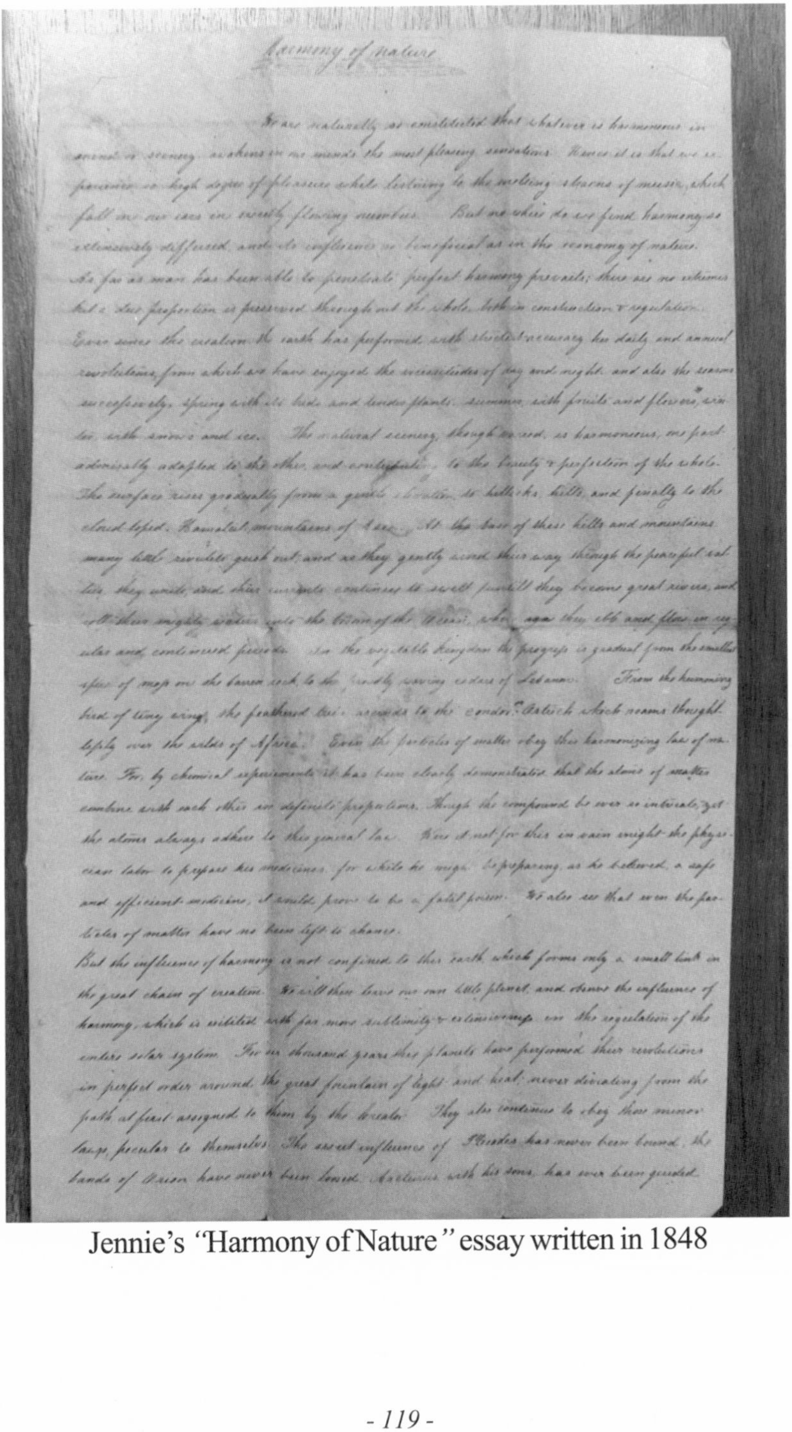
Harmony of Nature

We are naturally so constituted that whatever is harmonious in sound or scenery awakens in our minds the most pleasing sensations. Hence it is that we experience so high degree of pleasure while listening to the melting strains of music, which fall on our ears in sweetly flowing numbers. But no where do we find harmony so extensively diffused, and its influence so beneficial as in the economy of nature. As far as man has been able to penetrate perfect harmony prevails; there are no extremes but a due proportion is preserved throughout the whole, both in construction & regulation. Ever since the creation the earth has performed with strictest accuracy her daily and annual revolutions, from which we have enjoyed the vicissitudes of day and night and also the seasons successively. Spring with its buds and tender plants, summer with fruits and flowers, winter with snows and ice. The natural scenery, though varied, is harmonious, one part admirably adapted to the other, and contributing to the beauty & perfection of the whole. The surface rises gradually from a gentle elevation to hillocks, hills, and finally to the cloud-topped Himalaya mountains of Asia. At the base of these hills and mountains many little rivulets gush out, and as they gently wind their way through the peaceful valley, they unite, and their currents continue to swell [illegible] till they become great rivers, and roll their mighty waters into the bosom of the Ocean, where they ebb and flow in regular and continued periods. In the vegetable kingdom the progress is gradual from the smallest speck of moss on the barren rock, to the proudly waving cedars of Lebanon. From the humming bird of tiny wing, the feathered tribe ascends to the condor & Ostrich which roams thoughtlessly over the wilds of Africa. Even the particles of matter obey this harmonizing law of nature. For, by chemical experiments it has been clearly demonstrated that the atoms of matter combine with each other in definite proportions. Though the compound be ever so intricate, yet the atoms always adhere to this general law. Were it not for this in vain might the physician labor to prepare his medicines, for while he might be preparing, as he believed, a safe and efficient medicine, it would prove to be a fatal poison. We also see that even the particles of matter have not been left to chance.

But the influence of harmony is not confined to this earth which forms only a small link in the great chain of creation. We will then leave our own little planet, and observe the influence of harmony, which is exhibited with far more sublimity & extensiveness in the regulation of the entire solar system. For six thousand years the planets have performed their revolutions in perfect order around the great fountain of light and heat, never deviating from the path at first assigned to them by the Creator. They also continue to obey those minor laws peculiar to themselves. The sweet influence of Pleiades has never been bound, the bands of Orion have never been loosed. Arcturus with his sons, has ever been guided

Jennie's "Harmony of Nature" essay written in 1848

The Falls at Providence

Flowers in Ann's Diary

Asbury Speer (1826-1864), oldest brother of Jennie and Ann, was a Colonel in the Yadkin militia c. 1850.

Asbury Speer, Colonel in Confederate Army c. 1863

Aaron Speer (1831-1856), brother of Jennie and Ann

Jennie and Ann's father, Aquilla Speer (1804-1888)

Jennie and Ann's mother, Elizabeth Ashby Speer (1804-1890)

Jennie and Ann's brother "Vet," Sheriff S. T. Speer (1837-1890), Sheriff of Yadkin County (1862-1866). (Photo used by permission of Ann Speer Riley, a great-granddaughter of Vet Speer.)

Jennie and Ann's aunt Nancy Speer (1796-1880), sister of Aquilla

Jennie and Ann's uncle James Jones Speer (1798-1853), brother of
Aquilla

Dr. Brantley York (1805-1891) was Jennie's teacher at Jonesville, N.C., in the 1840s. Duke University had its beginning in a school organized by Dr. York in 1838. (Photo used by permission of Charles Mathis, a great-great-grandson of Dr. York.)

Lyman Beecher, father of Harriet Beecher Stowe

Horace Greeley, Editor of the *New York Tribune*

Jennie presented her father, Aquilla, with a copy of this temperance
book the year it was published in 1851.

Mount Holyoke Female Seminary c. 1870 (Photo used courtesy of
Mount Holyoke College Archives and Special Collections, South
Hadley, Mass.)

Mary Lyon, founder of Mount Holyoke Female Seminary in 1836 (Photo used courtesy of Mount Holyoke College Archives and Special Collections, South Hadley, Mass.)

Gertrude Sykes, class of 1853, was Jennie's roomate at Mount Holyoke. Gertrude taught at Mount Holyoke from 1853-1858. (Photo used courtesy of Mount Holyoke College Archives and Special Collections, South Hadley, Mass.)

Jennie's receipt from the Howard Hotel in New York City in August 1853

Dr. Charles Force Deems (1820-1893) was President of Greensboro Female College (1850-1854). (Photo used by permission of Greensboro College.)

Theophilus C. Hauser (1810-1887) owned a large plantation in what is now the Yadkinville, N.C., area. (Photo used by permission of Lucille Hauser Miller.)

Bethania Hauser was close to 100 years old when she died on Nov. 11, 1934. She was head housekeeper for T. C. Hauser. (Photo used by permission of Lucille Hauser Miller.)

(LtoR) Cousins Peaches Hauser Golding and Lucille Hauser Miller at the Hauser Family reunion. Black and white descendants of T.C. Hauser have gathered for reunions since 1952. (Photo used by permission of Lucille Hauser Miller.)

Peaches Hauser Golding, great-granddaughter of Bethania Hauser, with Prince Charles of England. (Photo used by permission of Dr. C.B. Hauser.)

Courthouse at Rockford

Ruins of the Burrus Hotel at Rockford. Rockford was the Surry County Seat from 1789-1850.

Jesse Lester Tavern at Rockford

Dudley Glass Store at Rockford

Speer reunion in 1920s. Jennie and Ann's brother James is in the wheelchair. Uncle James Speer, the child fifth from left, is the grandson of James.

Nellie Speer (1886-1980), neice of Jennie and Ann, with her father, James Speer (1843-1928)

Captain James Speer at home during WWII. Uncle James received the following recognition for his time in the service: the European Africa Middle Eastern Service Medal with two Bronze Stars, the American Service Medal, the America Defense Service Medal and The Victory Medal. Uncle James died in 1999.

Graves of the Aquilla Speer family on Cemetery Hill. (LtoR) Mother Elizabeth, Aquilla, Aunt Nancy, Asbury, Ann, Jennie, Aaron, Sylvia, and Grandmother Elizabeth.

January 4 - Ann's Diary

The sun arose in unwonted grandeur this morning. A few fleecy clouds veiled his face, but he soon dispersed them, throwing a most brilliant light. The scene surpassed anything I ever beheld for splendor and sublimity. The wind was blowing strongly and rocked the trees to and fro, and when the sun had risen so high as to be seen through them, the whole appeared one vast sea of liquid gold, moving in the heavens. The light clouds that floated in the east were tinted with golden light, and appeared like huge monuments, arches and colonnades rearing their proud heads above this sea of gold. O how beautiful and rapturing the sight! I have spent the day quite pleasantly.

January 5 - Ann's Diary

Nothing particular has occurred this morning. Nature assumes her usual aspect. The great king of day rolls on his accustomed route; the stars hide in the chilly blue sky, and the earth revolves as usual. I arose this morning full of cheerfulness. Read a portion of Thompson's lesson. He gives a glowing and accurate description of winter. I like his writings. Poetry constitutes much of my reading. It adds a new charm to beauty, increases sublimity, and gives life and energy to description. The earth is full of poetry. There is nothing but will admit of description, nothing but is connected with mystery. We begin to solve the mysterious but the mind recoils aghast at its own littleness. Tho the earth is fraught with such endless numbers of poetical objects, it is something rare to find a truly poetical genius, one of nature's truly favored poets.

January 6 - Ann's Diary

Some people met here have engaged in a lawsuit. Why should there not be deep principles of honor stamped on the heart sufficient to prompt each one to act uprightly? I have been reading Young's *Night Thoughts on Life, Death, and Immortality*. How sublime his imagination. How glowing his descriptions. A solemn sense of awe pervades my mind when reading his works. He asks "Where are his departed hours?" He exclaims, "With the years beyond the flood." How affecting the thought! What does each passing moment bear to the "Recording Scribe of Heaven" of me? What is continually recorded of me? Do I improve each golden moment of life and cherish it as I would sublunary pleasures?

January 7 - Ann's Diary

I seat myself at my little table, raise my window, and the cool morning breeze rushes into my room, fanning my cheek and adding vigor and cheerfulness to my spirit. I look abroad upon the beautiful earth now lying dormant enveloped in the hoary frost of winter, and ask myself, who created it? Where is its great Author? I look again; all the earth responds, "The hand that made me is Divine." He is present everywhere and at all times, sees all my actions and knows all my thoughts. How careful should I be.

Same day - January 7 - Friday Afternoon - Jennie's Diary

I am sad and lonely. What makes me so? It seems impossible for me to shake it off. Yesterday was to me a sorrowful day. This morning I felt some better, but now this loneliness comes over me again. I want to [fly] away to some desert spot where I may be all alone. I sometimes fear it presages some sad news from home. But no, I will not think so. Oh that I could shake off this melancholy, and be cheerful and happy. What shall I do? I know not. I love to flee away from every human being. To be alone, alone. I want to make my roommates happy but how to do it I know not. I want to be a comfort to them. But how shall I? They are kind.

January 8 - Ann's Diary

I have no time to write much this evening as I did not spend the day at home. Nothing interesting has occurred.

January 9 - Ann's Diary

Time with its swift [?] again brings me to my desk. Another holy Sabbath has dawned and while some retire to the church, others to their revelry. I withdraw to my little chamber to read, write and hold communion with my own heart. Few know the value of Sabbath days, and never till eternity's sable curtain is withdrawn shall we know what responsibilities cluster around its moments. We should spend it [devoted] to God.

January 13 - Ann's Diary
Last evening I returned from the wedding of one of my cousins. Many people were collected to see the marriage ceremony performed. We had a fine ride of 14 miles. A portion of the road was beautiful, and other places were wild rugged hills. The Yadkin River was very full and as our prancing horses cleaved the sparkling waters, the reflection of the sun on the waves was splendid. The wedding party was quite agreeable. I enjoyed myself very well.

January 14 - Ann's Diary
We so often meet with people who pretend great friendship, and employ a number of sweet words to convince one of their sincerity, while at the same time their hearts are entirely foreign to their expressions. They carry a heart black with wickedness, while at the same time they employ artful words and winning smiles as a mask for their deceitful hearts! I will beware of such, for a friend possessing such qualities is like the dazzling nectar composed of deadly poison, or the alluring song of the Siren. Give me a simple loving heart, devoid of deceit and envy, where I may confide without fear.

January 16 - Ann's Diary
Another golden Sabbath is swiftly passing away. The bright sun is lingering in the western horizon, as if bidding "adieu" to nature. Night envelops herself in her sable mantle, and walks forth beneath the twinkling stars and pale moon. I love, in the deepening twilight, to walk out and behold the earth as she sinks into repose. I love to think of the past, the present, and future. The future! What hope and fear cling to that word! What mystery it conceals. What destiny awaits me in the inevitable future? — Where has this day fled? Alas! It flitted away on the swift wings of time; it has been borne to the Grand Scribe of Heaven. Each moment with its acts has there been registered. What good thing has been accredited to me?

January 17 - Monday - Jennie's Diary

How rapidly these days pass away! The term has closed and vacation, with all its dreams of rest and happiness is here. Most of the young ladies have gone home. Happy children they, who have a home so near that they can go and spend these days with all the loved ones there. About 80 remain here. We have pleasant times. Dear Miss Spoffard, Miss Jessup, and Miss Walker [teachers] are with us doing what they can to make us happy. My roommates, Miss Sykes and Miss Darling, have gone to Suffield to spend the vacation with friends there. Dear Ellen and I are all alone. We have a nice quiet time. She is a dear, precious child. I want to be able to make her happy. I wish I had a heart so pure, so holy, that all who associate with me would be made better. But alas! Alas! My heart is so wicked, my life so imperfect, that I sometimes almost despair. I have seen more and felt more the depravity of my heart of late than ever before. May it humble me, and lead me near the cross. I would live at the foot of the cross. I would ever bear in mind the great love of God to sinful man.

January 21 - Ann's Diary

Last evening I returned from a visit to my friend Emily - I spent quite a pleasant time - an evening and night at her home, and next morning we called on Old Mr. and Mrs. Cruze, two aged people. They live alone. While we were there some people passed bearing the corpse of Mr. Reynolds to his last long resting-place. "The lot of all living mortality is doom." I returned home in the evening just before sunset; just in time to see the last farewell of the departing King of day.

January 24 - Monday Evening - Jennie's Diary

My section sisters, Miss Poor, Miss Prauchar and Miss Kelly have made me a visit this evening. We had a pleasant time. **8 o'clock.** Vacation will soon be gone. How it has sped away. I have accomplished but little. I have attended reading circles. We are reading Homer's *Iliad,* and Edward's *History of Redemption.*

January 25 - Ann's Diary

The temperance cause is creating a great excitement in the country. The papers are filled with accounts of the interest taken in this great moral reformation. Lecturers are traveling the State to enlist people in the heavenly work. We hope soon to see our beloved country break the bonds that bind us under a despot's power. The yoke of Tyranny has long been laid upon our unresisting necks by alcohol. Many brave hearts have been crushed. Many glittering talents are buried, and many, very many happy hearts have been rendered desolate by the demon intemperance. But a dim twilight is dawning upon the land. We look upon "Temperance" as our guiding star, as the deliverer of our sex from the galling yoke of Bacchus. A wreath of glory, eternal glory, encircles that word. It enters the lowly cottage bearing truth, love and mercy on its wings. It sheds a "sunbeam" of happiness and peace in the heart of many a widowed mother. It irradiates the beaming countenance of youth. It adds new luster to talents, forms a new diadem in the crown of the hero, and adds a never-fading laurel to the wreath that twines around the brow of every good and brave man.

January 26 - Jennie's Letter to her Mother, Elizabeth
Mt. H. F. Seminary, Wednesday evening
My own dear precious Mother,

Your letter mailed 17 January is now in my pocket. Miss Roberts [student] brought it to me a short time ago. I have hastily devoured its contents, and pocketed it as I always do. And Mother, I feel real sorrowful when I see that you do not get my letters sooner. I have written to you and father long enough for you to have received [them] before yours was mailed. It does make me sad to know while I am writing that long weeks will pass away before it reaches my home.

I commence this letter this evening and will finish it soon as I can. I mailed one this morning to Sister Ann. But when will she get it? Letters from home have generally of late come directly on. They are about a week on the way. But I will not grieve if I can avoid it. Maybe you will get mine sometime. But if letters do not come to hand as often as you think they should, do not think it is because I am not faithful in writing. I write almost every week.

Saturday 11 o'clock - Mother, I am feeling the cold severely — my feet are so frosted and lame I can scarce walk, and my hands are so chapped they have cracked open and bled profusely. I do not suffer with the cold otherwise. My body is well protected. We have snow in abundance and ice. I think this cold climate will do me good if I am careful.

Vacation is passed and we are now upon the duties of another Term. We have had a pleasant vacation. I have enjoyed it much. You will learn something of it in my letter to Sister Ann.

The letter continues on February 8 but will be kept in chronological order. This next diary entry by Ann is most revealing. Her words clearly indicate a sentiment among some people in the South that slavery was barbaric and unacceptable.

January 29 - Ann's Diary
This has been a busy week. The estate of Mr. G. P. [?] is being sold, and we have had company nearly every night. Some Speculators came by here; they brought some Negroes. One was handcuffed and his feet were chained together. It looked too bad. A man, one that God created, endowed with rationality, and possessing feelings like us, chained like a brute. That Speculator must possess a heart of steel that he can engage in a traffic so sordid and debasing.

January 30 - Ann's Diary
This holy Sabbath has opened beautifully. Tho it is the middle of winter, the day is as bright and warm as a spring day. I have been reading all day. I love to spend Sabbaths alone in reading. I have but little use for Sunday visiting.

January 31 - Ann's Diary
Night with her sable mantle has enveloped the earth, and I sit me down and trim my lamp in order to transcribe a few of the thoughts of the day upon paper. I have been thinking of my early school days - when I moved, free as the morning air, through the quiet groves that surrounded the academy. When, to the merry ringing bell, I bounded

with delight - when with attentive ear, I listened to the voice of instruction from my teacher. When, arm in arm with some favorite companion, I strolled through the shady glen, and with the dewy daisy and beautiful violets, listened to the carol of love from the birds of the forest, or watched the gorgeous sun as he lingered in "the gates of the west," and the golden tinted clouds that reveled in his light. Ah! Then were pleasant days, but I knew it not. It is natural for us to consider the past more delightful than the present. A halo of attraction encircles the past, which the present cannot attain. The phantom of happiness ever dances before, and we let the present moments slip away, while contemplating the future. Hope ever urges us forward, in pursuance of something more enticing. But perhaps when age shall have stamped his signature on our brow, when our locks are sprinkled with hoary hairs, and the buoyant step of youth is exchanged for the quiet dignity of age, then we may look through a different glass upon things of the past, present, and future.

January 31 - Monday - Jennie's Diary
The last day of the month is here. Oh how rapidly time flies, how little I accomplish. I really fear I do not make that improvement of my time which I ought. I am enjoying the freedom from care which I now have, but I would not sink down into idleness. I want to be industrious. I have had some thoughts this morning of remaining here until I graduate. If I had funds sufficient I would. I sometimes think I ought. I do wish I knew what would be for the best. But will it be right for me to take up so much of my time in my own improvement? May I not make the same improvement, and at the same time, be communicating to others? I want to do what is for the best. May I have wisdom.

February 2 - Ann's Diary
Uncle James Jones Speer now lies perfectly insensible. He was thrown from his horse last Sunday evening and badly, if not fatally, wounded. He was found by his sons after night, groaning piteously. He was carried to Mr. C's [the Crummels lived in the Providence area. This may be where he was taken.] A physician was called who

examined his head and body, but found no sign of broken bones. There is no hope of his recovery. He has never opened his eyes or spoken. He was returning from his appointment. He was a faithful minister and attended many churches who will mourn his loss. He was a member of the Old Baptist church and labored as a minister in that church.

February 4 - Ann's Diary

Death has done his work. Wearied nature yields, an easy prey to the Monster. We were called to witness the last struggle of my Uncle. Calmly and silently his spirit took its flight. Weeping children and friends crowded around his bed, but all was over - the soul had ascended to its God - and the clay tenement became the dwelling of Death. "That eye is fixed, that heart is still - how dreadful in its stillness! Death, new tenant of the house, pervadeth all the fabric; he waiteth at the head, and he standeth at the feet, and hideth in the caverns of the breast." Another soul has been taken to the courts of heaven. Another inhabitant has lodged in the city of the dead - "mortals say 'a man is dead,' angels say 'a child is born.'" Uncle James' example was worthy of emulation. He was ever kind, and many many times has he prayed for the dying - a most attentive nurse for the sick - and doubtless he now receives that reward for the righteous in heaven. May we all "live the life of the righteous, that our last end may be like his."

February 4 - Jennie's Diary

This is the first day of the series. I am studying history yet. When I finish it I think I shall spend the remaining time in reading. I want to attend lectures on Chemistry and Philosophy. Mrs. Upsom, a teacher from Alabama, is spending a few days in the Seminary. She led in devotions this morning in the Hall. She made some excellent remarks to us. This is the time for changing domestic work. Many are quite sad because of their work. Mine has not been changed yet. They have been very favorable to me. I have been on the miscellaneous circle and it is quite pleasant. We meet in Room B and sew an hour and ten minutes. I am glad that Ellen has her work changed. She now makes the early fires. She is pleased and I am glad. She is a dear precious child and I love her much. The question often comes up, am I improving myself, my time as I ought. May I have wisdom. **Saturday evening**. I have just returned from our usual missionary meeting. Miss [?] gave us several interesting items about the Moravian Mission in Greensboro, commenced by three young men in 1732. Our usual exercises in the hall were very interesting, as they called forth several remarks from Miss Chapin. This week Mrs. Tolman has been changing the Domestic work of the young ladies. Many have been very unwilling to take work that is hard or unpleasant. This led Miss Chapin to speak about being selfish. She told us she wanted us to watch ourselves and see how often during the day we were guilty of selfishness. She also spoke about our teasing our teachers for things which we wanted; especially about our studies, and being dissatisfied with the decisions of the teachers. We had some notes of criticism about selfishness. Miss Finny and Miss Avery [teachers] were in to hear our compositions. Four were read; "The Home of My Childhood," by Miss Scofield, "Time," by Miss Scribner, "He Knows It All," by Miss Sloan. "My Grandmother," by Miss Spofford, and "The Power of Thought," by Miss Sleeper. I feel that I have spent this day almost uselessly. This morning I tried to write a composition, but I could not write anything with which I was satisfied. This has been a damp, dark day. The vapor is so dense that we cannot see the church steeple.

February 5 - Saturday - Jennie's Essay - Untitled - Mount Holyoke Female Seminary

This is composition day, and a dark day it is too. A dense fog has shut out all the sunlight, and even hides the church steeple from sight. The snow is fast melting away, and the roads are so wet I cannot go out to take a bit of fresh air, and quicken my sluggish thoughts.

The whole building is quiet as a convent, except now and then the bell gives a few strokes, but these are dull and heavy, as if, at last, even it was tired of striking. I cannot see into the rooms of others, but I reckon if I could I should see many a sober face bent over a bit of paper and a motionless pencil. What a sad thing it is to have to write, and nothing to write about. My roommates are in about the same sad case as myself. One is sitting on a cricket at my feet, and from the manner in which her pencil moves just now, I presume some happy thought has come to her relief. Another is sitting by, one foot on the stove hearth, trying to fix in her mind some Geological facts. Now she presses the textbook to her head, and the long sigh, and contracted brow says how fruitless is the attempt. The third has gone into the bedroom, if perchance solitude may lend some assistance.

And here I sit. A piece of paper, on a volume of Mrs. Hemans' work, is before me and says, "come and write." [Felicia Hemans (1793-1835) was a nineteenth century poet, playwright, and composer of hymns.] But what shall I write? That is the trouble. I do not lack for subjects; they are many as sands upon the seashore. But there is not one of this multitude but what has been written upon time and again, until the heart is sick of hearing them mentioned.

I love to write composition, but I want to write something that has not been written a thousand times already. Sometimes I have finished a composition with some self-satisfaction, thinking sure I have something new now. But the next day I have gone into the reading room, and, as if for very spite, there is spread out in the papers almost a facsimile of what I had written. Then again, I have had my subject selected and a plan formed for a composition, when someone mentions in conversation that Miss [?] has written a splendid composition upon "[?]", and all my hopes for something new have been blasted.

Now what am I to do? One of two things. I must not write at all, or else be content to follow the footsteps of others. The first I cannot do, for I would be disobeying the regulations of the Institution, and that would not be right. I must do the second and be content. This then shall be the last time I will throw my time away in needless repining. Henceforth I will try to write something that will be of some profit to me.

While Jennie is having a difficult time writing, Ann joyfully goes about her own documentation.

February 7 - Ann's Diary
How delightful to shut me up in my little study. My books around me for companions and instructory friends, my pen in my hand ready to

obey my will, and my paper before me waiting to receive my simple thoughts. 'Tis when thus retired from mortal view that I spend some of the most delightful hours of my life. With nothing to disturb the impressive serenity. The low chirp of the cricket, the sweet notes of the forest birds, and the cool morning breeze, all conspire to render the scene more attractive. I pity the gay and thoughtless that never enjoy the peace and happiness of being alone. They know nothing of the charms of solitude. The most interesting part of my time I spend alone.

The letter continues that Jennie began on January 26 to her mother.

February 8 - Thursday - Jennie's Letter to her Mother Continues

Dear Mother, my pen has been idle some time, for my head and hands have been busily employed in many other things. But I now find time to write a little. I am quite well this morning. I do think my health is improving very much. I have not felt as well since last winter. One great reason is, I believe, that I have no anxious cares as I have had during the past two years. If I ever go back again to my duties at the College I think I will not take so much to heart as I did while there before. I now believe it did me more harm than all my work.

Mother, I had a delightful walk this morning. I did up my room work early, and started out. I went alone. One of my roommates was working and the others were busy studying so I went all alone, but it was delightful. The sun was just rising above the mountains, the trees on the mountains were covered with ice; these reflected the rays of the rising sun, and appeared like a silver forest. As far as I could see the mountains rose gradually, their trees covered with ice looking like boundless hills of light. It was grand, grand. I enjoyed it wonderfully. I walked almost an hour. The mountain air here is so fresh, so bracing. We have but little snow now; the rains have taken it away.

I have not anything very new or interesting to write you, Mother. We are quite shut in from the outer world and know but little of what is going on. If I say anything it must necessarily be local — about the Seminary — and that I fear will interest you but little.

I can tell you of a little promotion I had last night. I was at my Domestic work, paring pumpkins. One of the teachers came to me and asked if I would be responsible for the cooking of it. I said I would if I could. She showed me where to find the wood to make the fire, and gave me other directions. When I had finished paring, I made up my fire (the kettles are put up in a furnace and the fire is made in the furnace) I then poured in some water and put in the pumpkin, and when I left it, it was cooking finely. I expect we shall have for dinner some pies made out of it. I will tell you if they are good.

I think I shall be quite a housekeeper by the time I leave. If I am ever called to that important station, Mr. Somebody may be thankful that I once came north. My home shall be in some respects a Northern home.

You speak in your letter of my being so far away. True I am far away. I can hardly realize that I am so far off. Yet I think I shall see my home in the sunny South once more. I am anxious for the time to come when I shall set my face homeward. I love to hear the car's [train] whistle, I think they will whistle for me some day.

You give me some strong inducements to come home, Mother, and I should love to do so if I did not think it was best for me to remain during the year, as I am here. I should love to enjoy some of your nice chicken pies, but I believe I want some good warm corn bread and butter and milk worse. Some nice warm corn loaf would be so good. And I remember Mother, how good you used to be to me in letting me cut a slice of the pone when it was taken out of the oven, fresh and hot. How I long for a piece now.

We have good bread here, but no corn bread. We have mush for a rarity sometimes for dinner. They call it "Indian pudding." Irish potatoes are all the rage. I do not recollect that we have made a single dinner without them since I have been here. And they are most excellent, just as mealy as ours are in the spring. We have but little meat except beef. I will give an example to illustrate. One day we had pork and beans. As pork was quite a rarity with us of course we valued it much. One of the young ladies said she came near losing her piece of pork for <u>one bean</u> got on it. From this you may imagine the size of our share. But our fare is very wholesome and good. It is better than at the College. I am satisfied with it. I do so much want some sweet potatoes. They are not raised here. I should indeed love to come home next spring and spend the summer at home with you all. I should love to do it for Father and Mother's sake, and also Brother's and Sister's sake, and for my own comfort. But I shall hardly ever come north again, unless I get married and come on a wedding tour, and maybe it will be best for me to stay.

February 11 - Friday Night - Jennie's Diary
I have just taken my half-hour. These half-hours are solemn seasons. I wonder how many misspent ones I shall meet in eternity. I have not been very successful in my studies today. My history lesson was a review, and part of it was some that I lost while sick last term. I had a headache, and my mind was all confusion. Our drawing class commenced today. Dear Miss Tolman is to be our teacher. I am glad. This afternoon in the Hall Miss Spoffard read to us some documents written by Miss Lyon, when the Seminary was first founded. They were very interesting. She mentioned the object for which the Institution was founded; that a supply of well-educated Christian young ladies might be given to the many destitute portions of our nation, that young ladies might be fitted for usefulness in any field to which the providence of God might call them. Miss Spoffard said she wondered how many of the present number were preparing themselves for teachers. We had a pleasant circle tonight. We pared apples awhile, and then picked ever nice. They had some merriment over some Southern phrases that I was telling them. Something is the matter with my dear Ellen. She has just gone in the bedroom to weep. I am sorry for her, but it is silent study hours and I cannot speak to her. I think I can <u>guess</u> the reason. And now I have got to

write composition, and I do not know what to write. I wish I did. Mary is writing hers now, and Gertrude is thinking about hers. I must be doing something too.

February 12 - Saturday Night - Jennie's Diary
I have just come home from Domestic work. I have been trying to make the pine burn, but it is hard to coax. Mary is studying her lesson. Her brother has been to see her today, and it has made her quite happy. I too have a dear brother, but alas, he is far away. Gertrude and Ellen are talking their half-hours. Ellen had a letter this evening from Mrs. Goodman, a former teacher of hers. She takes so much interest in Ellen. What would I give if I had some kind one thus to care for me, and write to me words of council and courage. But such is not my fortune. No dear teacher have I had thus to love me, thus to seek my good. I have struggled alone. But One cares for me. I have felt sadly when I have thought that I have no one who has an interest in me.

Jennie is so melancholy in the above entry that she has forgotten the strong connection she has with her family. Below, Ann makes the family ties quite clear.

February 13 - Ann's Diary
Attended church and heard two good sermons, one delivered by Rev. W. G. Brown, the other by Rev. Naylor. I do not think we fully appreciate our privileges. We have preaching almost every Sabbath, and we have become so accustomed to attend preaching that I fear we sometimes go more from habit than proper motives. Night, dusky and silent night has settled around; we draw near our cheerful blazing fire to spend the evening of this lovely Sabbath day. How blessed the influence of such holy Sabbath evenings! It tends to unite the family chain that links our hearts in love around the domestic hearth. Methinks, when age has furrowed these cheeks, dimmed my eyes, and sprinkled with fleecy snow my jetty tresses, when the buoyant step of happy youth has relaxed into the firm steady step of womanhood; I shall recall, with pleasure, these now delightful evenings spent in the family circle.

On two cold February days both sisters embark upon excursions.
Ann describes a walk to a natural waterfall on the farm, while
Jennie walks to a mill where the water has been tamed.

February 21 - Ann's Diary

I walked to the [water] "fall" a few days ago in company with
Miss E [probably a student], and we found some sweet little flowers
growing in the ledges of some rocks. A liver leaf, cemlea and violets
all peeping up, reveling in their luxuriant beauty and native wildness.
They forget the icy hands of winter are not yet unlocked. O I love
these little predecessors of beautiful spring. They seem to have just
arrived from their blissful dreamland. Angels eyes beam from their
[?]. They bow their sylph-like form and the wild tempest passes
over lightly. They drink the finest dews distilled from heaven. Rest
peacefully sweet little flowerets, in your rural home. No destroyer
shall harm you, emblems of innocence, faithfulness, love. Forever
retain the purity you now display. Brighter skies, warmer sunbeams,
more genial dews, and merry, beautiful companions are in reserve for
you. And may I learn from you that modest worth is superior to
showy [and] glittering, but empty and vain pretentions.

February 26 - Jennie's Essay

Mt. Holyoke Female Seminary
February 26, 1853

A Morning Walk

It was one cold morning in February that I put on my rubbers,
shawl and hood for an early walk. Such a morning I had seldom been
out, for it was very unlike the mild pleasant mornings of my Southern
home. But I was fast becoming acclimated to these New England
breezes, and thought I might venture out. That I might enjoy one of
nature's most beautiful exhibitions, the rising Sun, I bent my footsteps
in that direction which would give me the best view.

I soon came to "the bridge," and tho I had often been there
before, yet I paused for a while that I might watch the stream below.

This stream, like everything else in New England, had been turned to some good account. Had it been a Southern brook, it might have been left free and wild to pursue its way to the great ocean. But here it was pent up by a wall, and made to turn a paper mill, which stood just above the bridge. Yet its waters, as restless as that utilitarian spirit which had thrown up this great wall in their way, after finishing their work of turning the mill, came leaping, foaming, and dancing on, as if for joy that they had at last broken away from their prison house.

A long time did I watch these waters, as merrily they chased each other over their pebbly way, and then turning themselves about, would take a thousand "mysteries" among the rocks beneath. I love the free, glad waters. But I could not linger longer. As I rose the hill, I met a little child perhaps going on an errand for its mother. It had a little tin pail on its arm. Its rosy cheek and light, quick step spoke of health, and its cheerful face said its little heart was all a stranger to care and sorrow. "Will you not freeze this cold morning?" I asked. "I am not afraid of that," it replied, and on it went to perform its little task, and I to pursue my walk.

In a short time I was at the top of the hill, and a scene opened before me, the like to which I had never seen before. The sun was just above the horizon, and his earliest beams were falling upon the forest all covered with ice. Every ray was reflected by a thousand icy mirrors. Here was presented in reality all that the mind is wont to picture, as one reads of silver forests, and enchanted groves. Far as the eye could reach, the mountains rose one above another in interminable succession, as so many hills of light. The valleys below were lit up with this new light, and I walked in the sunlight, and the light of the forests.

Feign would I have lingered to drink in all the beauty of that lovely scene, but other duties bade me hasten. I followed the road as it wound around the hill, and soon came to a farmhouse. An old woman was out in the yard feeding her feathery tribe. With no small delight did she survey the group at her feet, now coming near, now stepping back, as if half afraid that some trick was to be played upon them.

A man walked on just before me, his dog by his side and an axe on his shoulder. He was making his way to the forests I presume, and some proud oak was doomed to fall before his stroke ere the sun went down.

Thus I walked on, and soon found myself upon the threshold of the Seminary. I would not take gold for what I enjoyed in this morning walk. It was well nigh worth a journey from North Carolina.

Though the sisters are far apart, they both battle melancholy on the same day.

February 26 - Saturday Evening - Jennie's Diary
I am sitting at my window. I feel sad and dejected. I feel as if I were doing nothing to make my roommates any happier or better. I feign would do it, but how to I know not. I love them, and no sacrifice that I could make would be too much if I could thereby make them happy and do them good. I feel that they are my superiors. Their advantages have been far greater than mine. They must know it too. One of them, whom I love better than all others, is sitting by the stove. (Yes, Ellen, if you knew how many sorrowful hours I have spent when I have thought that you too did not think of me.) She was kind to me when I was sick, and I shall never forget her. She won my heart. Such kindness I had not received since I left my home in the sunny South. What wonder then if I should love her best? She will go again to her home, and thoughts of her humble roommate may never come into her mind. But I shall love her and pray for her. I trust we may know and love each other in the Spirit Land. "Thy will be done," oh Father. The shadows are lengthening. Soon the sunshine will leave the world to darkness and solitude. But the morrow cometh, a day of rest.

February 26 - Ann's Diary
Another week has fled. How many hearts have been saddened during its passing moments? I feel unaccountably sad this evening. The future bears weightily upon my mind. The gulf—the abyss of futility—how

much is encircling its dark recesses. Yet I hasten on to its brink not knowing what awaits me, what hidden mystery may be explained. None can solve the future, yet with wild eagerness we sometimes merge into its depths, but we only learn more of our own littleness.

February 27 - Ann's Diary
The day has been cloudy and sad. The sun veils himself in thick portentous clouds. And in my heart hangs a heavy cloud of gloomy forebodings. I know I should not cherish such feelings, but they press into my heart and I sometimes delight in them. May Heaven guide me aright.

March 2 - Ann's Diary
Bright beautiful spring has arrived. Her airy robes flutter and wave in the fragrant breeze. She scatters bright refreshing dews on vegetation, and the little flowers will spring up to greet her at every step. The icy hands of winter will melt and hasten away at the touch of her breath. Let my heart be in unison with the smiling earth. Let it be prepared to enjoy the beauties of spring and alternately look from nature up to her great author. May it be susceptible of His goodness, and receive the stamp of his image indelibly.

March 3 - Ann's Diary
"Open the casement, and up with the Sun!
This gallant journey is just begun:
Over the hills his chariot is rolled,
Bannered with glory and burnished with gold,
Over the hills he comes sublime,
Bridegroom of Earth, and brother of Time!"
What a bright beautiful morning. Mother Earth arose from her transient sleep, to revel in the warm sunbeams. Awake my heart, and join with mountain, rivers, and all creation in ascribing to the "great first Cause."

March 3 - Thursday Evening - Jennie's Diary
This has been a great day. All the forenoon it snowed rapidly. O it is splendid to see it snow so. We have no such scenes [in the] South.

About 2 o'clock the sun shone out, bright as a day in June. We attended "Preparatory lecture." Tonight I have more time than usual. I worked today in Miss C's [a student] place, clearing tables, and so I do not have to work tonight. I have been trying to learn some useful lessons from the past few days. I believe Providence has given me a warm heart. I find myself very much attached to my friends. But this may be cultivated to extremes. Now I think I have proof of this in my own experience. For example, here is Ellen sitting by me studying algebra. She is dearer to me than anyone here. But I restrain my feelings; it may be even to coldness. It has cost me a greater effort, and more tears than anything else I have met with in the Seminary. She is kind to me, yet I do not think she has any particular regard for me. Now this, trying as it is, is all right. Did she love me as I do her, I might make an idol of her, and so do wickedly. I am trying to say "thy will be done." And I do want to guard against any spirit of envy or jealousy. She has a right to love others better than me. It is all right. I will be submissive. I want to remember all this when I go again to teaching. I may turn it to some good account. I am now reading Abbott's *Teacher*. It is a most excellent book. I shall learn some useful lessons from it. I do want to be a teacher worth the name.

March 4 - Friday Night - Jennie's Diary
This evening I am again at liberty. Nothing very marked has taken place today. All things have passed on smoothly. I have had some success in my studies. President Pierce has gone into office today. It has been a delightful day. What a busy time it has been in Washington. May the blessing of heaven rest upon the President and his Administration. I had a good letter from my dear sister this evening. They are all alive, well and happy. I am thankful. Now I must go to writing composition. I wish I could write something more improving to myself.

March 5 - Ann's Diary
We have a beautiful snow today. The first of any consequence this winter. Winter has been remarkably warm. We have hardly been

aware that heavy ironfooted winter was present. I heard of Mrs. Hert's death. She died yesterday and leaves a family and many connections to mourn her loss. She was an excellent lady. She will be greatly missed in her circle of life, and many a poverty-stricken child of mortality will shed the tear of gratitude on her early grave. Her memory will be cherished in the finest affections of her acquaintances, and her name and example will be enshrined in the hearts of her relatives, till the relentless hand of death stills their throbs, and arrests their pulses.

March 6 - Ann's Diary
Sabbath dawns remarkably beautiful. The earth is robed in white and the sun smiles down on his charge. May my heart join in the song of praise to Heaven's King.

March 8 - Tuesday Night - Jennie's Diary
We took our first lessons in the review of France today. I studied until my poor head was all confusion. This morning I went to Miss Chapin asking permission to attend the Chemical lectures. She kindly gave me leave. This evening I attended. I was pleased. The Professor took up most of the time in experiments. He does not <u>talk</u> enough; does not tell the <u>reasons why</u>. I wonder that instructors do not pay more attention to the reason why. I care little for an experiment or operation if I cannot know why. I'm about half-sick tonight with a cold. I have a severe cough. I should love to go home. I have not spent a spring there since 1847. My dear home.

March 10 - Thursday Night - Jennie's Diary
This evening I have quite a treat. The mail brought me two letters one from Mr. Deems, one from Miss Hagen. I am thankful for such friends. May I ever be worthy of them. Mr. Deems wishes me to learn of all the arrangements here that they may be reproduced in North Carolina. I do want to feel more freedom to go and talk with the teachers. I know my time here is precious and I want to improve it.

March 15 - Ann's Diary

I feel unaccountably sad this evening. Yet I have no particular cause for such feelings. Yet they haunt me, and I almost willingly abandon myself to their control. I love to indulge in melancholy. I love to wonder, in pensive musings, in the region of fancy, and picture to my mind beings and scenes of imagination.

March 16 - Wednesday - Recreation Day - Jennie's Diary

Missionary meeting at quarter past two. It was very interesting. Miss Balentine [daughter of a missionary in India] came in dressed in the costume of the women in India. She then read a part of her mother's journal, kept while on the voyage to India for the comfort of her children. It gave us some idea of the sacrifice missionaries must make. After missionary meeting I took a painting lesson. I am somewhat pleased with it.

March 17 - Thursday - Jennie's Diary

This is a cold, cloudy day. I do not feel in humor to study much. I have laid aside my books to write a bit. I have been thinking much of late about going home. It seems to me it would be better for me to go home and get rested, than to stay here. I might take the money I should use here and buy books, go home and read, then the books would be there for my sister and brothers. I do not feel as if I am improving my time as I ought.

Ann's poem "I Love" expresses her passion for pensive musing. It seems that this was her favorite pastime. She must have felt the muses strongly, because she wrote a new poem each day.

March 18 - Ann's Poem

I Love

I love to watch the setting Sun
Slowly sinking in the west,
And his journey almost done,
He spreads abroad his golden crest.

Now dancing on the dimpled lake
Now lingering on a turfy grave
The sunbeams say a short adieu
And sink into the western wave.

I love to gaze upon the streaks
Of varied tints upon you, Sky;
And see the rose and yellow flakes
That mingle with its azure dye.

I love to watch the glittering stars
Peep forth from 'neath their spotless veil,
And deck the eve with brilliant gems,
And bid the Queen of night - all hail!

I love the pale glance of the moon
When forth among the stars she rides
And veils herself in fleecy clouds
Or in full majesty she glides.

I love to gaze upon the heaven
Adorned in pearls and jewels bright
And the west - to beauties given
"Sits blushing in the arms of night."

But most I love the pensive thoughts
That flit across my youthful mind.
The calm, deep musings of the heart,
When on some grassy bank reclined.

When nothing breaks the quiet night,
But low, sad murmurings of the brook,
The wild hoots of the boding Owl,
The chirping cricket in his nook.

'Tis then my fancy plumes her wings
And soars, aloft, in wild delight,
To realms of everlasting things,
To regions of celestial light.

March 19 - Ann's Diary

The day has been beautiful. Not a cloud dims the splendor of the King of day. O! It is a lovely spring day. I have spent it so very pleasantly. May my heart be in proper pause for the coming Sabbath.

March 20 - Ann's Diary

Sabbath has again been ours and fled. The dusk of evening gathers around, and this day is numbered with the things past. I walked alone to the Churchyard. How many I once knew and loved now lie pale and motionless in the quiet graveyard. Rest peacefully, all ye blessed dead, till the last trumpet shall arouse you from your slumbers. The body shall rise in immortality - worms shall no more destroy the flesh. It is something worthy of note that not one wicked person is buried in that graveyard. Every grown person was a professor of religion.

The above passage is dear to our family since there are so many of our ancestors, including my father, uncles, aunts and grand-parents who lie there. Ann's words "not one wicked person is buried in that graveyard" still ring true to us today.

Same day - March 20 - Ann's Poem

Fragments

> Perched on yonder lofty oak
> A flock of merry black birds sing
> But now they've gone to the forest brook
> To lave their beaks in the cooling spring.
> What looks so bright in the morning light
> When the sun casts abroad his warming rays
> 'Tis a sparkling dewdrop - a gem of the night
> That tints of rose color and yellow displays.

Same day - March 20 - Ann's Poem

This poem remembers Ann and Jennie's sister Sylvia, who died at age four. Ann had just visited the graveyard that day and came home to write this remembrance.

To a Periwinkle From My Sister's Grave

Beautiful flower, from whence did ye come?
From the silent glen on your mountain home?
From the mossy bank or grassflat fair?
No! O No! My abode is not there.

Beautiful flower, from whence did ye come?
From some jutting crag or moldering dome?
From the purling brook or river's bank?
No! O No! My home is not so dank.

Beautiful flower, whence did ye come?
From the forest's shade or cataract's foam?
From the grassy mead or lovely cave?
No! I came from your sister's grave.

March 21 - Monday Morning - Selection From Jennie's Diary
I went to Miss Chapin this morning to ask her if I might leave off reviewing history. But she would not give me permission. I am sorry. Miss Chapin does not know through what I have struggled to reach my present position. I should love to tell her something of my past history, but then she does not seem to have any sympathy for the young ladies. I do wish I could go to her, as I want to. I do feel that I am not spending my time as profitably as I ought. I think I shall go home soon. My head aches, and I feel discouraged. What shall I do?

March 22 - Thursday Night - Selection From Jennie's Diary
I feel tired and dissatisfied with myself tonight. What have I accomplished today? But little. Tonight I have been writing to Mother. Oh that I could see my dear mother.

March 22 - Ann's Diary

Yesterday I received a dear nice letter from my estimable friend Mattie Hauser. She is a darling girl. I know of no one of my friends whom I more dearly love. I have known her from childhood. We have been classmates in the schoolroom for many months. And I have formed for her an attachment which death alone can extinguish. NO! Not even death! For it shall be the gateway, the passage to another life where our love shall increase and ripen to perfection, and no cloud of disappointment or sorrow shall arise to chill the pure flame in our immortal hearts.

Jennie is clearly feeling inferior to her Northern schoolmates. She has neither the material, nor educational advantages that were enjoyed by those around her. Several of the diary passages in 1853 refer to this.

March 23 - Wednesday - Jennie's Diary

Dinner is over. I am now seated in room B. I see Prospect Hill, and the clouds in the distance are fine today. Some signs of rain. One of the young ladies is practicing in the adjoining music room, and it does me much good. Oh I love music. It sooths my ruffled spirits, it quiets this troubled heart. I do wish I understood it so as to play well. I love music, painting, drawing and poetry. I believe one ought to study them. Just now that young lady has struck up "Thou Has Wounded the Spirit That Loved Thee." I have often heard Miss Hagen play it. It calls up many associations. I shall be thankful to that young lady for this music. It has made one little bright spot in my heart. Upon what a fickle thread is human happiness suspended. We are truly creatures of circumstance. Now Miss Jessup [teacher] comes in to hear two young ladies recite. I wish I was as smart as Miss Jessup. Oh she has solid worth! I have felt some workings of my old spirit repining. My roommates were talking this morning about their friends and homes. How great the contrast between my early life and theirs. While I was busy in helping my father in the field, or my mother in the house, they were enjoying all the advantages of refined society; books and schools. How eagerly did I long to have books then, but I had them not. With [?] did I devour what books I could get. But it was all right. A kind Providence ordered all for the best; I do not want to complain. My lot has been far above many. I would not complain. I would not. I only ask that I may have grace and strength that I may fully improve all the present. I want to trust in God. He will guide me in the best way. Truly he has led me in a way which I knew not. Instead of complaints I would constantly raise hymns of praise and thanksgiving. Father forgive me the thoughts of my heart.

March 24 - Ann's Diary
What a bright lovely morning! Next Monday I am to commence a school at Providence. May I be successful. Some of the young ladies are calculating largely. I intend to do my best. I will give them all the instruction I can. O! Thou, who guidest the hearts of mankind, be thou my Instructor. Teach me aright. And may I not only teach them to love knowledge, but to adore thee, the Creator of Earth.

March 24 - Jennie's Diary
I have decided to leave for home. I trust the decision.

March 25 - Ann's Diary
This is "Good Friday." This day is consecrated as the anniversary of the crucifixion of Christ. It is wonderfully strange! The coming of the Son of God into the world to suffer the most cruel tortures that a deluded world could devise! How amazingly strange! How sublime to think that Christ should give his life as a ransom for our sin polluted souls! May I never forget the duty I owe to my Redeemer! O! Almighty Father, for the sake of Christ, wash my soul in his blood and it shall be cleansed from all impurity.

March 27 - Easter Sunday - Ann's Diary
Easter Sunday. The sun rides high in the heavens, darting his fiery beams to the earth. Old Boreas [the North Wind] comes howling from the caves of the north. The trees of the forest bow their lofty heads in solemn grandeur. The fleecy clouds float in the air, and all nature adorns herself in robes of beauty to welcome, to celebrate this

day, to pay divine homage to the King of Heaven, and bow in awful reverence to the Son of God. Did Christ indeed suffer the agonies of the cross? Was it for my soul? Oh my Redeemer that thy body was lashed with the cruel scourge - thy tender hands and feet pierced with rough nails, that thou bore the vile mockings, buffetings, and at last the ignominious death of the cross! Yes! For me, the vile worm of earth didst thou shed thy blood on the cross. For a sinful world thou left the glories of heaven and suffered death. Even God the Father seems to have forsaken Christ at this awful event, for he cries, "My God, My God, why hast thou forsaken me?" Many Angels strike the mournful dirge and stand aghast when they see their adored Lord subject to the cruelties of fallen man. But the art of man, combined with the powers of hell and the devices of Satan can't confine Christ in the tomb. Man's redemption is secured; God is reconciled to man through the intercession of the son, and He now shows to a wondering world the full extent of his goodness. He "will not suffer his holy One to see corruption." Accordingly, he sends Angels to remove the stone and Christ comes forth. He has conquered sin. He has taken the sting from Death, has gained the victory over the grave, and deprived hell of its victims. The choir of heaven strikes up anew the praises of God, and those thrilling melodies echo and re-echo through the heights of heaven. I think the redemption of man will be one of the most wonderful themes that shall employ the saints in heaven. Oh Lord, from this time may I wholly devote myself to thee. Let the love melt my heart. May my soul be entirely absorbed in the love and admiration of thy goodness. May I aim at nothing less than sanctification.

March 29 - Thursday Afternoon - Jennie's Diary
How changeable are all things here. The other day I thought I should go home, but a conversation with Miss Spoffard caused me to decide otherwise. I am glad I did. This has been a sorrowful day to many here. This morning Miss Tolman left, and her sections were very sad at her departure. This afternoon Miss Gilbert [teacher] leaves, and her sections are well nigh inconsolable. Poor children, I am sorry for them. Miss Gilbert is a dear precious good woman. I do love her

and would mingle my tears with her sections. I shall never forget Miss Gilbert. Oh if I could be as good, as worthy as she. The scenes today remind me of the time I left college. This morning in the Hall Miss Spoffard selected a hymn and lesson appropriate to the occasion. Many tears were shed.

March 30 - Wed. Afternoon - Recreation Day - Jennie's Diary
How fast Wednesdays come. I have done but little. This morning I took a painting lesson, then did my extra work, and dressed me for dinner. Since dinner I have been preparing a history lesson. This is our last lesson in history, and I am truly glad. My roommates had quite a discussion this morning about independence of character. Mary and Ellen had had a little dispute about some trifling matter, which gave rise to the conversation. In this I feel I am deficient. I know I am too much disposed to give way and yield my opinion to others. But I am determined to turn my thoughts to it more, and if possible cultivate independence of character. I may correct these defects yet. I have a disposition to think that I am not worthy of the love of those around me, and I reckon I am not. But then I ought not to dwell upon it so much as I do. I will try to act right, try to make my roommates happy, and if I do not succeed I cannot help it. I shall have done my duty. Now, I love my roommates very much, and I often feel sorrowful when I think that they care for me no more. But I reckon it is all my fault. I am not lively as they would like. Neither am I gifted or rich. But then, it is no matter; I can love them, and do what I can to make them happy. One thing I know, there are those at my dear home who love me and care for me. I am thankful for that. I will not repine. My dear Ellen is sitting at the window studying algebra. She is a dear good roommate, but it is with her as with others. I have concluded it best not to love anyone too well.

April 1 - Ann's Diary
I had a dream last night, which made a deep impression on my mind. I dreamed that the quarterly meeting at Providence had commenced, and there were hundreds of people there. I saw many of my old acquaintances, and many, many strangers. Among the latter was a

young gentleman of the most exquisite beauty I ever beheld. I dreamed Rev. Naylor was preaching, and his father —an aged minister who died some time ago— was sitting by the stand and he commenced shouting. [He] walked the house, clapped his hands and exclaimed "Hallelujah - hallelujah," and his countenance lit up with a heavenly smile and holy serenity, that so often characterized his former career. I was so deeply impressed with the scene that I burst into tears. I sobbed so loud I awoke and my pillow was moist with tears. I was so overpowered that it was sometime ere I could regain my composure.

April 4 - Jennie's Diary
I have just come from "setting tables," and I have a few minutes to write. This morning I did my washing. I think I shall be able to do it hereafter, and thus I can save some money for something else. The workmen have commenced pulling down the old wooden wing, and soon we shall see the new brick building going up in its stead. I like the way the Yankees go at things. This is a trying time with us. Last Thursday, Miss Spoffard was called away by the sickness of her brother. Yesterday Miss Chapin was called home by the death of her father. He was killed in a sawmill Saturday. A severe affliction to Miss Chapin and we would all sympathize with her. Miss Jessup and Miss Titcomb are most sick. Several of the girls have turned teacher today, and have been hearing the recitations. All things have gone on about as well as usual. This demonstrates the efficiency of the system here. Almost any other institution would have been almost broken up. Oh it is a gloomy day. It rains and rains. **Tuesday Night - 9 o'clock** Tonight we had a chemical lecture. Some experiments were made, but little explanation was made. Why is there such a universal failure on this point? I have been to recess meeting, taken my "half hour," and now I feel very much disposed to commune with my journal. I come to it as to a faithful friend. I can here unbosom myself as I cannot to any one of my companions. There is one now sitting by me to whom I should love to go and tell her my joys and sorrows, but then she does not enter into my feelings enough. I would not trouble her with my tale of sadness. Little does she know through what I

have made my way up to the present. But it is all right. I am foolish
for dwelling on this so much. We shall know each other better in the
Spirit World. This evening's mail brought me a letter from my cousin.
How much have I to be thankful for when I contrast my condition
with hers. She has no father or mother to care for her. She has not
had the advantages of education as I have had. I sympathize with
her. May I know how to do her good. And now I go to rest. May
tomorrow be a profitable day.

April 5 - Ann's Diary
I have commenced my little school at Providence. I am constantly
employed so that I have but little time to write. May I perform my
duty to those interesting children.

April 7 - Ann's Diary
I find the situation of a teacher very confining but I like it. I love to see
the youthful minds expanding beneath the genial rays of instruction.

April 7 - Jennie's Diary
State Fast. School duties suspended. Went to church twice. Funeral
of Mr. Moody this evening. This is the last fast day I shall ever spend
in the Seminary.

April 8 - Ann's Diary
This is a bright cool spring morning. The great Sun scatters abroad
his numerous rays. The little birds sing merrily. May my heart be
in unison with bright happy nature.

April 9 - Saturday - Jennie's Diary
I have just come from sections. This afternoon we had a lecture on
chemistry, and that made some changes in our arrangements. We
met in the Hall before we met in sections. Miss Jessup met with us in
the Hall. She made a great many remarks worthy of being treasured
up in our hearts. She spoke in a very pleasant and kind manner, and
all seemed pleased. Some notes of criticism led her to make some
remarks on politeness. I do love Miss Jessup. I wish I was as good

a teacher as she is. This is Saturday. I am tired. I am glad tomorrow is the Sabbath. Just now since I have been writing, I turned the ink over on Mary's table spread. I am sorry, very sorry. And more so because I suffered myself to get angry, because of some remark she made. I did not think that I would thus give way to my feelings. So true is it that we know not what we will do until we are tired. I am sorry that I have set such an example to my roommates. May I be forgiven, and may it not have any bad influence upon them. Oh shall I never do right? Shall I always be thus sinful? What shall I do?

April 11 - Tuesday - Jennie's Diary
The tardy bell for silent study hours has just struck, and as my tongue has to be silent for a little while, I will let my pen be the busier. I have one hour before I go to drawing, and I do not feel in a reading mood so I will write. I have been writing to my sister today. Dear Sister, how I wish I could be with her. She is engaged in a little school at home, and is quite pleased with her duties. I am so glad that she is doing something. I do feel anxious for her. May she have much success. My dear Ellen is sick this afternoon. I am sorry. I do want to sympathize with her; she was a dear good child to me when I was sick. Miss Walker has been in to see her. Mary and Gertrude are studying. All is quiet. One would scarce think a dozen girls were in the building, much less two hundred and fifty. The workmen are preparing the foundation for the new Wing. Now Augusta Tupper comes in our room, her [room is full of] smoke so she has to leave it.

April 11 - Ann's Diary
I have again met my school. May I be able to instruct them aright. Yesterday I went to church [and] heard a sermon by Rev. G. Brown. Attended a singing in the evening. The singing was delightful. I love to hear the thrilling melodies of our churches well sung. They create within us feelings of love.

April 13 - Thursday - Jennie's Diary
What a cold cloudy evening. I am so fidgety I do not know what to do. We commenced reviews today preparatory to the spring examinations. I like the way they do things up here. It is with a finish.

This afternoon in the Hall Miss Jessup gave us some advice about studying. She did not want us to be over anxious about our studies, but do the best we could and leave the rest. She did not want anyone on any occasion to ask for permission to be tardy in retiring, or to rise before the first bell, for we needed all the sleep we could get. [She told us] that the teachers did not wish us to recite any better now than we did before. [She told us] that they did not want us to appear any better than what we really were. She made some other pleasant remarks. We have been somewhat disappointed that Miss Chapin has not come today. I am sorry for Miss Jessup; she has so much to do. She hears fourteen recitations, besides attending to many other things. Some of our Southern Teachers would learn some useful lessons from the devotedness of teachers here. They work. The power of abstraction is cultivated wonderfully here. Sometimes two or three classes will be reciting in the same room. I had a good illustration today. At the hour bell I went down to set tables. Miss Scott's History class recited in the dining Hall at the same time. I said to her if I could attend to my work while the class recited. She said yes. And I went to setting tables and she to hearing recitation. And no inconvenience was given. **9 o'clock.** I have just returned from recess meeting. We had a pleasant little meeting. How often shall I remember these recess meetings. I am thankful for them. And also for the half-hours at morning and evening. How good it is, when weary with earth, and the cares of the outer and busy world, to have a kind Father to whom we can go and tell all our sorrows. I am glad it is written, "cast all of your care upon him, for he careth for you."

April 14 - Ann's Diary
The quarterly meeting will commence the 16 April. I expect to commemorate the death of our Lord and Savior. By the drinking of wine and eating bread, which are types of his blood spilt for us, and his precious body which suffered the pains of death for our redemption, we do show forth his love till his coming. May I have my heart cleansed by divine grace for the event.

April 18 - Ann's Diary

The quarterly meeting closed last night. We had some good preaching. Dr. Carter did not get here Saturday. He arrived yesterday morning. Preached at 11 o'clock from 1st Corinthians 21, 22, 23, 24. O! He did preach so well. After the second sermon we took the sacrament. By that we proclaimed to the world that we were servants of God. We renewed our vows with God and promised anew to love and serve him. May I go forth from this time shielded anew by divine Grace. Dr. Carter preached last night. O may I never forget it. He spoke of the death of the good man. He said, "God was with the good man in life and in death he was his support. Weeping friends might gather around his dying pillow to receive the last farewell, but they would avail nothing. The spirit of the good man saw bright winged Angels to conduct him over. The cold death damp gathers on his brow - - - an icy coldness seizes his heart."

April 18 - Monday Evening - Jennie's Diary

These evening hours have been delightful. The sun set behind Mt. Tom so beautifully. I do love New England sunsets. After supper I went down and did my rinsing. I am glad I have health and strength to do my own washing. I feel so independent now. My friend N. returned this evening to be at the reviews. I am glad to see her. Her health is much improved, and she hopes to be able to remain. Mr. Lyman's family remembered me, and sent me some nice walnuts. I and my roommates are enjoying them much. Today I have felt a pensive and melancholy mood stealing over me. I have quite a conflict in this matter. I do love to indulge in these states of mind. I have even sometimes thought they made me better. And yet I fear it is not right to indulge them. I may have cultivated the sensibilities too much. I find little things affect me greatly. A word, a look speaks volumes. And often has a simple expression or act deprived me a whole day's enjoyment. This ought not so to be. Maybe nothing was intended. I would I knew what was right. It is well I do not meet with the sympathy I long for. My heart clings too fondly to these whom I love. I should do wrong.

April 19 - Tuesday Night - Jennie's Diary

I am tired tonight, though I scarcely know for why. I am weary of all things earthly. But stop, here comes that indefinite longing after the ethereal, the spirit like, the unknown. I must not give way to it. I have a constant proneness to indulge this disposition. My time has been fully occupied today and yet I have accomplished but little. I get weary going over the same thing so much. I shall be glad when reviews are over and vacation is here. Mary and Ellen have gone to bed, for they are tired too. Mary is sick and I am sorry for the dear child. Tomorrow is recreation day. I must get up early and try to accomplish something.

April 20 - Wednesday Afternoon - 3 o'clock - Jennie's Diary

Wednesday is here again. It seems as if Wednesday came oftener than any other day. I have spent the morning in doing extra and domestic work. I have felt quite tired. Since dinner I have been in the Reading Room, much interested in a work [on treatment] of the Indians. There is much to be learned in it of the manners and the cultures of the Red Man of the forest. I am now alone in our room with my dear Ellen. I should be glad if Ellen knew how much I love her, if the knowledge would be acceptable. I wish I did not love her so much, unless she realized. I ought not. Well, my time is going on, and it is precious. I want to improve it. Soon I shall leave here. I want to gather up that which shall do me good in [the] afterlife. One thing I have learned, how little I know. **Evening. 9 o'clock** - One thing I do not want to let pass, (though it is now getting late) yet my pen must fly fast to record my wishes. This has been a rainy cheerless day. While at devotions at the supper table this evening, just as we were singing the last verse of the beautiful hymn, "When I Can Read My Little Dear," the last rays of the evening sun shone in most beautifully. Then in the prayer Prof. Haver mentioned the circumstance. After devotions I went up in the Upper Hall to see the sun sink behind Mt. Tom. Oh it was beautiful, beautiful. I love the setting sun.

April 21 - Thursday Evening - Jennie's Diary

"The day is done." How rapidly they flit away. This afternoon I had a delightful ramble with my roommates and two section sisters. We found a few flowers, and some winter green berries. I came back through the churchyard, and stopped a while to look upon the inscriptions. I love the quiet churchyard; the peaceful resting places of the loved and lost. I want to go again and commune with its silent monitors. After supper I sit down by the window and give myself to meditation. Ellen was sitting by me studying algebra. Mary was taking her half-hour, and Gertrude was down at Domestic work. Ada Catline played and sang some airs, which carried me back to scenes long gone by. I then took my "half hour," and the bell rang for "recess meeting." It was a pleasant little meeting. I shall always be thankful for these half-hours of prayer and meditation, and these recess meetings. I would I had a pure heart. I am so prone to place my affections upon earthly objects. They are not elevated as they should be. I do not cultivate that nobleness of spirit which I ought. I do not realize how much time is worth. Would that I could. I will strive for more spiritual mindedness. Alas, what is man! Now, I believe the greater the attainments we make in this world, the greater will be our attainments in the life to come. Yet, how little do we live in reference to that life. Shall I not be more thoughtful, more diligent in the future? My life is passing rapidly away, and what I do must be done quickly.

We chose to place Jennie's undated, untitled essay after the above diary entry since it continues to explore her thoughts on the afterlife and how humankind will be judged. She describes an art gallery where man and God view paintings. Jennie's various illnesses probably caused her to wonder about her own mortality and where she would fit into the spirit world. The essay has the aura of a "Dorian Gray," as she infers that art represents the ugly or beautiful truth. The piece sounds autobiographical, alluding to such events as the death of her sister. On the other hand, events such as the explosion of the steamboat and being thrown from the carriage were never mentioned in her writing. The sixteen-month period missing from her journal might have included a description of her travel to Mount Holyoke. The steamer incident could have happened as she was en route. The first part of the manuscript is missing.

c. 1852-1853 - Jennie's Essay - Untitled

...We paused nearby, but not so as to disturb the wretched one. From my guide I learned the following history of this man. In early life he had been thrown upon his own efforts. He was ever busy, active and energetic, and by his industry he gained untold wealth, and men praised him because he did well for himself. He lived to old age, and accomplished more than any of his fellows - hence the great canvas, and numerous pictures.

He gave abundantly to charity, and men extolled his benevolence. When he died it was said, "a great man has fallen," a nation mourned his loss, and a costly monument was reared to his memory, and his deeds inscribed thereon.

But how different the record of his works on the canvas before us. The motive and not the deed had been noted by the angel artist. In the left column were large paintings of his works as looked upon by men; in the right was written the estimate of the Almighty Judge. Against one was written "selfishness," against another "pride," against another, "to ease a guilty conscience."

At the bottom of the canvas was the closing act of his life. It was a huge representation of his noble Institution, founded for the friendless ones. Around stood admiring crowds wondering at the unheard liberality of the donor. To it he gave his name, and endowed it richly with gold and learned men, but from its classic halls all fear of God had been excluded. Against this great picture was written, "to be seen of men." Long and intently did he gaze upon the canvas, now and then exclaiming in all the bitterness of deep despair, "It is just, I am ruined, I am lost."

Near by stood one whose countenance beamed with holy joy as he looked upon the picture before him. On earth he had been a servant of this great man, was oppressed and despised. He was smitten by the same foul disease and followed his master to the Spirit Land. He now stood viewing his life as the heavenly artist had painted it. It was represented by little pictures, simple, yet so beautiful, showing a life spent in little acts, good and kind, of which the world never knew. At the bottom was written, "<u>well done</u>."

Time would fail me to tell of all that great multitude. There was the minister from his pulpit, the statesman from the Senate chamber—the lover of fame from his career of ambition—the rich man from his princely mansion, the slave from his galling chains, each absorbed in paintings which told of his life and destiny.

Many were there whom I had known on earth, and yet how changed. Not only did the canvas represent their lives differently, but themselves how changed. Some, whom I had known as fair and beautiful on earth, were now unsightly and even hideous. Others, who had been shunned on earth for their uncomely person, were now fairer than man can conceive. This I learned was owing to the different thoughts and dispositions which they had cherished in life. I recognized one who had been a companion of my early years, and had been envied by many, and admired by all for her beauty, grace of manner and accomplishments. But now her form all contorted and disfigured, she stood horror stricken before the almost blank canvas, which spoke of a useless life.

Another I remember as an old friend, whose body had been drawn and emaciated by intense suffering, and at whose patience I had often wondered. She was now a spirit perfect, pure and of loveliness divine. A multitude of others were around me, and I longed to learn their history, but my guide now hurried me on. We proceeded but a little way when he suddenly stopped before a canvas, and, turning to me with a look of deep meaning, said, "examine this," and he left me alone. Feeble is the pen of mortal to describe the emotions of my heart as I now saw my whole life spread out before me in perfect miniature. There were many things painted out in my own life that I had failed to see in others, and which I learned could be seen only by the one whose life, from [my] earliest infancy, was pictured [along] the train of Providences which had attended my pathway. Many of these [events] represented times when I had been exposed to imminent peril and had been rescued by an unseen hand. Some I remembered with distinctness. Once, I had been thrown from a carriage, and must have been instantly killed had not a guardian spirit saved me.

At another time while sailing in a beautiful steamer, a sudden explosion sent many to a watery grave, and I should have shared the same fate had not that invisible friend been near. Many things, which in life had been hidden mysteries, were now made plain.

Once I was about deciding upon a course of life. I now saw it would have led me to an early grave. My friends were surprised I did not choose it, and I wondered at myself. I also now understood plainly why a little sister whom I most tenderly loved had been early taken from me. But from studying these Providences, which were deeply interesting to me, I turned to the paintings of my actions. And here began a mournful picture. Actions which I and others thought done from pure motives were defaced by selfishness, envy, pride and ambition...

The next diary entry reconfirms Jennie's fear that she would die young.

April 22 - Friday Evening - Jennie's Diary

It's night again, and I am at my accustomed seat, my journal before me. I have just come from recess meeting. I love my section teacher and section sisters. May I be a comfort to them. This has been a rainy day. This afternoon we have had some thunder. The weekly account of exceptions was taken in this afternoon. More had exceptions than I have known since I have been here. There was but one perfect section. Miss Chapin seemed grieved at the number, and made some remarks. I am daily becoming more and more in love with the Seminary. I should love to remain here another year. I do so wish that I could graduate. Yet I am glad that I have the privilege of being here as long as I have. It will be a lasting benefit to me I trust. But I fear I shall never be able to go out and work as I wish. I fear a fatal disease is secretly wasting away my life. I shrink from the cares and responsibilities of a teacher's life. But surely my work cannot be finished. I long to go out and do something for the world. I am glad for the quiet night. It is a holy time. Care is done.

President Hitchcock [on the board of trustees at Mount Holyoke and president of Amherst College] was at devotions this morning and read the 37 Psalm. He called our attention particularly to the text, "Delight thyself in the Lord, and he shall give thee the desires of thy heart." His comment was cheering. And now I am going to bed. Good night.

Jennie, at the beginning of the year, defended the simplicity and reticence of her upbringing in the South but now sees fault in its lack of attention to refined culture. This farmer's daughter has come to admire the amenities of Northern high society.

April 26 - Tuesday Afternoon - Jennie's Diary

We have just left the Hall. Miss Jessup gave us some directions about cleaning our rooms; some remarks produced some merriment. Mary has gone to walk, and Gertrude and Ellen are down in the washroom rinsing. Our room is cold, for we have no fire; and to be alone and in a comfortable room I have to come to the Chemical Hall. The sun is shining brightly on Prospect Hill. Very many of the young ladies are out walking. The spring is opening delightfully; the valleys are fast being covered with a rich green carpet. I feel in a contemplative mood this afternoon, and my thoughts go back to other days. I love to think of the past, yet I would not dwell upon it too much, only to take courage and be faithful. I am sorry to remember that so many of my relations and friends are deprived of the advantages which I enjoy. But few of them have had any educational advantages. Would that light might break in upon my natal place. I have felt since I have been here more than ever, the unspeakable value of good society, and intelligent companions in early life. Not that I would despise the humble, by no means. But there is no one so humble who may not cultivate taste and refinement. The tone of morals and general good breeding in common society could and should be far more elevated. Courtesy and morality are not limited to the circles of the wealthy. But common people, since they are not bound by the rigid formalities of polished life, indulge in a rude familiarity, which tends greatly to lower the standard of manners and morals. May I know how to do good to mine own class.

Jennie was a tormented person who never felt comfortable in her own skin. Note how she changes her mind dramatically from the above journal entry. One day she wishes she could be more like Northern gentility, the next day she berates herself for excessive pride. This pattern of inner conflict and indecisiveness continued throughout her life.

April 28 - 2 o'clock - Jennie's Diary

This is a delightful day. The sun shines so brightly and the grass is so lively green. I am reminded of my own sunny home, far, far away. I long to be there. I sometimes think I have done wrong to leave my home. I have left the circle of my birth, and I may yet repent it. Every day makes me more and more sensible [as to] how much I lack in the formalities of higher society. Some I would not know, others I should like to know. Yet I know there is much vanity, pride, selfishness, and sin hid under a graceful exterior, and accomplished manners. I do not know why, but I have had one continued struggle for a few days against my discontented heart! I long for a refined and noble nature. I want to take a more elevated course. I am living for eternity. I am working a work, which shall be tried in the day of judgment. I shall then stand not according to my wealth, or learning, or position in society; not according to the politeness of my manners, or gentility of person but <u>according as I have known and done my duty.</u> Now I do want to do right. I would not murmur. I have ten thousand reasons to be constantly thankful. I want to live for something, and to do that, I must have a decided and energetic spirit. I must have some independence. Oh what, what shall I do? I am almost crazy. I feel sometimes as if I should surely go crazy. Oh what, what shall I do? Have I no control over my feelings! It is not right for me to feel as I do, I wish I could shake it off.

April 29 - Friday Evening - Jennie's Diary

This has been a day of suffering to me. My jaw has pained me very much, but feels some better just now. I see from what I wrote yesterday, that my spirit was sad indeed. Now I know what made me feel so. Gertrude and Ellen's cousins were here, and they were very happy. Seeing them enjoying themselves so, made me realize my utter loneliness and how far separated I was from my home and friends. Their cousins were very genteel; I remembered I could claim no such cousins, and I was sorrowful. But this was wrong, very wrong. I am sorry I have such a spirit! I have striven against it, prayed against it. I do hope I may never feel so any more. I want to overcome it. It is sinful. Though my dear parents have given me no titled name, no stately mansion, yet they have given me an unsullied name. I would be thankful.

May 2 - Monday - Jennie's Diary
I did have a precious letter from my sister tonight. I am thankful for such a sister. She is pleased with her schools. Tomorrow the examinations commence.

May 3 - Tuesday - Jennie's Diary
The examinations have gone off finely today. I have been much interested in seeing how the teachers do up things now. I shall get some valuable ideas for the future. Seven classes are examined each half-day. There is no humbug in these examinations. But few failures today. We are requested to be in the Hall four hours per day. During examinations we cannot speak in our rooms above a whisper.

May 4 - Wednesday Evening - Jennie's Diary
Another day of our examinations is gone. There have been some most excellent recitations. Miss Jessup's class in [Paleontology] passed finely. Miss Jessup was so pleased. All the teachers have been in good spirits; they appear so cheerful and happy. Many hearts are growing buoyant at thoughts of going home. Oh that I could go to my home so easily. But alas, it is far away. "Happy Home, I am sure I love thee."

May 5 - Thursday - Jennie's Diary

Well, examinations are now over and right glad children are we. Some have gone home, some are going in the morning in the early stage. Many are going. I am glad for quiet vacation.

May 12 - Thursday Morning - Jennie's Diary

I employ my pen this morning in noting down some scenes in which I have been during the past two days, the impressions of which I do not wish to fade away. Last Monday Miss Scott proposed a visit to Miss Lyon's home. Many of us were anxious to go, and we made up a party of about thirty. We were busily engaged Monday afternoon in making arrangements for our journey. We took our provisions and so we [were] quite independent. Early Tuesday morning we set off, a merry company, for Buckland. We passed through many pleasant villages along the banks of the Connecticut, among which were Hadley, Sunderland, South Deerfield. We halted at the foot of Sugar Loaf and a party went on top of the mountain, the others went to the Hotel in South Deerfield. Here we rested a while, took a lunch, and in about an hour were joined by the mountain party. Soon the coaches were ready and we were off again. I enjoyed the afternoon but little because of a violent headache. We passed through different towns, the principle [one] was Greenfield, quite a place. The evening was very warm, and we traveled slowly. We reached Shelburne Falls about six o'clock, and stopped for the night. Found very good accommodations, and after a quiet night, set out next morning for the place of our destination. The morning was fine, and the scenery was grand beyond description. Wild rugged mountain heights, covered with rich evergreens, towered up each side of our pathway. After climbing mountains, and winding through ravines we came to a steep ascent, at the top of which we were to find the object of our journey, Miss Lyon's home. We got out of the coaches and walked up. And sure enough, there upon the side of the mountain was a little obscure dwelling with two small rooms; the home of Miss Mary Lyon, the founder of Mt. Holyoke Female Seminary. We walked through the rooms, wandered over the grounds, which had witnessed the childish sports and youthful exertions of that wonderful woman. We felt as if we were on hallowed ground, and a reverence bound us to the spot. After visiting the different places of interest, we spread our dinner on the green grass beneath a tree, under whose shade she had probably played. After finishing our meal we sent some cake and biscuit to the family living in the house. They were very poor, and seemed overjoyed at such supply of food. We gathered many relics, and after spending about two hours, turned our steps towards home. We passed through Ashfield and visited the Academy in which Miss Lyon taught school. Our journey homeward was one of the most delightful rides I ever had. It was a gradual descent from the mountains to the valley of the Connecticut. For the greater part of our journey down the mountains, a brook of crystal waters made its way. It came leaping and dancing over its rocky bed so wild and free. The mountainsides were covered with rich evergreens, fine hemlock, fir and etc. From the wild romantic scenery of the mountains we came to the quiet valley of the Connecticut. Night was fast coming on, and the village farmers were winding their way home. For about seven miles our way lay along the Connecticut. Someone has said, "this earth has many a beautiful spot as poet and painter may show," but here was a scene that would laugh to scorn the best efforts of the greatest "poet or painter." The sun set behind Mt. Tom, and the deep gold of eventide was richly reflected on the silvery bosom of the Connecticut, whose quiet waters were unruffled by wave. The stately elms along its banks were mirrored with the most perfect exactness in the waters below. Soon the daylight was gone, and the red light faded from the West. The new moon unveiled her modest face, and one star, and then another, came out, and looked down so peacefully upon us; all nature meanwhile looking so lovely, that we feign would have detained the hours, that we might feast longer on the delightful scene. Thus fades away a day never to be forgotten by one of our happy number. We reached the Seminary about 9 o'clock, and found a nice warm super carefully prepared by our companions here. This we enjoyed, and then uniting with Miss Scott in returning thanks for the blessings of the day, we went to our beds with glad and thankful hearts.

Back at Providence, Ann's poem mirrors Jennie's mood as well as her all-embracing love of nature.

May 13 - Ann's Poem

To a Vase of Flowers

Beautiful Vase! Thy mission is glorious,
Thou art laden with Nature's loveliest gifts.
Thy inmates are roses and honeysuckle odorous;
Which is culled in the forests and rocky cliffs.

Wild woodbines and jasmine gracefully twine -
Laurels and Ivy encircle thy brow -
Daisies and Daffodils confiding recline,
Cedars and Evergreens fantastically bow.

Half concealed lie the glittering dewdrops of night
In the fragrant and delicately blushing rose,
And the morning sun so radiant and bright,
Lends a ray to salute it - how lovely it grows!

Beautiful Vase! May no harm befall thee,
No thistle or thorn on thy margin repose,
But fanciful wreaths in drap'ry conceal thee
And thy brow richly thy beauties disclose.

May 16 - Ann's Diary
Why does my heart hang heavily? I feel so serious and melancholy.
O! How I long for more Christian love. A subject, which I thought
overcome, has, for the past two days, harnessed my mind. Why do I
feel so solemn about it? O! Wisest of the wise, if I have decided
wrong, help me. I acted as I thought for the best. Be thou our stay
and comforter.

May 17 - Ann's Diary
While listening to a lesson read by one of the girls this morning on the
Omnipresence and Omniscience of the Deity I was strongly impressed.

Not one atom of the whole creation but bears the impress of a divine hand that made it. Not the least space but his presence pervades it. O may I take heed to my ways for God is ever present.

May 19 - Ann's Diary
I have been engaged in school all day. I find delight in my new occupation. It is delightful to see the youth mind expanding under instruction.

May 19 - Jennie's Diary
Vacation is done. The young ladies have returned. But some have been hindered by the rain. Some came wet, and we could exercise our benevolence in giving them some little aid. Tomorrow we commence studying, though vacation has been very, very pleasant. Miss Scott has done her best to make us happy. She said she had never spent a vacation so pleasant as this. I am glad to see the girls return; and I shall be glad when our duties commence and all things move on harmoniously as usual. I do love to have things done orderly.

May 21 - Jennie's Diary
This has been [an] almost useless day to me. This morning I tried to write compositions, but my poor brain became so confused and crazed that I had to stop. So the day has passed away and I have written not a word of composition. Thus have I added to the number of my misspent Saturdays. I have been sad and thoughtful all day. And I am sorry for it, for I fear I make my roommates unhappy. I know I love them very much, but I cannot think that they do me, and I do not blame them. I have thoughts of petitioning that they put me in another room when we change rooms. I have sent many thoughts home today, and much wished to be there. This lovely springtime I should spend so pleasantly there. The scenery around South Hadley is now growing delightful. The first trees are in full bloom, and the trees are leaved out. It is beautiful but still I am sad and lonely. It is wrong for me to indulge such feeling, but it seems as if I cannot help it.

The next five entries are quite fascinating. Jennie writes in her diary, then writes home to her mother. The letter is filled with information which sheds light on the mechanics of washing clothes and the dangers of traveling. Sister Ann reveals in her diary that she has a headache. Jennie has one the same day. The entry on May 25 will be Jennie's last diary notation until February 1854. We have to piece the information together in order to close this gap in the story.

May 23 - Monday Night - Jennie's Diary

Just now I am all alone. My roommates are at Domestic work. I have been washing this evening since supper, and am somewhat tired. Ellen has been talking about going south. I should so much love to have her with me at the college. I believe she might do good there. She is a dear roommate. I should love to tell her my own history, but she might not feel any interest in it. The teachers are making arrangements to change our rooms Wednesday. There will be some sorrowful hearts I expect. I will not be anxious about my room. I love my present roommates, and if it is for the best I should love to remain as we are. Sometimes I think I might do other roommates more good. I have of late been trying to look into my own heart. And I find it so sinful, and full of worldly thoughts that I am almost discouraged. I would grow more heavenly-minded day by day. I would have my conversation in heaven, and my treasure there.

Same day - May 23 - Jennie's Letter to her Mother, Elizabeth

Holyoke Seminary
23 May, 1853
Monday evening

My dear Mother,

I have need to make apology to you for my long silence, but as you have heard from me in my letters to sister Ann, you will be disposed to excuse me. I have for some time been looking for a letter from you. Sister Ann said in her last [letter] that you had the will to write but was hindered by company.

Had I not been silent so long I might not have commenced writing tonight for I have a headache and am somewhat tired. I have been washing this evening since supper, and tho it is but small washing, yet I have not much extra strength. I enjoy washing very much, and have done it with but little trouble except getting tired. We have every convenience for doing it that we could ask. There is a large wash room in which near one hundred can wash at once. The water is heated in immense kettles in large furnaces. Two of the young ladies attend to filling the kettles, and keeping up the fires all the time. The tubs in which we wash are fastened to a framework. When we have [filled them] with the water, all we have to do is to pull out a stopper in the bottom of the tub and the water runs off in a pipe with which the tub is connected. When our clothes are ready to boil, we put them in our clothes bags and place them on a bench, and look after them no farther for the time. A young lady attends to the boiling of them, and at a certain hour we go down and rinse. But you would think that among so many it would be difficult for each one to find her own bag, and it would if the whole was not reduced to a system. The owner's name is written on the bag. A paper, with a list of our names, and the number of the tub in which our clothes should be put, is hung up in the wash room. By looking at this the one who takes out the clothes knows where to put them, and looking at it we know where to find them. We have our clothes on a line marked with the number of our room. We iron Saturday morning.

I like the fun of washing, but I do not succeed in getting my clothes very white sometimes. And now I have told you a rather a long story about washing, and after all it does not amount to very much. For it is of little moment to Southerners how Yankees do their washing. I often wish while enjoying these conveniences that I could transfer some of them to my home. I should love to see my mother [the mistress] of a nice farm house such as I have seen in New England.

Same Day - May 23 - Ann's Diary.

Yesterday was my birthday but I spent it badly. In the morning I attended [a] Temperance meeting and after that I had the headache so badly I could neither read nor write. I had intended to read and write much but I was so unwell I could not.

The incident in the papers that Jennie refers to in this next letter was a New Haven Railroad accident in Norwalk, Connecticut, on May 6. The conductors somehow missed the signals and the train rushed up a drawbridge while it was open, and the cars fell into the opening. Of the 218 passengers on board, twenty-seven were wounded and forty-five were killed. It was considered the worst accident ever recorded in U.S. railroad history.

May 25 - Jennie's Letter to her Mother Continues

Wednesday night. This has been a busy day Mother. We have been changing rooms, and we have all been in a great hurly-burly. I have changed my room from No. 93 to 84. I have the same roommates, and a very pleasant room, much more pleasant than the one we left. I wish Mother could come into my room and see how nicely all things are arranged. I am becoming quite accomplished in housekeeping. I am learning to do up many things with neatness and taste.

I have had my Domestic work changed also. My work heretofore has been setting tables. I now work on the "White Crockery Circle." I wash bake dishes, bake pans, and bowls one hour after dinner. It is rather hard work, for some of the vessels are very large, but I do not mind it if I can do it, for they have been very kind to me all the while and [have] given me easy work. I shall keep this work if I am able until the year closes, and that will not be long. Oh mother, when I think that in so short a time as ten weeks I shall be homeward bound I can scarce contain myself. And yet ten weeks is a wide gap between me and home. And as the time comes on I ask myself more earnestly how shall I get home alone? Railroad and steamboat disasters come to us in almost every paper. You have no doubt seen in the [papers] the account of the terrible accident at Norwalk, Conn., and that was only a part of the many heart-rending scenes which have of late been acted. But the same strong arm that protected me here can take me safely home. Glad as I shall be to place my foot in the cars that shall take me home, yet I shall somewhat regret to leave the Seminary. There are some pleasant associations here which I shall regret to break up. I am quite attached to my New England home, and to my roommates. I shall part from all these to meet no more. But then I would not be very sad for all this, for I have many dear interests in my Southern home, and there are those there who love me better than anyone here can.

So far as worldly prospects are concerned, the future is as bright as I need ask it. But for all that, I flee, I feel dissatisfied. I am not so much weary of the world as of myself. I do not so much wish for friends, as that I may be worthy of those I already have. I know there is much expected of me; I tremble lest I fail to meet the expectations of friends.

One thing I will tell you Mother, but as it is rather a confidential matter just now, you will not say anything about it outside of the family. Mr. Deems wrote me the other day telling me the former faculty was broken up. Of all the lady teachers, he did not expect any to return except Miss Hagen and myself. That I should head the list of lady teachers hereafter, with a salary of $300 beside board, and other attentions. The session commences 28 July [and] he is anxious to have me there as early as possible; I may be there by the 15 of August.

Mother, I have long been looking for a letter from you but none has come. I know I have written poor uninteresting letters of late, but I have done the best I could. The correspondence has mostly been between Sister Ann and I [sic], but I hope Mother has not forgotten me. I need your letters very much. I have hard work sometimes to keep up my spirits. I have sad attacks of melancholy. And yet I have nothing to make me sad but my own bad heart. Oh Mother, if I were only good and wise I should be satisfied.

I have not heard from home so long, but I think I may have a letter from you soon. If papa could steal time to write me a little line I should be so glad. Much love to all. I must close for tonight. I think I will do better next time. I am sorry to send away such a poor scrape as this. My health is good as usual. Tell Sister Ann to write me often.

I should love to write Aunt ["Blind Aunt Nancy"] but my time will not allow me now. It is growing late.

> Goodbye, Mother
> Your daughter
> Jennie

Same Day - May 25 - Wednesday Evening - Jennie's Diary

This has been an unstirred day. We have changed rooms, and many have changed roommates, and many are sad because they have not the rooms and roommates they wanted. I am very well satisfied. I have the same roommates, but have changed my room for No. 84. It is a very pleasant room on the south side of the wing. We have a good view from our windows. I hope we may be very happy together, and do each other much good. I sometimes wish they had taken my dear Ellen away. I fear I shall do wrong in loving her too much. (She is now sitting by me writing a letter, little thinking what is passing in my mind.) I am glad all things have passed off so pleasantly as they have.

As for the next entry our best guess is that Ann was experiencing unrequited love. Her passages of forlorn point to the idea that some man had proposed to her, then broke off the engagement. This unfinished letter was found in her 1853 diary. We do not know the specific day or month.

c. 1853 - Undated - Ann's Diary

In compliance with your request, I will answer your letter, though it may not be so soon as you requested. The question contained in your letter should receive a decided answer, at once, but this I am at present unable to give you. I am sensible of, and appreciate the honor you confer upon me by offering me the first place in your affections, but I cannot engage myself to any young gentleman without first consulting my parents. For I could not marry without their consent, even though my affections were blighted by their refusal. And as they, of course, must know and be consulted sometime, it is proper that I know their opinions first. I have had no opportunity of seeing them;

you will excuse this delay, which is unavoidable. You may think it strange that I should defer my decision on account of my parents. If so, I can only say that if I had not had one of the best of fathers and an almost perfect mother....

June 8 - Ann's Diary

My mind is all turned this morning - I feel sad. I almost repent my decision in regard to _____. [?]. O God, have mercy on me. If life's young hopes are blasted, be thou, O Father, my stay. Thou art my only refuge. In thee will I trust.

Long before ecology became a buzzword of the twentieth century, Jennie was warning against those who use the land for profit without referring to the "depths of the soul."

June 11 - Jennie's Essay

The Beautiful Lies in the Depths of the Soul

The world in which we live gives evident marks that the Builder intended its inhabitants should be happy. If not, why these towering mountains and fertile plains, rising hills and far spreading valleys; these rivers, lakes and oceans? Why this endless profusion of flowers and fruits, these ever changing seasons, with their varied loveliness? Yet one half of mankind lives and dies without ever suspecting that there is anything attractive in the scenes around them.

It is true a love for the beautiful is the gift of God, and lies hidden deep in the soul, but it is our duty to cultivate and strengthen it. He who has it not, looks upon this world as one great mass of earth, rocks, water and vegetation, heaped together for use only. He values a beautiful plain only as it will bring him so many dollars and cents per acre or foot, or yield so many bushels of grain. The most majestic river in all its winding course is naught to him; he is interested only in the rich meadows along its banks, or the amount of merchandise which may be floated upon its bosom. He builds an elegant mansion by the roaring, dashing, whirling waters of proud Niagara, not because the scenery is grand and imposing, and may exert a happy influence upon the character of his family, but that he may gain the gold of the visitor.

But if the soul be turned to harmony, all things else will be beautiful. Everyone has proof of this in his own experience. When I have been sad and lonely, I have seen or heard nothing pleasant, tho a friend pointed out the most lovely prospect in nature. But, again, when sunshine has been in my heart, all things lit up with a glory unearthly; and though the day were dark and stormy, there was music in the patter of the rain drops upon the window, and in the whistling winds.

Upon the banks of a noble river sat a weary student, just come from his study to bathe his fevered brow in the cool evening air. The sun had gone down behind the distant mountains, and the "last red light, the farewell of the day" was on the western sky. Some majestic elms standing on a little island were mirrored to the life in the waters beneath. A noble steamer was bearing leisurely up the river, and music from a joyous band was borne upon the evening air. A few clouds of snowy whiteness, tipped with the deep gold of eventide, were reflected in the quiet waters. There sat the youth absorbed, lost in admiration. Passers-by wondered at the intensity of thought and feeling that was pictured in his countenance. But they knew not that the beauteous scene had so bound him to the spot. They saw nothing uncommon; they felt no delight. "The beautiful lies in the depth of the soul."

As the oldest in the family, Asbury was not allowed the educational advantages enjoyed by Aaron, Jennie and Ann. While a colonel in the Civil War, he would write frequently, but it appears that he was reluctant to write in the 1850s because it was difficult for him. We have only one letter from Asbury during this time. In this letter he tells Jennie that he will not be able to accompany her home from the North. We will leave misspellings and grammatical errors as he wrote them to demonstrate the contrast.

June 17 - Asbury's Letter to Jennie

Dear Sister,

      I am like you were in your letter. I have neglected answering your letter I received some two weeks ago. I hope you will excuse me.

      I am well and trust this may finde you injoying all the blessings of health. I was very glad to hear from you and that you were well.

      Sister I have but little news of any importance to write though I will make my letter as interesting as I can. We have very dry weather now - - - no rain to do any good and everything looks very dry. Wheat is good and the people are done cutting. Oats are very short. Corn looks very well. We have beans and potatoes - - - lots of them. I eat potatoes down the country four weeks ago. We have had plums for the last three weeks. Pares and June apples will soon be good now. The examination [at Jonesville Academy] is now over and the scholars have all gon home. The next session commences the eighteenth of July. There were a grate many people here at the examination, and were highly pleased. Your old friend Miss Higgin [Hagen? Miss Hagen was in the music department] from Greensboro was here and is here now. She gave us some splendid pieces on the forty foot instrument.

      The people in this section are inclined to be rather sickly at this time. There has been two deaths in two days in this neighborhood. One of them is buried today. Miss Sally Pinyin is at home. She graduated this session.

      You write that you will be ready to start home in August and that you would like for your Brother to accompany you home. Well, Sister I would like very much to come and come home with you. If nothing happens I espect to go to Pha. [?] this fall about the first of September. But I suppose you will want to come home before then. I would be highly pleased to come where you are and see the country. Your pictures of the surrounding country has excited my curiosity but if you come in August the time will be very bad for me to come as I will have to go in September.

I was at Fathers last week and they were all well. The apple trees, garden field and meadow all look very pleasant indeed. O! They bring back the thoughts of the past when we were all there injoying all the blessings of Parental affections and cear. These are days I dare not speak of as I am all most compelled to shed the tear of regret that I ever left my Father's house. But everything is for the better to them that do right. I will bring my letter to a close. Excuse haste and bad hand. I hope to see you - - - will write soon.

Your Brother,
W.H.A. Speer

July 4 - Jennie's Letter to her Mother, Elizabeth

Mt. Holyoke Seminary
Monday noon 4 July
My dear Mother, the letter I promised to write last week has not been begun until this morning. I have risen early this morning, combed my hair, spent half [an] hour in devotions, taken the clothes off the beds that they may air, and I am now sitting by the window writing to you. You see from the date above that one year ago today I was with you. That to me was a happy day. This [day] will pass in the usual routine of school duties, as the teachers do not think it best for us to observe the day. I think it is a shame that we cannot celebrate the greatest anniversary of our nation. But I am glad that the people around here think differently from the teachers. Cannon have been firing around in different towns ever since midnight. And just now a stage load of men went by going to Springfield; it is a high day there. The day is rather unfavorable tho, for it has been raining, and still is dark.

July 6 - Jennie's Letter Continues

Mother, the "fourth" came and went, and two more days have come and gone, and you see how my letter progresses. Something interrupted me just as I was getting ready to write and I had to break away. I do indeed get discouraged, and were it not my duty I am not sure that I should try to write any more. My friends think strange of me that I do not write more, but if they could only look upon me and see the numerous demands upon my time, they would wonder no longer. But I will not trouble you with complaints longer.

I have just come from domestic work, and have half an hour before I go to drawing, which I will make the most of. I have learned that they had a splendid time in Springfield and Northampton on the "fourth." We could see something of the fire works in Springfield, a distance of ten miles. Yesterday was recreation day, and I went to Easthampton to see Miss Lyman. I had a pleasant visit, tho I had a bad headache all day. Last night I dreamed of going home. It did seem so plain. I could scarce believe it was not a reality. I had only gone home to stay a few days and then to return, but I felt sorry that I had not waited until the term was out, and then I would not have had to return. But waking I found it was but a dream. A few weeks and I hope it will not all be a dream. Four weeks from today and the school closes. I shall be glad.

I received a letter from sister Ann Tuesday night. I think there must be a letter which I have not received, for she speaks of some things as tho she had written them before. The trip to the "Pilot" (Mountain) I am left to conjecture. But I can make allowances for her; I know she is busy. I am glad that her school closed up so pleasantly, and also that she has another made. [Ann went from teaching at Providence to teaching at Jonesville Methodist Academy.] Can it be that I am yet to see what I have so long wished for —— my sister a teacher. But I see from something she says that she is tending to a mood that has given me untold sorrow and trouble. I will say a word to her if I possibly can. She mentions Cousin Joshua's School. I am ignorant of it however, as I have not heard about it. [First cousin - Joshua Kennerly Speer III was teaching at Yadkin Institute in 1853.] Where is it located and what size? I wish I could go home and have a good long talk about things in general. I am well nigh a stranger to the people of my own neighborhood. I should love to renew the acquaintance. I have by no means forgotten them. It did me some good when Annis said the people of Center inquired of me, not because I want people to think a great deal of me, but Mother, there is something refreshing in the thought that one lives in the affectionate remembrances of friends. I sometimes think I value this more than I should as it makes me sensitive to things I should not mind. But it is my misfortune and not my sin.

I received a letter from brother Asbury the same evening that sister Ann's came. He is a good brother to write me. If you see him directly, say to him he shall have an answer as soon as I can find time to write. The pictures, which he and Sister Ann give of fruits, beans, potatoes, and etc., are really provoking, unless one could get them. Here we have yet had but three dinners of peas, a few cherry pies and dumplings. I shall miss them all this summer, for I shall leave here before they come on, and when I get home they will be gone, but never mind that if I can only get home, I shall be thankful.

Night. Mother it is now near bedtime. I am tired and can only say to you and all, "good night."

July 8 - Jennie's Letter Continues

Friday After Dinner. Again I have just come from domestic work. I had some hard work, and am somewhat tired. Miss Scott said the other day that she thought it the most unpleasant work that is to be done. I console myself by thinking that it will soon be done. If you could see my hands you might think that they belonged to some washerwoman - they are so big and black. But it all may do me good in the end.

Mother I need some comforting from you today, for I feel quite discouraged. I have undertaken to draw a head [portrait] but have not succeeded well, and I feel very much disappointed. I wanted to draw a nice piece to bring home but shall fail at last. So it seems with everything I undertake and I fear after all, that life itself will be a failure and if so, what a failure! I must need someone to tell me what to do. I am often sorry that I have such longings for sympathy, for there is not much to be found in this world, and one ought not to expect it. And yet to me it is the half of life. But Mother, these vague speculations are not appropriate for a letter, tho I find myself so prone to indulge them. I fear my letters must be insipid, for I see no meaning to them after they are finished. I might as well sit down and write of letters received, and that I am well, for if I go beyond this I may write something which I have written before. I hope, ere long, to have a better means of communication. But I do not know that I shall come home until winter, as they expect me at the College, and I could not stay long. And it may be better for me to stop in Greensboro and rest during that time, than to come home. I do remember what father said last summer, that he hoped I would give myself some time to rest when I come from the North, but I see little chance for it. I should dearly love to come home and stay until New Year, but when one gives themselves up to the public, they must do as the public demands, and not as inclination would lead them. You have said Mother, that you had given me up never to be at home any more, and I am thinking I might as well be reconciled to the same. Mr. Deems says my situation at the College shall be more pleasant, as there will be a greater number of teachers, and I shall not have so much to do. I intend also not to set my heart so on my duties as to affect my health. Yet I fear. Mother will you let me hear from you if there is time for [you to write] me before I leave? I have not heard [from you] in a long time. I cannot expect to hear much oftener as the time is so short. I will write when I get to Greensboro and let you know of my state. Love to all.

Dutifully,
Your daughter Jennie

As she studied at Mt. Holyoke, Jennie began to realize that no matter how much she studied or read, she could not attain the whole of knowledge. She left the seminary realizing how little she knew. This undated and untitled essay was probably written while she was in Massachusetts.

c. 1853 - Jennie's Essay - Untitled

When I was a child my father spoke of my commencing to study Geography, Grammar, etc... I was very much pleased with the idea of studying Geography, for I thought I should like to know more about the great world in which we live. And I was not a little elated with the thought of possessing so large a book as an Atlas. As for studying Grammar or anything else, I thought it quite absurd. Already I knew more than any of my class, could write as well, read better, and had read more books. What else did I need?

Long years have passed away since then, and today I am infinitely farther from knowing all than in my childish fancy. Days, months, years I have spent in study. Text-book after text-book I have devoured, until my heart has grown sick, and my head distracted with the toil, and now I must confess, "how little I know."

And must it always be thus? Shall the knowledge I gain day by day serve only to light up the boundless fields yet unexplored and set my ignorance ever before me? I am as one coming out of a deep dark ravine, whose ideas of the world have been limited to the surrounding mountains. As he ascends, new light breaks in, and a widening prospect spreads out before him. Higher and higher he ascends, his astonishment increasing with the increasing distances, until he stands upon the mountain top and looks off upon interminable fields of hills and plains, of mountains and valleys.

I might proudly enumerate the sciences I have studied, which have told me of the starry hosts above, of the earth beneath, and of the animals and plants upon it. But yonder roll those worlds of light effectually defying my feeble efforts to comprehend their times and seasons. The tiniest seed has hid within it a secret I cannot unravel - its living principle.

I can trace many effects to their causes, and from a given cause reason the effect, but why those causes should produce such effects I cannot tell. Of the empires that have risen and fallen, of the nations and kingdoms which now exist, what do I know? And what do I know of myself? Whatever Mental Philosophy may have revealed, I am still a stranger to myself. I should indeed despair, were it not for the hope that when I stand amid the realities and in the broad sunlight of eternity, I "shall know even as also I am known."

July 15 - Ann's Diary

This is Saturday; a beautiful lovely day. O! That I had Angel's wings. I would cleave the rustling air, and reach the summit of gorgeous clouds and rest there on its snowy bosom. I would pillow my head on its vapory cushion and look aloft at the glorious sun and free blue sky. The eagle itself should not outstrip my flight.

From a receipt from the Howard Hotel in New York City, we know that Jennie was en route home and stayed at the hotel August 12. Ann's diary entry suggests that she is still mourning the loss of her suitor, and it also serves well to summarize the 1853 year. This is the last diary entry we have for that year.

August 26 - Ann's Diary

What charm does this life afford to prolong our stay? What joy unmixed with sorrow? What cup replete with sweets but has a draught of bitterness mingled with its contents! The protestations of undying love and fidelity made today, tomorrow are scattered to the winds of heaven. Things flattered and caressed today are objects of disgust tomorrow. Today we may bask in sunbeams of gladness, while friends throng around and add an attraction for us to _____, our hearts are deluged in sorrow, adversity's pains may wither our souls, former friends forsake us, and we have no refuge but heaven. Oh! What blessedness in this trying hour to have access to God's mercy.

CHAPTER THREE

JENNIE AND ANN

1854-1855

From late August 1853 to February 1854 we have no documents from either sister. We do, however, know that Jennie returned to Greensboro Female College and that Ann is listed in the catalog as a teacher at Jonesville Female Academy. From a letter that Ann wrote, it would appear she was also taking classes. We do not think Ann kept a diary during 1854, so our only records are her letters and essays, some of which are only dated "1854." Jennie mentions several authors, including Margaret Fuller, a noted transcendentalist, who wrote for Horace Greeley's New York newspaper, The Tribune. Her journal entries become short and to the point. Of interest this year is a visit to the dentist, her move to Rockford, North Carolina, and Ann's beautiful essays. While Jennie slides deeper into melancholy, Ann is able to sustain her passionate exuberance of language and is simply more secure than her sister. She never dances around her emotions but meets them head on.

February 7, 1854 - Tuesday Evening - Jennie's Diary

I have finished another manuscript of my journal, and begin a new one. I want to make this still more true and faithful. My journal is my friend. I want it to be a true one. I had a nice treat tonight from one of my section, Miss Williams—she is a little child, but a smart child. It is pleasant to have these tokens of affectionate remembrance. May my Father bless my dear section, and make them his own.

February 8 - Wednesday Afternoon - Jennie's Diary

Mr. Deems told me a little while ago that Miss T. [student] would be in my section. Thus I have another responsibility added to my already full list. I hope I may be able to do her good. This is a dreary day. I feel it much. What creatures of circumstances are we! My classes drag heavily, and sometimes I feel quite discouraged. Today composition [class was] a trying day to teachers and pupils. Oh how it rains!

February 9 - Jennie's Diary

The sun has come out all bright and beautiful this morning, and when the earth shakes off the dewdrops, it will be a pleasant day. I am glad for this sunshine, how refreshing after the dreariness of yesterday. As in the natural, so in the social world; one day is gloom and darkness the next, sunlight and gladness. I have work to do today. I want to do it well. Tomorrow I hope we shall have rest day.

February 11 - Saturday Morning - Jennie's Diary

This morning I have been down Street Shopping. And now I am waiting for Dr. Howlett to come and work upon my teeth. This is a severe business, but then it is for my health and comfort, and I ought to go to it bravely. I have one tooth to be taken out, and I can bring myself up to it only by remembering that it is my duty. And though it is a little matter, yet I can do even this for the sake of my Heavenly Father. This is a beautiful day, and if it were not for my teeth I would have one nice, long walk. **Saturday evening -** And now the day and week are done. And I do feel much relieved. This afternoon I went through the trial - - - had Dr. H. to take out my tooth. But oh the shock. He had three trials before he could take it out. It was severe. But I do feel so thankful that it is out. Tomorrow is Prof. Wallie's birthday. We have thought to make him a birthday present. I have added a writing desk. And now may the quiet, peaceful Sabbath come on. May it be a day of profound rest and Holy Communion to us all. Hasten on, blessed day.

February 12 - Sabbath Evening - Jennie's Diary

The quiet Sabbath is gone. We went to church this morning, heard Mr. Wilson. This afternoon had a profitable prayer meeting, I hope. Tonight some of the young ladies have gone to church. I would give the evening to quiet meditation and prayer. Tomorrow I begin afresh the duties of another "Seven Weeks." I ask for wisdom to direct me. May I do right. My Father, help thou me.

February 14 - Tuesday Morning - Jennie's Diary
I am discouraged this morning. After all, am I doing any good here? My classes seem so slow to take hold of what I tell them. But maybe some good seed will fall in a favorable soil, and produce fruit. I must not suffer such desponding thoughts to come into my mind. I must work on faithfully. I would I could give my pupils a love of knowledge. My strength, my hope is in my Father.

Jennie tries diligently to look to a brighter future but reverts to a bleak melancholy that seems to periodically overpower her. Sister Ann is much more optimistic. In this essay, written at the Jonesville Female Academy, Ann sees the future and past as collections of fond memories. These sentiments, at times, are foreign to Sister Jennie.

1854 - Undated - Ann's Essay

The Past
Jonesville 1854

Memory, in her wild wanderings, loves to linger amid the pleasures of the past, and recall those scenes of blessedness in which we once delighted. How indelibly are stamped upon the memory the gaieties of childhood, and the innocent rambles of our earlier days. We trace each winding of the grassy mound where, in infant carelessness, we flung ourselves, with nothing to disturb the quiet but the low lulling winds and singing birds; the tall grass waving around the old oaks and blue sky above. We wander, free as the mountain breeze. We pluck the fairest flowers and chase each phantom of hope that lured us before. What splendid scenes were pictured on the mind, untarnished joys filling the deep wells of the heart! But delusive fancyings were doomed never to be fully realized.

But the past hath a charm the present can never attain; with magic wand it paints in splendid hues, and we gaze in pleasure on her fabrications. Should some unpleasant scene intrude upon our minds, how soon we turn away. Could we but blot from the tablet of the past those scenes of wrong, which, through ignorance or willfulness, we acted, we might go forth upon the pathway of life with a firmer step and a loftier brow.

Tho scenes unpleasant are sometimes mingled with other days, yet we love to dwell in their unforgotten haunts. Each familiar face, each kind look and word are treasured up in the heart. How often have we pictured the future. We looked with confidence into the abyss of the future and traced a life of joys. The fairest flowers of earth were fancied to cluster about our pathway. We looked upon life as almost a fairyland, replete with the richest hours of earth. But what a fall were these air castles doomed to receive! What a wreck of imagination!

But we partially view life through the same glasses yet. Hope still flies to the future, and points to the heights of happiness with winning smiles, and we, entranced, plunge where we vainly imagine real bliss may yet be found. 'Tis well for the human heart that memory brings up treasures from the oblivion of the past, and that hope pierces the dim future, otherwise our courage might fail us in life's fitful journey.

February 15 - Wednesday Morning - Jennie's Diary
Oh what a rainy, dreary morning. And [to] Miss Simpson [student] all is dreary. Yesterday she had sad news from Cal. [California]. It is thought her brother Isaiah is lost at sea. She is sick and sorrowful.

February 20 - Monday Morning - Jennie's Diary
The week has commenced rainy and stormy enough. These rainy days make me so dreary. The week is before me, what I shall meet I know not. As my day, so may my strength be. I would dwell this week upon the subject of perfect holiness. O that I might attain it.

February 21 - Tuesday Morning - Jennie's Diary

The sun came out all bright and beautiful this morning. Truly it is a pleasant thing to see the sun, and now I am in my recitation room again. The duties of another day are before me. I know not how severe. My first and earnest prayer is that I may be kept from sin this day. I want to be holy. I shall meet with many things in my classes to try my patience, but I will look to my Father for help. By the grace of God this shall be a profitable day. I want to make much self-improvement so that tomorrow I may be a better and wiser teacher. May I be a conscientious teacher. I know I must often be misunderstood, but if I do my whole duty I may cheerfully leave the event to God. *The New York Times* for the 18 brings a sad news of another distressing shipwreck; "The Taylor," a fine British vessel. Thus another is added to the almost unparalleled list of wrecks. One would think the world might put on mourning. Truly the ways of Providence are mysterious. This cannot be mere chance.

February 26 - Sabbath Evening - Jennie's Diary

'Tis the holy Sabbath evening, and the quiet hours are rapidly passing. Soon another Sabbath will be numbered with the past. This has been a blessed day. This morning Mr. Deems preached for us in the Chapel, for the great rains prevented our going to church. His sermon was eminently practical. After services were over the clouds had broken away so that some of us went down to church. Mr. Barringer preached a very excellent sermon. So has the day passed away. I trust I have been made better by all the exercises of the same. But still I must mourn my want of entire consecration to God my Redeemer. I, who am striving to teach others the right way, do fall so far short of doing right myself. My spirit is oft bowed within me when I remember the waywardness of many around me. And many is the time that I feel my spirit ready to sink. But then comes the thought that maybe this very discipline is necessary to fit me for the duties of the Spirit World. I want to be prepared to do a great and effectual work in Eternity. I would take no mean part in the grand concerns of the Spirit World. My Father may intend to make me a ministering spirit to some other world, or to take the over sight of the "little ones," but whatever my work shall be I want to be well prepared for it.

March 1 - Wednesday - Jennie's Diary

Spring has come. Spring has come. This afternoon we had reading of Compositions in the Chapel. Mr. Deems read a letter on partiality, which he intends leaving with Winnie [daughter?] when he takes her away to school. After he was done Miss Reamy [student] asked that the senior class might read this on the same subject. The request was granted. But oh! There were some severe things said. I scarcely thought that pupils could write so bitterly against their teachers. Poor children! May riper years lead them to wiser reflections. They little think of the heartaches which come to their teachers often, as their care for their pupils come to mind. May I have more wisdom and more moral courage and strength for the duties of my station.

March 2 - Thursday Afternoon - Jennie's Diary

I am now alone in my Recitation room. It is pleasant to have a room, to which one may come and be alone. I love to be alone, and commune with my Spirit. I grow wiser and better. And yet I like company too. Mind sharpens mind. I believe that rooming with Miss S. [?] will make me wiser. She is a great judge of human nature, and her remarks do me good. I look at things differently. But in a world so full of mistakes, I shall often err. Yet may I not be mistaken about eternity. **Thursday night.** Tonight a burden of sadness is upon my heart. I long to be at rest. I know not how I am to bear up under the weight of care and responsibility which rests upon me. Again the question comes to me, is it right for me thus to wear myself away? I feel as if my Spirit was being crushed. Alas. Alas! I know not what to do. I have much inclination to go home. Surely it would be better, than thus to be oppressed with self-consuming care. And yet I would contend right womanly with life's bitterest trials. I would not shrink. I would "be a hero in the strife." If I did but have strength for all— but my nervous system becomes so unstrung that I feel I must give way. O for strength—for wisdom—for discretion. May I know and do my whole duty, and then leave the event to God. The great day of final accounts will bring all things right. I must trust in my great and powerful Father. He is able to sustain me.

Jennie constantly wonders if she is doing the right thing. Although she says she will trust in God, she never is able to let go. She believes that she is somehow evil and cannot receive God's love. Ann's next essay, also written at Jonesville, shows that she is much more secure. She sees God's angel with her as troubles arise. Moments of decision and fear are laid aside because there is always someone there. Jennie, on the other hand, is eminently alone. In her essay Ann uses an allegorical character named Candace Connelle.

1854 - Undated - Ann's Essay

Candace Connelle, or A Picture of Human Life

Jonesville 1854

The morning dews yet tumbled on the bending flowers. Zephyrs wafted the carols of the forest songsters, as their early [calls] swelled out from the deep shady glen and all earth seemed breathing a hymn of devotion to its Creator. The sun boomed from the east in all his wonted grandeur and magnificence, piercing the somber forest with his life inspiring rays. A few clouds idly floating in the western horizon, tinged with gold and purple by the first morning sun rays, seemed a couch on which, perchance, some angel, returning from his missions of mercy, might be borne to the portals of heaven. Earth was arrayed in her robes of richest beauty as tho to celebrate the anniversary of her creation. Such scenery was well calculated to awaken in a youthful heart, emotions of cheerfulness; and with such enticements no wonder Candace Connelle sprang from her room to enjoy the freshness of the early day. Her heart seemed overflowing with life and activity. She sipped the dew from the blushing rose, she sprang from flower to flower till life seemed ebbing in that hour of bliss. Now she bent over a brook to watch the fishes glide in the depths of the cleaving waves, and now flung herself on a moss-clad bank and listened to the warblings - the woodland minstrels. Nature, to her, had never appeared as beautiful. If she had been wandering in a fairyland, she would not have been more enchanted. Thus carelessly and happy she wandered till evening's shades. She looked for the first time and saw a dark cloud arising in the west. Quickly she turned and thought to retrace her steps, but she was bewildered and knew not where to go. A deafening peal of thunder startled her, the cloud rolled up hurriedly and thunders echoed and reechoed till it seemed that heaven and earth would rend with their force streams of lurid lightning flitted hurriedly through the fearful arch, and earth reeled with the force of contending elements. In the scene of confusion Candace flew in agony through the gloom, but when the last hope of aid vanished she sank powerless to the earth.

A gentle hand touched her, and a voice sweet as the tones of some seraphim's lute whispered "Candace, arise, I will deliver thee." A gleam of lightning revealed to her a being bright and beautiful as an angel, a robe of snowy purity veiled her fair form, a crown brilliant with the gems of heaven encircled her brow. Candace had never formed a conception of any creature half as beautiful. She half imagined that some angel of light had descended to shield her from the coming storm.

Again she spoke and the accents strangely contrasted with the confusion of nature. "Come with me and I will lead you to a place of security; I will find a retreat from the confusion of this hour," and taking the hand of Candace, she led her to a cave that was near. When Candace was in the cave she exclaimed, "Beautiful angel, tell me whence thou art? By what means didst thou discover me? Art thou a goddess of some fairy land?" "I am no Goddess," replied she, "my name is Euphelia. I am thy guardian angel. I linger near thee ever. In the deep still night I preside at thy pillow. I direct thy dreams. I guard thee from every danger. When thy footsteps stray from the path of virtue I bring thee back. I saw thee in the morning when life seemed to thee composed of every beauty. You were deluded. Bright and beautiful may be the morning, but clouds overspread the sky in the evening. Remain here until nature shall have gained her usual serenity, till the blackened clouds shall have rolled away, and the sun once more beamed brightly. I will then guide thee home. And whenever life appears so bewitching, as to involve thy whole soul, remember this day and be wise."

March 3 - Friday Morning - Jennie's Diary
Again I am entering upon the duties of another day. What trials are before me I know not. But my trust this morning is in the Lord most mighty. I will strive to do my duty. May I not be blinded by passion or prejudice. It is an easy matter for one to deceive one's self. I pray against it. I may make mistakes, for it is human to err, but may I not be deceived as to my character, my qualifications as a teacher, my conduct as a friend, a daughter, [and] sister. I have thoughts of writing a book for pupils, and [to] try if possible to do away with some of the prejudices, which seem to be deeply fixed in the minds of most pupils.

March 6 - Monday Morning - Jennie's Diary
I begin the duties of another week this morning. I am quite hopeful and cheerful but how long I shall be, there is no telling. I know not what trials may come to me; I would not know. My only care shall be to look to Jesus. I want very much the moral courage to do my duty very well, and very firmly. There is quite a feeling in our school about partiality of teachers. Our pupils are watching us. I pray for very much wisdom and strength to do right. Upon a paper spread out before me on the table I see the following lines which I will copy.

> "He who checks a child with terror,
>   Stops its play and stills its song,
> Not alone commits an error,
>   But a great and moral wrong.
>
> Give it play and never fear it,
>   Active life is no defeat;
> Never, never break its spirit,
>   Curb it only to direct.

> Would you stop the flowing river,
> Thinking it would cease to flow?
> Onward it must flow forever—
> Better teach it where to go."

May I have the wisdom that will enable me thus to train my pupils.

March 7 - Tuesday Morning - Jennie's Diary
This morning it is raining. My first Arithmetic Class have recited but poorly. Poor children, they find it a difficult matter to understand Arithmetic. But I remember the seed does not spring up in a day. I must wait patiently. It may be that some fruit will be gathered many days hence. Yesterday I had a letter from my dear sister. It was a comfort to me to hear from her.

March 13 - Monday Morning - Jennie's Diary
Again the labors of another week are before me. I have but little heart for the work, and but little strength. But I must trust in my Father. He will give me the strength and wisdom. I have to work only a minute at a time, and as my need, so shall my strength be. I pray that I may be kept from sin this day and this week [and] that my heart may be staid upon God my Creator. **Night.** A line in my Journal before I retire.

> "The day is done and the darkness
> falls from the wings of night."

This has been in some things a day of trial. I have not been well, and my classes have been a drag. It does require much patience to be a teacher, and then I am such an imperfect one. I cannot see into the hearts of my pupils. And sometimes I may be severe where the pupil is not to blame, and then I may be indulgent when I ought to be strict. Oh who is sufficient for these things!? But then I must strive to do my duty. I will seek aid and wisdom from the Fountain. Today I have finished reading "Home Influence." I do think I have gained some useful lessons from it, and I shall try to profit from them. In all things

I will remember my dear papa's advice, to do all, aiming it for the best and leave the event to God. As I grow older life seems to me more, and still more, wonderful. Life present, and life to come. To live, to live now, and to live forever is surely the one all absorbing thought of the immortal spirit. Let people speak of dying, but what is death to life? Death is but passing through the gate, but stepping off the cars after a long journey. Oh it is more terrible to live than to die. Who can live as he ought? Many may dare to die, but who will dare to live? And with all its responsibilities I thank my Father for life; for warm, religious life. even for a life of trial. 'Tis like the refiner's furnace. And especially do I give thanks for an endless life; a life with God in Eternity. Thanksgiving to my Father for immortality. Blessed thought, I shall live forever. When a thousand ages are gone I shall still live, and look back upon these years of toil in this world. May it not be with regret. And what shall be my attainments then? When my spirit is freed. Who may say or measure its capacities? And then with the increased and gathered strength of a thousand ages, I shall plume my wings for far nobler flights, over still more boundless fields of investigation. And thus I may go on for millions of ages more, and still have no fear that the end cometh. And oh, how much I shall know of the Almighty Creator. I shall have seen Him—known Him—and shall love Him infinitely more than I now can think. I shall be near Him, shall be like Him. My Father, save me. Save me.

March 16 - Thursday Morning - Jennie's Diary

One does not know what a day may bring forth. Yesterday morning I commenced writing, but the bell called me to recitation, and I could write no more. Last night I received a letter from my brother Aaron. Poor dear brother, he writes so affectionately and so longingly for home. He is far away, but may a kind Providence protect him. **Night.** This afternoon we have had a fine thundershower and now as the deep darkness is upon the earth, the lightnings shine out away in the south. I love to watch these great lights. I am taken back to the days of my childhood, when I was seated in the piazza at my own dear home, watching the clouds piled up far away in the south, and the broad flashes of lightning darting from cloud to cloud, and yet so far away that only now and then could I hear the tones of thunder. I love the thunderstorm. I love the utterings of his mighty voice, and the bright shining of his countenance.

"When shall I see my Father's face?"

I am now alone in my recitation room. I am thankful for this life and health. I am thankful for health. Three of my section are sick. Poor children. And now I have a nice time to read and study. I want to improve my time; may I not be idle or flighty. Oh, for wisdom. For wisdom!

March 21 - Tuesday Morning - Jennie's Diary
Once more I am in my recitation room. Uncle Davie has made me a nice warm fire. And I hope the day will be a successful one. Whatever I do today I would do as unto the Lord. I thought that all I do, even the commonest duty of life I may do, for God my Creator gives me strength and cheers my heart. Yesterday brought me a letter from Rockford, requesting me to take charge of "Rockford Female Institute." This is a matter of some importance. I have written to the Secretary stating my thoughts upon it. And now I wait an answer. I will trust this matter to my Father. I want to do right. May I not be influenced by any unworthy motive.

March 22 - Wednesday - Jennie's Diary
I am working away this morning, but my thoughts go to Rockford. The idea was not pleasant at first but the more I think of it the more am I anxious to go. I think I might do more good there. I hope all will be ordered for the best.

March 23 - Thursday Evening - Jennie's Diary
Tonight I have been out with my Astronomy class tracing out constellations. We did not stay long for the cold, but traced out Taurus, Orion, Canis Major, Canis Minor, Lepers, Great Bear

and c + c and saw Saturn and Mars. Now I have been to see Miss Reamey. She is sick. She is a dear girl to me. There is much of the ethereal in her nature, and she is destined to suffer very intensely in this world. She has a heart yearning for sympathy, more than will ordinarily be found in this world. She is frail, and may not stay in this life long. I only ask that she may be prepared for the Spirit World. I must soon part with her, and maybe see her no more. I am much interested in all my section, but we must soon part. When I think of breaking up here, and going to Rockford, I find it a trial, but then I shall soon be interested in others. If I can only feel that I am doing much good I shall be content. And the more I think of it, the more do I want to go. I feel very sensibly that I am wearing myself away here, and maybe for very little profit. I want to go.

Eclectic Magazine *was published in New York and began publication in 1844.*

March 24 - Friday Afternoon - Jennie's Diary
In my recitation room. Upon my table is a beautiful bouquet which one of my section brought me. It is beautiful, and so fragrant. These little gifts are precious; they are offerings of loving and grateful hearts. Who does not value the love of a human heart? "How strong it strikes the sense." I sometimes fear I crave too much the love of my pupils. And now I am again all involved in mystery. Life is mysterious all. When I watch the workings of the deathless spirit, when I feel its strugglings after light, and knowledge, and immortality, I am lost in wonder. And I long to rush into the freedom of the unimprisoned spirit—but may not this be wrong? I will stop—I will pause—I will wait patiently all the days of my appointed time. Today while reading the *Eclectic* I came across the following stanza, which is very beautiful I think:

"Faint not, o spirit, in dejected mood,
   Thinking how much is planned, how little done;
Revolt not, heart, though still misunderstood;
   For gratitude of all things 'neath the sun,

> Is easiest lost, and insecurest won'
> Doubt not, clear mind, that worked out the right
>   For the right's sake; the thin thread must be spun,
> And patience weave it, ere that sign of might.
> Truth's banner, wave aloft, full flashing to the light."

It is from the writings of Hon. Mrs. Caroline Norton. Lord Byron said that he was "doomed to be misunderstood in this life," and maybe he was. I believe there are many who are.

March 29 - Wednesday Morning - Jennie's Diary

I am not very well this morning, but I hope I shall have the strength for the duties of the day. This is review week, always a trying week to teachers, but I pray for wisdom and discretion to do right. I shall not [be here] but one more such week I think. I have made my mind to go to Rockford, if they will give me my salary. I look upon the call as providential, and if it is best for me, I shall go. It will be hard to break up all the ties that bind me here; to say "good bye' to my college home. But then I go to work, and soon I shall form a loved circle around me, for whom I may live as now I do for these. I want to go, and yet I regret to part with many who are here. This morning, Miss Sundy, one of my pupils, came to me to tell me of the comfort and peace, which she had, in trusting in her Father. She has sometimes been in very great darkness, but now the bright light shineth. I rejoice with the dear child, and hope she may, in all coming time, be faithful.

March 31 - Friday Night - Jennie's Diary

I must write tonight to say goodbye to March. This is the last day, the last night. O shall I ever see another March!? May I be better and stronger than I am now. I see and feel many weak points in my character. I long to correct them. I wish I had some firm, sincere, and enticing friend, who would tell me all my faults, then I might correct them. Alas, alas for poor human nature. It is human to err. When shall I go to the land where the sinless are? Oh my Father, save me.

This next entry implies that a trustee of Greensboro Female College was involved in some sort of scandal and left home.

April 1 - Saturday Night - Jennie's Diary

Tonight I would unburden my mind to my journal. I have spent most of the day in drawing and thinking. What a world this is. How full of disappointments and deceptions. Friends in whom I confide most implicitly may deceive me in an hour when I think not. I may trust no one only so far as I have tried that one. The case of one of our Trustees has lately made me feel this more than ever. He has ruined himself, and his children are heartbroken. Poor S. Only yesterday she was so proud spirited, now she has not a home —but I need not dwell upon this. I have today thought much about my going to Rockford. I hope the question will in some measure be solved before next Saturday night. Sometimes I shrink from the responsibilities, but then, no position of usefulness is without responsible duties. I would not shrink from the trying and stern realities of life. Here my spirits are often times deeply and sorely tried by the young ladies. But so the life of a teacher must ever be. I shall find the reckless and the wayward everywhere I go. I must expect it. I must nerve myself up for it. O there are times of trial in this life, and now and then I feel that I can no more bear up under them. When, oh when, will the storm of earthly life be over? I would learn to suffer and to wait.

April 3 - Monday Morning - Jennie's Diary

This morning we start straight to commencement. How soon it will be here. Last evening I had a call from Mr. Van Eaton. [The Principal of Jonesville Male and Female Academies] He is in great distress about his schools. Mr. Reid has taken his wife away from the school and he is without a teacher. I am sorry for the man. There is nothing certain in this world in the affairs of men. I may not trust any one not [even] myself.

April 4 - Tuesday Morning - Jennie's Diary

My mind is again turned to my anticipated change. Yesterday brought me a letter from Dr. Folger, but it was not decided. Now I must write saying precisely what I can do and what I cannot. The matter must be settled by the next. I hope I shall be able to do just what is right. It will be a trial to break up here, and come back no more. And just now it comes over me that I must leave my recitation room; this dear old room, sacred to me on many accounts. Here I have met my classes, my Section, in Sections, and in Section meetings; my Sabbath class in class meeting. Here I have studied and thought, suffered and enjoyed, but to all I must say "good bye." And then again has come the thought, who will love and care for these whom I leave behind? But some one will. I am not indispensable to the prosperity of the college. I will not think so.

April 5 - Wednesday Morning - Jennie's Diary

This is a beautiful morning. So spring-like. I feel much of good humor this morning, and hope I shall be able to do good work today. Last night I spent with Mrs. Deems; Mr. Deems having gone to Lexington. I shall not regret to say "good bye" to Mrs. Deems. But then I think Mr. Deems will hardly be here next year, and if he is not I shall be glad that I am going away. I shall hardly ever be with Mr. Deems again, and now I am thankful that I have been with him so much as I have. I owe much to him. I owe much to the college. Here I have been educated for the great work of the future—for I trust there is a great work for me to do yet. The future shall witness me making greater exertions for self-improvement, and to make myself more useful than the past has been.

April 6 - Thursday Morning - Jennie's Diary

I have this morning heard that Mr. Deems intends to remain here only five months longer. If so, then I am glad I am going. What a breaking up there will be at Commencement. And now I remember that it is only six weeks from today that the present drama winds up. **Thursday Afternoon.** I am all moody this afternoon. This is one of those spring days that make one feel lifeless and restless. The winds are sighing mournfully thro the pines, and now and then a warm breath comes in at my window. Mr. Jones has gone to walk with the young ladies, but I am all alone in my recitation room. My thoughts turn upon my departure. I want to go — and yet the pain of parting. I shall ever love the college, and long for its welfare. But my days are numbered here. And still I think it will be for the best for me to go. In Rockford I shall be in society more, and yet it will be more simple.

April 7 - Friday Morning - Jennie's Diary
This is the last working day of this week; so fast does Commencement come on. Only five weeks more, and then . . . . I want to be more cheerful and active this day than I was yesterday. One has not time to be moody in this world. I am often given to these fits, and yet I want to shake them off. Now I will try to be cheerful and glad today, and work with a right good will. The little birds are singing merrily.

April 12 - Wednesday Morning - Jennie's Diary
I have just been round to see the sick children; some are very sick, some are getting better. Now I go to work. I want to work wisely today. May I not do wrong nor be weak in anything. What I do I would do in a masterly manner, do it for my creator. The longer I live the more am I impressed that one makes one's self. That no one was ever great or good in an instant. I believe this is eminently a working world, and I would not spend my time idly; now the bell rings for arithmetic.

(Sarah) Margaret Fuller (1810-1850) was an American social reformer and author, who espoused Transcendentalism and advocated equal rights for women. She married an Italian marquis and the couple became involved with the political unrest of the period as French soldiers invaded Rome. Her husband fought the invading forces while she helped in the hospitals. Both escaped with their infant son when Rome fell to the French. On their way back to the United States, their ship sank and all three were drowned. Margaret Fuller was a pioneer for today's feminist movement.

In spite of her Christian beliefs Jennie was drawn to Transcendentalism as is evidenced in this next entry.

April 19 - Wednesday Evening - Jennie's Diary

I am now reading *The Life of Margaret Fuller*. I am absorbed in it. I feel that a new life is dawning upon me. I like many of her thoughts and opinions, and some I do not. She had a great mind, but I do not think it was sufficiently imbued with Christian principles. I cannot say much yet, as I have not finished the first volume. I anticipate much from it, and yet I pray that I may not be led off into excesses of transcendentalism. I believe that my mind is somewhat inclined in that channel now, and I would guard against it. I am strongly impressed with the spiritual. I am a spirit. I live the life of a spirit now, and this spirit must live on in another, and, I trust a higher life. I would be careful of this spirit.

Ever since I was a little child I have felt the strugglings of my encaged spirit, and an insatiable longing for something unattained. I feel the same now, only over and over I get a glimpse here and there, and think that some of the darkness is breaking away. But there is still a thick cloud above me pressing me down. I feel it and I long to break through it—to throw it off—and merge into the full sunlight of truth and beauty. I feel that above this all is bright and beautiful, that there I may see and know more of my Great Creator.

April 20 - Thursday Noon - Jennie's Diary

My recitations for the morning are done. My astronomy class has just gone out. I am very tired. I fear after all, that my labors with this class will be almost in vain. But I must be faithful.

> P.S. At the close of the session, one of the class said she never had understood anything she studied as well as she did astronomy. Rockford. July 1854

The above footnote would indicate that Jennie was reading her diary in July while she was at Rockford and made a comment that a student did get something out of her astronomy class. This remark reveals that Jennie often re-read her journal and added commentary.

April 21 - Friday Forenoon - Jennie's Diary

This is a beautiful spring day, more like spring than anything we have had yet. Now I hope it will continue to be pleasant. This morning I have been reading the "Old Brewery," a volume illustrating the labors and successes of the Ladies Home Missionary Society at the "Fire Points," New York. The story is thrilling and truthful. May abundant blessings and successes attend the efforts of these Christian women. I have been somewhat tired this morning by the noises in the college. I am worn out by college life, and I hope that the present session will terminate my connection with the institution. I do not think that I have any right to wear myself away here when I may do as much good somewhere else.

April 22 - Saturday Night - Jennie's Diary

Another week is done. I feel tired and worn tonight. Many thoughts rush upon my mind. Life with all its living realities comes upon me, and I shrink—alas! Who has not at some time felt weary of living, a certain undefinable longing after "the far off, unattained, and dim?" What heart sickness comes to the heart when it first learns that "man may smile but to deceive," that there is here such a want of human sympathy for human woe—a want of brotherly love. That here sensitive hearts must be wrung and crushed—natures be misunderstood—that long and deep shadows must fall upon life's pathway. But amid all this gloom there comes a ray of sunlight. There is rest for all the weary. I would have a heart brave and be hopeful. May I not despond. The Sabbath draweth on. May it bring to me joy and calmness. I will trust in God.

April 24 - Monday Morning - Jennie's Diary

This morning is a sad morning to us all. Mr. Deems leaves for Gen. [general] Conference, and many of us shall see him no more. Yesterday he preached his farewell sermon in the church from these words, "I have glorified thee on earth, I have finished the work thou gavest me to do." John 17:4. It was a powerful sermon. At 4 o'clock he preached his farewell sermon to the college in the chapel. It was an effective time. And now this morning he leaves us. I shall hardly see him again, especially if I go to Rockford. But I shall ever remember my connection with him as a teacher. Next to my father I owe more to Mr. Deems than any living man. And it is painful to have this friendship broken up. But so it must be with all human attachments. Yet there cometh a time when there shall be no more partings—no more sorrow. In that bright world may I be near Mr. Deems. Miss Reamey is almost inconsolable at Mr. Deems' departure. She has been very much attached to him, and now must part with him feeling that in some little matter there must be a misunderstanding. I have just been in to see her, and she is all in tears. Poor child! I expect a letter from Rockford this morning saying if I should go. And now with much faith and hope I must begin the duties of another week. May I have success such as shall be best for me. I will go to all my work "in the strength of the Lord God."

April 25 - Tuesday Noon - Jennie's Diary

I have been much tried this morning by the dullness of my Astronomy class, and then by the utter disregard of study hours by Miss N. and others. Alas! For the life of a teacher. Surely I shall sink under this weight after all. Is all this anguish of spirit necessary to fit me for the life in time, and life in eternity? But I would not complain.

April 26 - Wednesday Morning - Jennie's Diary

Another beautiful spring morning this; oh so rapidly does time fly. And I cannot say I am sorry. I would not be tired of life, but I do feel sometimes as if I would hasten to finish up its work and go home. I want to do my work well, but I would do it rapidly. But what an experience I am gathering up. I have lived near a lifetime in the last two years. I have awaked to a new life—a more vigorous life. I am glad for this experience tho it has been gathered up amid so many heartaches, so many great trials. I trust all will go to fit me better for future life. I am looking anxiously to hear from Rockford. I will trust all to my Heavenly Father, believing that all will be right.

April 29 - Saturday Night - Jennie's Diary

With these lines I wind up the doings of another week. It has been a week of care. As all the remaining weeks must be, of the present session. I dread these weeks. But when they are done I hope to be free from college. I am worn out here, and I do think it best that I should leave. If I do not go to Rockford I do not know what I shall do. But I do not wish to return here. I think I may not be here another year. One year of rest at home would do me and my friends much good. But amid all this perplexing business I would not be over anxious. I would trust all to the wise direction of my Father. It may be best after all for me to stay and suffer and labor on a while longer. The more I think and see of colleges for girls, the more I do not like them. And if the public will demand such institutions, I do not see that I am under obligations to wear myself away in them. This afternoon I have finished reading Margaret Fuller. Hers was a great and strange life.

May 1 - Monday Morning - Jennie's Diary

This is a delightful May Day. It is cold, yet so clear and sunny. The young ladies sent in a petition for holiday, and the Faculty thought best to grant the request. I hope now they will be happy and enjoy the day. And now I must write some letters, and do up many things. I am anxiously waiting a letter from Rockford.

May 2 - Tuesday Morning - Jennie's Diary

Yesterday the long looked-for letter came, and all arrangements are made for my going to Rockford. I have now to do up my last work here. And I want it to be done well, so that at the close I may say conscientiously, "I have <u>finished</u> the work Thou gavest me to do." Some are expressing deep regrets that I am to leave, but yet I will think my going is for the best. I have tried to commit all to the direction of my Heavenly Father, and believe he has over ruled all. I now pray for much wisdom that I may discharge the duties of my new position. I shall need strength of body, of spirit, of mind. But I will not be anxious.

May 3 - Wednesday Morning - Jennie's Diary

I have my work before me this day. I feel more like working than I did yesterday. And I hope I shall be able to do more. My Astronomy class tries me much—I must be patient. My work will be done after a while. And I hope well done.

May 3 - Wednesday - Letter from Jennie to Dr. Deems

May 3, 1854

My Dear Mr. Deems,

I have now sit me down all alone in my recitation room to write you "good bye." Now that I am to go away and see you no more, there are some things I want to say before going.

First of all, I shall always be thankful that I have had the privilege of being associated with you as I have. To you, next to my father, I owe more than to any living man. And you will not wonder then that to me it was hard to part, and that I felt I never could say "good bye". It was hard to know that ever hereafter I must be cut off from all your influence — but all this had to be.

And now I go to a new field of labor; go from my College home. And this will cost me much, for there comes to my heart ties from every room; all these must be broken, and my life almost must be rooted up, for it has gone through and through the College until there is not a room or nook that brings not some pleasant memories. And the College where I have labored long and suffered much must become a strange place to me. I am to be your humble co-worker no longer. I have been with you in my weakness. I should have been glad to be with you in more strength. But no one has been more charitable to my faults than yourself; you have been to me a brother, good and kind—would I have been a more worthy sister. Nature did not give to me a very demonstrative manner, and my regard for my friends has never struck them very forcibly. So it has been with you, Mr. Deems. While my regard for you has been almost unbounded, even as a sister cherishes for a brother beloved, yet I have been doomed to see others do and say the very things I had in my heart to do and say, but could not find the way.

For some things I am glad that you are to be away when I leave, for sure I could not say farewell. But I would not enumerate these things. "Bygones must be bygones," and I must rouse myself up to all of life which is before me. You will work on as well when I am gone as before, for the sun could not miss the moon. And I will work on the best I can and when the great working day is done, there may be a happy home gathering.

My sister, my only sister, may be with you next year. I would not ask anything more for her than another, but I would have you watch over and train her for the future. Do not pass by her faults, she will understand you, and be thankful for reproof, tho severe.

And now Mr. Deems, that I am going away, there are some things which I may say with freedom, for I am no longer personally interested, and they may be of advantage to you in the future. The first thing coming to mind now is shopping, which I have just wound up. This is a task more taxing than any one, except the unfortunate teacher, can imagine. And I think candidly that few teachers will bear it long unless receiving greater remuneration. Now as I think of it, I almost wonder that I have gone thro it so long. I have been and am willing to work, but it does seem to me that this is more than any parent in justice can ask of a teacher. In addition to all our professional duties, we are required to carry out what parents want moral courage enough to do, or else inclination—that is restrict their daughter's expenditures. I know that this is a perplexing business, and I have studied how it might be remedied. Among different plans coming up, the following seems plausible at least. Let the deposits be made as now. Let the young ladies do their own shopping, paying strictly for every article purchased, receiving a receipted bill, which the Section Teacher might keep at discretion. Let all purchases be made in the presence of the Section Teacher. Surely parents could say decidedly to their daughters, "you may not have accounts. You may not over go the deposit." For the sake of my successors I wish some new plan might be adopted. All the teachers have felt it as heavily as I, tho they may not say.

There is another matter. You know of the trouble we have had at prayers and at the table. I have uniformly observed that there has been more quietude at prayers when all the Faculty have been present, and that in <u>no</u> instances has a young lady left the table without permission when the teacher has been present. At prayers and the table are the only two places in which we meet as a family; all times else we meet as teachers and pupils. Then we say to young ladies "we want you to go to prayers because it <u>is right</u>." Should we not set the example? At home I remember the table is not half so pleasant if father and mother are not there, May it not be so with teachers? If the hours for prayers and meals are so unreasonable that teachers cannot be there, they must be wrong hours. Because it is right and because it is teaching the young ladies by example as well as precept I do think that all the Faculty should be present at prayers and table.

At this point Jennie's letter to Dr. Deems comes to an abrupt conclusion. No doubt the second half of the letter has been lost. Deems would leave Greensboro Female College in 1854.

May 8 - Monday Morning - Jennie's Diary

This morning I commence the duties of the last week of the Session. It is a delightful morning, and I do hope this will be a successful week, a time when all will strive to do what is right. I need much wisdom and strength for these last two weeks. And I do look forward with some anxiety to my new position. There will be trials there which I little think of now. But then, I must trust in my Father. Has he not directed it all? It is hard for me to part from the Faculty. I shall miss their sympathy, and stimulus. I must go to my work with a brave heart. If severe trials await me, they will do me good. I will not be discouraged. I will be strong in "the strength of the Lord God." I now ask for wisdom, strength and discretion for my duties here.

May 14 - Sabbath Night - Jennie's Diary

This is the last Sabbath night which as a College we shall ever spend together. Commencement week is upon us, and a time of trial it is. One week hence and many who are now very dear to me will be far,

far away from me. But these partings will come. And I am trying to school myself so that I shall be as glad at parting as meeting. O I am glad for this year's experience, for all this labor and care. I am glad for all the pleasant friendships formed here, tho they now must be broken up, yet I am glad for them. Many, many regrets are expressed at my departure. I hope it is the best for me to go. May I be guided aright.

Ann is at Jonesville studying and perhaps even teaching when she writes this letter home. We know she taught at Jonesville during the 1853-1854 school year because she was listed as a teacher in the school catalog. This next entry, however, would indicate that she was also studying. Note her more open style. While Jennie is controlled and careful, Ann is uninhibited. Where Jennie will take on the troubles of the world, blaming herself, Ann will place the blame squarely where she thinks it belongs.

Same Day - May 14 - Sunday - Ann's Letter to her Mother
My dear affectionate mother,
      It is a rainy Sabbath and I feel so bad I have declined going to church today, and I hardly think it would be unpardonable if I were to write you. I have consequently seated myself to commence. But what shall I write? Shall I give you a history of our daily course of duties? If I do they will be uninteresting to you for they are nothing but everyday occurrences. If I were to send memory flower gatherings through the beauties of the past, and collect all the rare and beautiful things that once gave a charm to life, it would only be a repetition of scenes and things that once passed before your eyes. And I might perchance touch upon things unpleasant. If we leave the past and present and step into the future, what is that but an unfathomable abyss that no prophetic eye can scan. If fancy exert all her power to trace some enchanting vision of the future, to construct an airy fabrication to feast the mind, these vain imaginings are doomed never to be realized and the pleasure they afford is as fleeting as the mind. But I am growing, as usual, sentimental, and dealing in things merely like thistledown; things that have no weight. But Mother, suffer me to

get ahead of time and fancy three weeks in the future. Yes Mother, three weeks from today, if nothing prevents, I shall be at home. At home! What a thrill of pleasure vibrates through my heart at the thought of being at home. With my father and mother, my little brothers and my only sister, how [can] I fail in being happy? Yet I shall leave here with regret. I have become so much attached to Brother Asbury that I cannot think of leaving him without a tear dimming my eye.

> Could we ever stay with those we love:
> For bright our hours would be.
> Each bounding heart would ever prove
> Calm as the slumbering sea.
> The tear, that dims the lustrous eye,
> Would change into a smile;
> The laughing hours fly singing by
> Untouched by care or guile.

But Mother when I suffer myself to dwell on these, a spirit of sadness mingles with my feelings, for I fear the pleasure may be alloyed by some evil. Bliss too strongly coveted, too eagerly anticipated, is frequently dashed from our extended hand ere it can be realized. So it may be in this instance, something may chance to turn our anticipated pleasure into sorrow. But we will hope for the better. You see I have run wild again, but turn over and I will try to talk like a rational being.

May 15 - Ann's Letter to her Mother Continues

Monday Night I am coming home next Saturday if possible. Aunt will come, and I think Asbury also. I reckon sister will be at home. I am almost obliged to see her before the examination. Brother has not come back yet and will not be [here] until tomorrow. He cannot go after sister, as it will be too late. I am sorry. I wrote to Papa last Monday. I hope he received it. Mrs. Van [wife of the principal of Jonesville Methodist Academy, William Van Eaton] and Mrs. Benham [wife of the owner of the Benham Hotel in Jonesville] want your butter.

Mother I had a good crying spell today. I heard that Dr. Wilson said that he intended to ask me questions at the examination that he knew I could not answer, that he would make me feel mighty little. Mrs. Reid told her girls of it, and one of them told me as a friend. I shall ever thank her. If Dr. Wilson said it, he is not what I thought he was. I intend to ask him. Mrs. Reid is exerting every power to injure me. She thinks I have no one to take my part. That was what made me cry. It is the hardest thing I ever had to do to keep cool. But I am resolved to do my duty, and if people talk, they must do it. If a teacher's path is ever this thorny I will quit its unenviable walks. I dislike Mrs. Reid more and more daily. And no one can blame me that knows how she has acted. I have not spoken to her in five or six weeks, and never will again if I can avoid it. One consolation; Mr. Van [Mr. Van Eaton, the principal] is pleased, and he is as kind as I could ask. Others have expressed freely their satisfaction with my efforts, but Mrs. Reid is determined to overbalance them if possible. I will tell you when I go home. But don't be in trouble for myself. I can cry awhile and then laugh it off, and I am conscious of having done my duty, and when I can feel assured of this, all Mrs. Reid can say shall not move me. I am well known here and any one is welcome to ask for my character. I am resolved to give no one room to complain.

I am looking for a letter from home tomorrow and shall be sadly disappointed if I do not get one. I am highly pleased to hear from Neal Bohannon and shall be more so to see him. I only fear he will come before I get home. If he does, give him my double (I had better say) triple, and trusted love, and tell him I wish him pleasant dreams. [Nine years from the time this letter is written, Neal Bohannon would become a statistic in the Civil War. As a lieutenant in Company I, Twenty-Eighth Regiment, N.C. Troops, he would serve under Ann's brother, Colonel Asbury Speer. Neal died of fever on June 20, 1863. His brother Simon survived the war.]

I dreamed a horrible dream about Noah Reece. I dreamed Old Scratch came and carried him off alive, and I saw him take a big knife and cut Noah's heart out and chop it up into bits. And he said it was because Noah had been a member of the church, and had gone to stilling to ruin the souls of his fellow men. I dreamed it so plain that for some days it seemed as distinct as a reality. I could not think of it without shuddering. May heaven save him!

But Mother I have written nothing of consequence at last. You must come to our examination. I will be at home Saturday if possible. Goodbye, dear Mother, until then,

Yours in endless love,
Annis

May 18 - Thursday - Commencement Day - Jennie's Diary

Tonight I see it has been a long time since I wrote a line in my journal. The Examination has come and gone. The Session has ended, and we are being parted. All the exercises have passed off finally. We could not ask for better. And now I am a member of the college no more. I am a teacher here no longer. My pupils are going, my Section is broken up, and I am thus bereaved. Oh these are sad, sad times; they make me wish to die rather than live. There are many aching hearts here; there are many far away.

By the time this next diary entry is made, most of the family is reunited. Jennie and Ann are home. James is age eleven. Vet, age seventeen, is attending Jonesville Male Academy but is home at present.

May 25 - Thursday - Jennie's Diary

One week ago we were in the midst of commencement [and] now I am at home. I reached home Tuesday morning. I am resting, so that I may be ready for the duties of the new position. Since coming home I learn that many high hopes are placed upon the school. I hope that I may be able to meet the expectations of the Trustees. I shall go to my work trusting in that wisdom which has hitherto directed my steps. It is good to be at home. My presence seems a comfort to my parents and brothers. I am glad, more than ever, that I accepted the invitation to Rockford.

May 28 - Sabbath Morning - Jennie's Diary

This calm, delightful Sabbath morning finds me at my own dear home. All the family are gone to church but Jamie and I [sic]. O! It is good to be at home. How shall I ever be thankful enough for these home influences? I owe much to my home; few have had such a home. May I ever be worthy of this home.

June 8 - Thursday - Jennie's Diary

So many things have taken my time since I have been at home that I have neglected my journal. I must be better. There are many things passing now, which are of interest, and I ought to note down. I am resting when I can, preparing myself for all the duties of the future. I feel a great responsibility resting upon me. I sometimes shrink from the cares, which are to come upon me shortly. But then I do feel this morning that I can commit all this into the hands of my powerful Heavenly Father. He will give me wisdom and strength for my day. I will trust him. A few days ago brought me a letter from Miss Reamy and Nannie Brame. I am thankful for their friendship; they are dear to me.

June 11 - Sabbath Afternoon - Jennie's Diary

This has been a rainy day. We went to church, but no minister was there. Came home thro rain. Today I am bowed in spirit. The future looks dark and dreary. I feel just now as if it was more than I could meet. How I shall sustain myself I know not. I am afraid after all, that I have too much disposition to seek position and ease. But O! I would not shrink from labor tho that labor be hid from the great eye of the world. Tho no man see me work, tho I labor on, die and be forgotten yet, let me never shrink from my duty. I will trust in God that all the future may be of his own directing. If he but work out my path, I can go therein. May he make my heart right; give me a teacher's spirit, make me strong in him — then shall all be well.

June 15 - Thursday - Jennie's Diary

I am homesick for college tonight. O it is hard to reconcile it to my mind that I am to be there no more. I do now forget the sorrow I there endured. I remember only the joy. I lived so much while there; no wonder I am attached to it. Blessings be upon the college. My heart is sad very much when I remember Rockford. Did I do right in leaving college? But I will not doubt. Has not Providence directed all? This I know. I tried to do right. I will be trustful, tho the future looks dark and dreary.

June 17 - Saturday - Jennie's Diary

This is the commencement of our two days meeting. May it be a profitable one. All my thoughts do go to Rockford. I am better reconciled this afternoon than for sometime before. I hope I may be able to go trustingly. May I do great work at Rockford. Why may I not? I am thankful for this much faith. All I do, I would do for my Father.

June 20 - Tuesday - Jennie's Diary

Our two days meeting closed last night. It has been a blessed meeting. Much religious influence was felt. Several were converted, and among the numbers was my own dear little brother Jamie. O it does seem too good to think all our family may now be numbered as the children of God. For all this I would be very thankful. Today is to us a day to be remembered. Ten years ago our little sister Sylvia left this world and went home. Ten years in heaven! What a blessed ten years. I have often been glad that our Father took her to himself so early.

June 24 - Saturday Morning - Jennie's Diary

Now I am in Rockford, in the little room I am to call my home for a long time to come. What conflicts, what trials, what heartaches shall here be mine I know not. But this one thing I do, I dedicate myself, my room, my labors in the Seminary, my all to my Heavenly Father. In this little room I will seek for the teachings of the Great Spirit, for strength to go to yonder Seminary, and labor for the prosperity of the school, and the good of this whole town. The future is not very promising, but no one knoweth what may be done. I am determined to labor to accomplish something which will be felt in all this country, and be a blessing to thousands. May I have wisdom and understanding.

June 25 - Sabbath Morning - Jennie's Diary

This is a beautiful morning. The cool wind is stirring among the shady trees. The roar of the Yadkin is never ceasing. I love it. The little birds are singing sweetly. The whole town is quiet. We have no church today, and I am sorry. I wish some religious service could be held in the town every Sabbath. There is much need of moral reformation here. I do trust I shall have wisdom for all things. **Evening.** The Sabbath is almost gone. It has been a peaceful day, and tho I have met with no great congregation I trust the day has been profitable. O! there is much, so much to be done here. I pray for wisdom that I may know how to do these people good—how to work wisely. I shall not go to my work in my own strength. My Father will now be my guide as I trust he has been in the past. I will not be over anxious, I will "have faith in God."

June 26 - Monday Night - Jennie's Diary

The first day of the school has come and gone. My heart has sunk within me today as I thought of the future. Who is able for the work here? How I shall succeed none knoweth. My trust is on high. May I have strength.

June 27 - Tuesday Night - Jennie's Diary

Now before going to my bed I must say a word for the day. I am thankful to my Heavenly Father that the day has passed in so much quietude in the schoolroom. I hope and fear. I would work believing. Is it possible that I may do something for good in this place?

July 1 - Saturday Morning - Jennie's Diary

A new month and a pleasant day. One week of my school has gone. I need not say, my pen could not tell the anxieties which have come to me during this week. Many times my heart has sunk within me, and I have been ready to despair. But now I feel stronger. All things considered, the first week has been as successful as one could expect. I am thankful, and want to be hopeful. I am trying to dismiss so much anxious care, and stay my heart on God. I would work for my Father. He will not require more than I can do and he will give me strength. It is a blessed thing we cannot know the future. I believe many a great work is accomplished that never would have been, if the difficulties in the way of its accomplishment had been seen before. I should not have been here if all the realities could have been seen from the beginning. But now I would not be faint-hearted. It is possible, after all, that I may do something here which will be a blessing to society.

July 2 - Sabbath Evening - Jennie's Diary

We have had church today. Rev. Mr. Brown gave us a very excellent sermon. I would trust more sincerely that a deep, precious and powerful work of reformation may be commenced in this town than ever has yet been known. And I pray for my school after all my efforts to lay care aside; my heart is even now oppressed with very great anxieties for the success of the Seminary. I would not be faithless, but I must hope against hope. There is that in my nature which causes me to suffer so much anxiety about the work in which I am engaged. I wish I could cast all on my Heavenly Father. I know he will not require that of me which I am unable to perform. I want to commit all the future to him. If it is well pleasing to him he will make this a good and great Institution. Into his hands I commit it with all its interests; now I feel I can rest in him. The future shall be well because God will direct it. I rejoice that at this holy evening hour I can thus trust all to him. I am glad for this strength. In days to come when my heart is weary and faint, I will turn to this page and read. Little did I think when I commenced to write that I should be able to commit my all so fully. Now I would doubt no more.

July 7 - Friday Afternoon - Jennie's Diary

Can it be that it is almost a week since I wrote a line in my journal? Surely the week has passed away rapidly. And O my heart is so thankful when I remember with what success the week has gone. All things have been pleasant, and I think a decided improvement in the school. My heart is stronger than at any time before. My trust is in my Father. He will make the school what it ought to be. I will surely never be desponding again. I am not weary this evening as usual. For all, O for all, I would be devoutly thankful.

July 10 - Monday - Jennie's Diary

This has been a day of much bodily weakness, but the day is now done, and the quiet hours of darkness are about me. I am thankful for the rest of the night. I have thought to myself this afternoon, why may I not go home and rest with my mother, instead of being subject to this life of care and anxiety. I see others at their ease—they have no cares upon them—they move about only to kill the "dull long hours." But here I toil on, prematurely growing old from these responsibilities. But then I would not change positions with them. No, no, no! I would not be a drone in society. Upon my tombstone I would have this simple line written, "She hath done what she could." Yes, give toil, life toil, heart toil, rather than a useless existence. Just now I do so much need wisdom to work rightly. I need wisdom that I may teach human hearts how to live. I want to know, to feel what life is. Then I want light and strength to teach others what it is—to educate others for living.

July 12 - Wednesday Morning - Jennie's Diary

This bright, beautiful, and invigorating morning, I must write a line in my journal to commemorate it. O it is so delightful. I feel a fresh life given unto me. And I would that it might be as bright and sunshiny in our schoolroom. I trust it may. I will try to take as much sunshine in my own heart there as I can. I will try to meet my pupils in cheerfulness. Oh I do want to do much good work today. Work for eternity. I am thankful that I have a great and Infallible Teacher who will teach me as I strive to teach others. May my Teacher be near me today.

July 15 - Saturday Night - Jennie's Diary

Another week is done. We have had peace and success in the schoolroom. I think things have a healthful appearance. O I would be thankful, so thankful to my Heavenly Father for all the blessings of the week. My own heart has grown stronger, and a great life work has come into mind. I will trust all to my Heavenly Father. And now I want to be prepared for the quiet, holy Sabbath. I had a nice good ride with my dear papa this afternoon.

July 16 - Sabbath Night - Jennie's Diary

The Sabbath day is bidding farewell, and leaving the world in peace. It has been a lovely day. We had no church. I am sorry we have not church on the Sabbath. I have tried to spend the day profitably. I would love the blessed Sabbath; may its light ever be to me a joy. And now I go to the peaceful rest of the night.

July 19 - Wednesday - Jennie's Diary

Oh what hot, hot weather. The thermometer has ranged from 100 to 108 in the shade; this is almost torrid. It is so warm we can do but little in the schoolroom. The prospects of the Seminary are still encouraging. But I want yet to put my confidence still implicitly in God. I know if the Institution is ever anything good or great, God must make it so. This is mail day. I do hope it will bring me some good news from afar.

July 23 - Sabbath - Jennie's Diary

Now I have said good bye to my sister. Dear Sister, when shall I see her again? It was hard for her to part with me—but I know the parting is for the best. Tomorrow she leaves home for Greensboro where she will remain one year and graduate. I have had a blessed little visit home. All were so kind, so affectionate. Oh it is good to be so that I can see home so often.

Dr. Thomas Arnold (1795-1842) was a British educator and father to poet Matthew Arnold. This is another passage that expresses Jennie's dream of making some contribution to society.

July 25 - Tuesday Morning - Jennie's Diary

I have just finished reading an article in the *Eclectic* on Dr. Thomas Arnold. It is most excellent. I am thankful for the reading. I shall go to my work today with a stronger heart for having read it. He was a great and successful Teacher. His theory was that all education should be based upon Christian principles. In this I think the same. How much do I wish that I could carry out my views of instruction. O shall I always fall short of accomplishing what I wish!

This much I can do. I can do earnest work. It may not be an extensive work, but it may be an earnest work. Surely my Heavenly Father will open the way for me to do a permanent work somewhere. My spirit struggles to be free, that I may work in a great and wide field. I so do much wish to write some word, to say some word, to do some work that shall live when I am dead. But now maybe this is selfish ambition. Yet surely it cannot be for I am not anxious that my name be remembered. I am anxious only that I work a permanent work.

Frederica Brenner (1801-1865) was a Swedish novelist who wrote about the manners in homes in Sweden. Her Homes of the New World *was a three-volume work that included her observations on homes in the United States, written between 1853 and 1854. Jennie must have had immediate access to books to have this at her disposal.*

July 26 - Wednesday Morning - Jennie's Diary
The bright sun has just come out through the thick clouds, which have hid it all the morning. Just so, I have thought, it is often in life a dark and cheerless morning has been followed by a sunny day. And now I must work today. I want to be cheerful and strong. I am trying to school myself so that I may go to my daily work without a feeling of dread. I have succeeded in part. I am now reading *Homes of the New World,* by Frederica Brenner. I find many things good and interesting. One expression has done me good. "A small work may be made great by being done perfectly." I hope to make this school great, for I will strive to do perfect work.

July 27 - Thursday Night - Jennie's Diary
Today the college has opened, and I am not there. So long have I been connected with it, but now I am there no more. I love the college and pray for its success, but I do not repent having left it. My situation here is far different, and yet I feel this new life is doing me much good. It is a great school time to me and I trust it is fitting me for the future. I hope the place and way will be open for me to do a permanent work somewhere. I am not anxious where, just so it is in

the place chosen by my Father. My dear sister Ann, I have often thought of her today. May she be happy. Things have passed on successfully in the schoolroom today. I believe these are favorable signs of improvement. There is an expression in the countenances of the pupils, which shows that they are not merely laying up words without ideas. For this I labor and I would patiently wait. If I can see an improvement in these few weeks, surely I ought to bless God and take courage. I commit all into his hands. He can dispose all things.

Evidently the McDonald girl was the daughter of the Greensboro Female College trustee who was involved in some scandal. The college records burned during the Civil War, so we do not know for sure.

July 29 - Saturday Afternoon - Jennie's Diary
A little note from Nannie Brame tells me of the death of Mary Frances McDonald. Poor child, she was a sufferer in this world, but I trust she is now at rest. She did not long survive the shame and sorrow brought upon her by her father.

July 30 - Sabbath Morning - Jennie's Diary
This is a Sabbath morning, so quiet, so peaceful. I would that all the world loved and honored the Sabbath. What a world this would be if all did. On the Sabbath there should be a universal cessation from all labor. A world would be at rest. All peoples of all lands would assemble themselves together in great and beautiful temples of worship, and in the midst of these temples, wise and holy ministers would stand up to speak to listening thousands the words of the Holy One, and the pure will of God would be written on every human heart. O what a world! And then men would go to their homes, the blessings of the Sanctuary resting upon them. And the last hours of the Sabbath would pass away, bearing up to the Great Eternal the sanctified evening sacrifice of a worshiping world. Oh! Why will not mankind "remember the Sabbath day to keep it holy."

July 31 - Monday - Jennie's Diary

July is upon us today with his fiercest heat, but this is the last day. What August will bring I cannot tell. Not hotter days than these I hope. Today I have made a new regulation in the Seminary. The most advanced class will select rooms and study in them, coming up to the schoolroom only to recite. I do trust this arrangement will be for the good of all. May my Father bless it.

August 1 - Tuesday - Jennie's Diary

I must say good morning to hot, sultry August. Here is it upon us. But oh, so oppressive one can have no energy for anything! Such excessive heat has not been known for years as we have this summer. But we must endure it. I hope this evening's mail will bring me good tidings from my sister and from Miss Reamey. I long to hear that Miss Reamey has found peace in believing. And now I must go to my school duties. What the day will be, I cannot tell. I have a bad headache, which with this heat will unfit me for vigorous work. But I must trust in God my strength.

August 3 - Thursday - Jennie's Diary

Today I have rest because of the election held here. So much noise is made that it was thought advisable to excuse school today. And it is a blessed thing for me that I can have a little rest. I am sick; symptoms I have feared of a fever. Last night I took medicine, which has left me quite feeble today. But while my body is feeble, my mind is strong and active, and I long for words and power to express what my heart feels. The object upon which I have had my heart fixed, that I might find a suitable place to settle down and do a permanent work, is I hope soon to be realized. [I received] a letter from Mr. Deems this week saying that he had a place for me in Bastrop, Texas, to take charge of a large female school. Texas is the state to which I have long wished to go, and if Providence opens the way I shall surely go. I have written Mr. Deems, and if not too late he will secure the situation for me. I shall be happy to go. I shall then be in a young and growing state, in which everything will be favorable to the establishment of a flourishing and permanent institution. I believe I can do it. And I believe there is a great future in reserve for me. Great, because it shall bring me the means of training human minds for Eternity, and to lend a helping hand towards spreading the kingdom of God upon earth. In this case as in all others, I commit all into the hands of my Heavenly Father. He can and will direct. I will wait patiently and see what the end be. In the meantime, I would be very diligent in preparing myself for great and vigorous action hereafter. May I have light and strength and wisdom. **Night.** This day of quiet rest has done me much good. My thoughts have gone to Mt. Holyoke Female Seminary. This has been Anniversary Day. One year ago I was there. I am here now; where shall I be one year hence? I [must be] careful so that I am in the place best for me. I long to feel that I have found a home, a place in which I may work the remainder of my days. I do not think Rockford is the place. When once I can feel this, then shall the great work of my life begin. I must make more out of life than I have yet thought. This life, great and precious as it is, must be no mean counterpart of eternity. I am glad for life, and I do consecrate my life to my Heavenly Father. May it be such a life as he would have it.

August 4 - Friday Evening - Jennie's Diary

The school duties of the week are done. The general improvement of the school is, I believe increasing. Sometimes I stop and wonder that in six short weeks the school should have worked itself to what it is. My faith is stronger that I shall one day be able to realize, in some measure, my ideal of a school for young ladies. But I hardly believe it will be in Rockford. And yet all the experience I am laying up here will be of infinite value to me when I come to that final position which I am to occupy.

August 6 - Sabbath Afternoon - Jennie's Diary

The quietude of another Sabbath is upon the world. It is a delightful day. We have gone to church. Rev. Mr. Brown gave us a good sermon. This was appointed a protracted meeting, but Mr. B. has no help, and is very feeble in health, and the meeting will close tomorrow. I had hoped that this might be the time when some of my dear pupils might be led to the Savior. But my Father can work in their young hearts yet and lead them unto himself. I pray for them.

August 8 - Tuesday Morning - Jennie's Diary

A delightful morning this. And then it is mail day, and maybe the post will bring me good news from far. And I can also go to my schoolroom and work for eternity. Some word I may say today may waken some mind to a new life and send it out on a great and blessed course of action. I do not know what minds I may be training here. I know not the future of these. I want to feel the importance of my mission and work faithfully. This beautiful day I would do a great work.

August 9 - Wednesday - Jennie's Diary

Last night's mail brought me some good news from my brother and from two of my section. I am glad for all this. I have risen early this morning, and I hope a day of useful work is before me. It is a pleasure to know that I may every day do something for my Heavenly Father. I will trust him today. **Night.** Now the nighttime is around me. The day has been pleasant and successful. I am glad and thankful. This evening my thoughts have gone out much towards the two great objects of my life; a permanent institution, and education made practical. I think I have gained some new ideas, which I hope to develop.

August 14 - Monday Noon - Jennie's Diary

A strange depression is upon me today. I woke with it this morning. A mist is before me, which I cannot penetrate. My heart goes to that ideal place and institution in which I may do a life work. I cannot think that Rockford is the place. It may be the stepping stone. I will trust in God.

August 15 - Tuesday Night - Jennie's Diary

Here are some beautiful lines, which I copied long ago. I will now transcribe them in my Journal for safekeeping.

Hope and the Rose

"Who shall die first," whispered Hope to the rose,
"Who shall sink earlier into the grave?
I by my fleetness, or thou by thy sweetness—
Which of the two is the future to save?
I by betraying or thou by decaying,
Who shall sleep first in eternal repose?"

"I said the flower-tho sweet is my blooming
Soon will my loveliness wither and die—
Lives that are sweetest are ever the fleetest—
Hours most happy most rapidly fly—
But Hope dieth never, it liveth forever—
Enchantment around the young bosom it throws.
In smiling or weeping Hope never is sleeping—
I shall die first," said the beautiful rose.

August 19 - Saturday Afternoon - Jennie's Diary

This has been a rainy day, but a pleasant day to me. I have few sad days now. Life to me wears a different light to what it once did. A few years back I had many dark and dreary days. Now I see and feel something so beautiful in life, something so noble in living and working for my Heavenly Father, that I do not get sad and weary as I once did. Daily does my spirit rejoice because of that higher, purer life which I may have in the Spirit World. O! I am glad, I am glad for this life and the life to come. Never in all my life did I seem so near my Father in heaven. Never such comfort in committing my all to his direction. I believe he will guide me in the future as he has in the past. I trust him for all things. O! can it be that this confiding is real; am I not deceived? My Father will not let me be deceived. I pray that I may be faithful, be humble, be wise. And now let me patiently wait until my destiny comes.

William Polk Dobson, husband of the "Mrs. Dobson" mentioned below, was a first cousin of President James K. Polk. Jennie knows the social and political implications of this invitation, but she is adamant that the Sabbath is not a day for frivolous visiting.

August 20 - Sabbath Afternoon - Jennie's Diary
This day has brought me a trial. Mrs. Dobson sent for me this morning to go and spend the day with them, and I could not conscientiously do it. I wrote her a little note asking her to excuse me. What influence all this will have I cannot tell. It may cost the friendship of the family, but I did what I believe to be right. I cannot spend my Sabbaths in visiting. I would visit the sick, and those whom I might benefit, but I must not make visits of pleasure. This is a bold stand for me to take here, where there is so little regard paid to the Sabbath.

August 21 - Monday Morning - Jennie's Diary
Beautiful Monday morning. A new arrangement is about to come up in our school. Rev. W. O. Reid is anxious to purchase the Seminary and all the engagements of the Trustees. How the matter will turn I cannot tell. I think the chances are favorable for him. I think when I tell the Trustees my thoughts for the future, they will be very apt to take him up. Should the engagement be made with Mr. Reid, I think I may resign in the winter, and go to college, and review Latin, study French, and attend lectures preparatory to my going to Texas or somewhere West. I trust my Father in heaven will direct all. I will trust in him. And now I go to my daily work. May I have the success best for me.

August 27 - Sabbath Evening - Jennie's Diary
Today I have said goodbye to Brother Vet. He leaves tomorrow afternoon for Greensboro, where he is to do business for Mr. Connel. Dear brother, my heart goes with him. This is his first step out into the world. It is a trial to him to go alone, and from home, but I trust it will do him good. Now our home-circle is almost broken up; none there but father and mother and little brother Jamie. Tomorrow morning I must go work afresh. The proposition made by Mr. Reid has failed and all things remain as they were. So I must work on here for the present year at least. I will strive to be cheerful and hopeful.

August 28 - Monday Noon - Jennie's Diary

This morning Col. Jarvis came to the Seminary and made a proposition upon which I must think. He proposes that the Trustees make a present to me of the Institution, with the piano and improvements, giving me a right to them so long as I may remain here, if for life. This is no mean offer. I must think of it.

August 31 - Thursday Night - Jennie's Diary

The last day of summer departs with these evening hours. What a summer it has been. While it has brought golden sunlight, beautiful flowers, and delicious fruits to all, it has also brought disease and death to many. But I live to work yet. And I trust to work a lasting work. I [have] almost made [up] my mind to settle in Rockford. If they offer me the Institution as proposed, and I can get my papa to come and take charge of a boarding house, I think I may remain. I do long to feel that I am engaged in that life work which I hope yet to accomplish, and I cannot feel this until I am settled.

September 2 - Saturday Night - Jennie's Diary

I have come this evening from a nice, pleasant visit to Mrs. Dobson's. They treated me kindly, and that will be a nice place for me to go. They are my friends. I have also had a good letter from Brother Vet. He reached Greensboro safely, and thinks he will be pleased. May the dear boy be kept from evil. My mind is still fixed on making Rockford my future home. I think all things are favorable. And I hope in this I shall be directed by that Infinite Wisdom which has ever guided me. And now the week is done. It has made its record. I found some lines in the *Poems of N.P. Willis*, which I think worth study:

> —the soul of man
> createth its own destiny of power;
> And as the trial is intenser here
> His being hath a nobler strength in heaven.

September 7 - Thursday Night - Jennie's Diary

I have just returned from a pleasant little visit to Mr. Crannon's. They are much gratified at the prospect of the school becoming permanent. The great question of my life is now very nearly determined. I have consented to take the entire charge of the Seminary in Rockford. The Trustees meet on Saturday and decide the matter. Now I feel happier than for a long time before. Now what I do is for life. There will be no more breaking up. I trust I shall have wisdom and grace to direct me that so I may be able to do my duty, and exert an influence here that shall last thro all time.

September 12 - Tuesday Evening - Jennie's Diary

How uncertain all things are. The question was decided just the reverse of what was expected. The Trustees have concluded to retain all in their own hands, so my stay in Rockford is all an uncertainly yet. I am content. I trust my Father in heaven will direct all.

September 17 - Sabbath - Jennie's Diary

Today is the quiet Sabbath, but we have no church. I regret much that so many Sabbaths should be vacant. But I pray that the Lord of the Sabbath may put it into the heart of some minister to come and settle among us. Again my prospects for the future are changed. The Trustees, or some of them, were unwilling to let the matter rest as it had been decided, and have made another effort to have the Seminary placed at my disposal. The effort will probably succeed. I have had many anxious fears about the whole matter. My heart has sometimes failed me when I have thought of the multiplied cares and responsibilities, which will thus be brought upon me. But I trust my Father in heaven. He will be the wise director of the whole. I do consecrate the Institution to him and I shall labor to make it a school in which his name shall be loved and revered, and from which an influence for him shall extend thro all this country. My prayer for this Institution shall be, "Father, let it live before thee in all future generations." The prospect for making this a permanent Institution of high character is not very flattering, but much may be accomplished by persevering energy and a firm trust in God.

September 25 - Monday Noon - Jennie's Diary

I am afraid after all, that I have done wrong to take the Seminary under my own entire control. I feel the weight of care coming upon me already, and I am sure my frail constitution will not bear up under it. I am sure I have come to a point in life at which two ways met, and I have taken the wrong road. My only alternative is to take some cross path that may lead me back into the right road. But alas, alas, it is not so easy undoing a thing as doing it first. I may have erred sadly, I believe I have, but now I do not want to be too much cast down. I shall not be able to do my duty to my pupils if I am. I hope to learn some useful lesson thereby. I will not hereafter act against convictions of my own better judgement, and without consulting my Father fully. I have not a heart to work now as I had before. I go to my work more as a task. What shall I do?

October 1 - Sabbath Evening - Jennie's Diary

I greet with a thankful heart this new month. I am glad for it. I am glad for this autumn. Today I spent at Mrs. Reeves. I went there Friday evening; had a nice pleasant time. Yesterday we went to the Pilot Mountain. The prospect from its summit richly repaid us for the toil of the ascent. This Sabbath evening does not find me happy. I am still unsatisfied with the new arrangement of the school.

October 8 - Sabbath Evening - Jennie's Diary

Another birthday I have seen. A birthday. A Sabbath birthday. I would record my thanksgiving to my Heavenly Father for all the mercies of the past year; for whatever of health, of happiness, of friends, of success in my labors that I have enjoyed. I do desire this evening to be devoutly thankful. And because of my many failings and follies and sins I would be deeply humbled before my Father. I would take careful review of all the past year, and tomorrow, as I go to my work I would go with new and increased strength. And this Sabbath evening I do earnestly pray that this year may be more useful than any of my former life. I pray a blessing upon the labors of the past year and with a firmer faith in God I would go to all the future. I know not what another year will bring, nor where I shall be. I am only anxious that all its events be directed by my Father in Heaven. More than half my life on earth is gone. I may spend my next Sabbath birthday in eternity. May I have wisdom to turn my present life to the greatest possible account.

October 10 - Tuesday Evening - Jennie's Diary

I am glad there is to be a judgement day, when all this perplexing maze of human life will be made plain. The farther on in life's pathway I go the more does my heart say, "vanity of vanities." How little I know after all these years of toil and study. I am glad Eternity is before me, and that, served by grace, I may go on thro endless ages in acquisition of knowledge. I pray for light— heavenly light. My Heavenly Father is my Great Teacher. He cannot err. I pray for purity of heart and life.

Almost out of nowhere a potential fiancé enters Jennie's life. He has not been mentioned before, and his name will never be mentioned. Jennie has the opportunity to travel, an opportunity she had always dreamed about.

October 18 - Wednesday - Jennie's Diary

I have serious thoughts of changing my manner of life. One who has long had a deep regard and love for me solicits me to share with him his beautiful home in California. If the way seems open I shall surely go. I may do as much good then as now. And there will be one human heart to share with me life's cares and toils. Oftimes I am in great perplexity. I feel I cannot bear up under the present arrangement and I regret to retract. I erred greatly when I went into the proposition. But I must not despair.

Ann, who later read Jennie's journal, would write "Poor child! she led a miserable life, just because she had no self-confidence, and because she thought no one loved her as she wished..."

October 22 - Sabbath - Jennie's Diary

Today I spend at home in my room. I have such a cold I cannot go out. It has been a pleasant quiet day to me. I do so enjoy the autumn days. Never in all my life have I valued this existence so much. I have not been happy for several weeks, on account of the school. I have despaired more than I ought. I have done wrong. I will try hereafter to be more hopeful, more cheerful. I may do something in Rockford. It will take much patient toil, but I must be brave-hearted. I ought to have more confidence in myself. May my Heavenly Father make me more hopeful. I pray for the prosperity of the Institution; that pupils, such as shall be best for us, may be sent to us.

October 25 - Wednesday Night - Jennie's Diary

I don't know why it is, but my thoughts have tonight gone away to California. I think of that quiet home. And then I would be making one man happier, and a better citizen. I believe the way will be opened for me to go. I hope in this I may not err. I will do as at all former times, commit my way unto the Lord. May he direct my steps.

Evidently others had told Jennie that she has a problem making decisions. Certainly her diary would bear that out. Here she is trying to decide whether or not to go to California. No move is made in her life without deep, soul-searching thought and much anxiety.

October 29 - Sabbath - Jennie's Diary

Now has the last Sabbath of this month gone. Blessed month this, my natal month. It came in on [the] Sabbath; my birthday on [the] Sabbath! It has been a month of much thinking, of much sadness, but I hope it is the dawn of a better future. I shall be happier when the California question is settled. This cannot be done for many months to come. And in the meanwhile I do not want thoughts of it to so take up my time that I may not do my duty. As this will probably be the last year of my life as a teacher, so do I want the work to be better than I have ever yet done. As each day passes away I want to feel that the work of that particular day is finished. I shall now work with better heart while I remember that after all this toil there is for me a quiet, beautiful resting place, where I may still do good, and make human hearts happy. I will trust in my Heavenly Father, knowing that he is able to direct all my ways. His powerful hand has ever been over me and led me. Tho I have been so unworthy, yet he has remembered me. In looking over my past life this evening, I have been sadly reminded of the great need in all my actions of <u>energy</u> and <u>decision</u>. I have long been apprised of my want of decision. I have prayed against it, struggled against it, but O shall I ever overcome it? I will struggle yet more bravely. I do pray my Father that I may see my faults as they are, and that I may be strong to overcome them. I pray for <u>wise decision</u>.

November 2 - Thursday Evening - Jennie's Diary

O when shall I be at rest! My mind has been much agitated for the past few days. I am this evening almost convinced that there is no quiet home for me in this world. I do not think it would be right for me to marry. I am thinking another mission is mine. If my Heavenly Father points out the way, I must walk therein. I dare not do otherwise. I must be content to spend my life as a teacher. O for wisdom.

As Jennie is mourning her decision to reject her suitor, Ann is writing essays at Greensboro Female College. Jennie has said, "There is no quiet home for me in this world." Ann, in this essay, celebrates the family home, which her sister has evidently forgotten in her grief. Had Jennie been able to read her sister's work, she might have been consoled.

November - Undated - Ann's Essay at Greensboro Female College

The Pleasures of Home

Away back in the treasure house of the heart is a little unexplored recess, sacred from the gaze of the world and the search of the curious. In it are buried the fondest affections of the past and of home. At the slightest touch, a thousand scenes spring from its sequestered haunts, and we see in imagination, the old homestead, the shaded by ways, the grassy sward, the tall waving trees of the dim old forests, the deep arching azure sky, the floating golden clouds tipped with the crimson of evening, the singing birds, the laughing rills that sparkle in the yellow sunlight.

Home! Around it spread the broad waving fields, the swaying trees that droop over and guard it, like hoary sentinels, that watch around the loved ones at midnight. Far above it, spreads the glorious blue sky illuminated by the mid day sun, or gemmed with the diamonds that have been interwoven with the tissue of this veil. There the zephyrs speed by, from this mountain home, rejoicing in their own happy freedom, and breathing the stories of other days. Beneath these same sturdy trees, we have flung ourselves on the rich green luxurious grass - - - flat - - - and peered up through their brawny arms and clustering foliage, on the far off heavens, and wondered if we really saw angels' eyes looking and smiling on us, if the moonbeams were lost, if we might not steal up this golden pathway and pillow our heads on the cushions of cloud, through which they gaze.

And there were the faint longings for something deep, holy and pure; something like God. But deep in the chaos of the mysterious past are immured those enchanting fairy scenes. Time has sped by, like lightning. Swiftness; his footprints are on earth, his signet on the brows of those we love, his records in heaven. But there is our home still, and we love it none the less, now that the vain imaginings, and the fancyings of childhood are past. We love it none the less now that we are away.

No! For the last fervent prayers of our parents still echo in our ear. The last look that greeted us was a look of love and anxiety, and their last kiss burns deep upon our cheeks and still deeper upon our hearts. It is not alone the glorious landscapes, the over hanging canopy of heaven, the singing rills, the dashing cataracts, the swaying forests, the proud massive hills and mountains that fondle green valleys in their huge arms, that make home happy. No! There are warm hearts, bound for us that smile if we are happy, and weep if we sorrow. There the reverend father presides with dignity and affection, and on every prayer that ascends to heaven the absent ones are borne, and an affectionate mother, sisters, and brothers smiling in the sunlight of gladness.

But perchance a seat may be vacant. Perhaps long years ago death stole in so quietly, and clasped one of the group so tenderly, and bore it to the land of spirits so peacefully that his presence was scarcely felt until his victim was secured. Or perhaps more recently, while we are speaking of the unbroken circle of happy ones around the home altar, death, pale and silently, has conveyed a loved one to the eternal house; and we, unconsciously, are left to mourn for the departed, ere we rejoin them in the Spirit Land.

Home! Why does the sunburnt sailor dash aside a tear as the last sights from land fade away, and last notes die in the distance? Ask the good man, ere the last tide of death sweeps over his departing soul, why he smiles such unearthly smiles? Ask the angels why they wing their passage from earth so swiftly.

The golden chain that binds us to our homes is composed of links, each of which possesses a history. If one of these links be lost, there is a blank page in the volume of our lives; if one of them be severed, a tie that binds us to earth is unloosed. These stray links severed and torn are strewn all along the pathway of our lives and there are sad sweet memories that linger around each. But they are reunited in the Spirit Land and form a chain more firmly wrought than any of earth, and bind our hearts to our homes in heaven. Sweet thought! That ties severed on earth are drawing us heavenward. If we so fondly cling to our earthly home, which is subject to blights and blasted hopes and loves, how much more should we love and cling to our home in the Spirit Land, which is undefiled by sin.

As Ann wrote, she thought of the plight of the American Indians. This essay was written at Greensboro Female College:

November 3 - Ann's Essay

Soliloquizing in the Wild Wood

Slowly and serenely to the west the day declines. Hills wait anxiously for the farewell kiss of their Monarch. I leave the busy world and seek the shades of the glen, and behold nature as she breathes her evening devotions. I see these forest trees, how their limbs wreathe together forming a fretwork so intricate that no finite mind may divine how those boughs, so proudly massive, ever laced themselves around a neighboring bough; how from that dark and uncouth branch sprung the tender stem, with the weight of rich, dark, green foliage. I scan the swaying screen that arches above, but I can not comprehend the power of that hand that wove the tissue of this woodland canopy. My heart does not reveal the mystery of the dark green carpet that spreads out at my feet, or the wild flower that nestles in its massive folds. There is not wisdom enough in the storehouse of knowledge to divine the sayings of the wind, or chant the strains the waters sing in this deep glen.

But look! A blast and the trees wave apart! Through this transient window the sunbeams glance, and illuminate the forest, ere his disk sinks in the west to renew his youthful radiance and vigor, that he may triumphantly begin the coming morrow.

On that sloping grass bank rise huge rocks, and on their gray and crumbling forms spreads the green turfed moss, child of the dying wood, vainly endeavoring to clothe their cold and pulseless bosom. Under their protruding forms springs the covey, and trembling, nestles in this retreat, until its pursuers pass howling for their lost prey.

Here are these oaks, pillars of this immense palace, where nature daily holds her evening festivals. Beneath their shade the Indian once roved, free and wild, sole monarch of these extensive domains, guiding his arrows with such unerring precision that deer and wild antelope ever cowered at his feet. Beneath the moonlit sky, they assembled around their campfires, or in their unguarded tents sang the requiem that bid their haste to the hunting grounds of their ancestors. Echoing over these hills clearly rang the war whoop that assembled the red men to revenge or victory. And here on this turf glistened the fallen tears when the pale face first peeped in upon this woodland palace and bade them go to their western home.

Dark eyed son of the forest, thy spirit still lingers in our ill-gotten bowers. Thy names are painted upon our waters and wrought in our forests. The swift deer that once sped before thy arrows, now are startled by the white man's death gun. But over the footpaths in the rock cliffs, briars and shrubs have laced their arms in impenetrable fretwork. Thy forest have been felled, thy campfires extinguished, thy war songs have ceased, thy ferocious yells died away. But thy memory, dark rover of the woodland, is engraved on the hearts of those who have wrecked thy all.

But the Great Spirit, who guided thy haughty chiefs and sealed their proud manly hearts with truth, (ere the white man set his sacrilegious foot on the Western world and guided thee to vengeance when thy forest home was wrested from thy grasp), shall watch thee still, tho now in thy far-off home thou rovest. And he shall teach thy exalted heart to bow in quiet submission to his will. Who shall guide thee to thy ancestors where thy brother shall meet thee, and extend the hand of peace, which thou shalt grasp, and all be the children of the great Common Father?

Once again Jennie is sick. Here she is at home, wondering if she should return to teaching and if her life should include marriage.

November 21 - Tuesday Noon - Jennie's Diary
Today finds me at home. It is vacation. I have been sick for more than two weeks, but am now improving. I have fears that I shall not be able to attend to my school when it opens again.

November 23 - Thursday Noon - Jennie's Diary
How rapidly time flies. One week more and my school opens again. I do not feel sufficient for all the duties of the next Session. Just now the next Session looks gloomy. I am more and more convinced that Rockford is not the place for me. I am sorry. I had hoped to settle down, and be at rest. O mysterious life is this of mine. I have always

felt that there was some thing in the future for me. I feel so still. But this may be a mere dream. Yet I do believe I am treading a path which is to lead me on to something which I have not attained to. An Invisible Hand guides my destiny. My Heavenly Father knows what is best for me, and he will direct. I do long to be a wise and powerful teacher; to wield an influence over minds, an influence that shall live for good thro all time and in Eternity. I am satisfied unless a very great change comes, that I shall never marry. I dare not do it with my present feelings. Tho it does seem to me I might be happier, yet I must not go contrary to convictions. It may be my mission on earth is simply that of a teacher. If so, I must be content.

November 29 - Wednesday Evening - Jennie's Diary
Tonight I am in Rockford and tomorrow school opens. I am sorry I have no longer [to] rest, but I want to go to work in right good earnest. I hope to be able to do more next Session than in all my life before. I look to my Heavenly Father for strength, for wisdom. I must do honest work and may the future be such as my Father directs. I commit all into his hands—myself—the school, and all whom I love.

December 2 - Saturday Night - Jennie's Diary.
I have been busy today fitting up my room; now it is nice and cozy. And I have been thinking of that time when I may fit up a little room in a distant state and call it my home for all future life. But that time may never come. Yet I often hope it will. I cannot see into the future. I know not what sorrows are yet for me. I cannot see the toil, which I yet must perform. My Father sees it all. He knows what heart aches, what agony of mind and body are reserved for me. I am now here quietly in my little room. Where shall I be one year hence? I feel more like a little child, than like a woman with weighty responsibilities upon her. May I have strength for this Session. I do so long for a good and right school.

December 14 - Thursday Night - Jennie's Diary
Tonight I have been out with Miss E. [?] tracing constellations. I think my Astronomy Class is taking some interest in the study. It

is one of my favorites. I am now much interested in my school duties. Things generally move on harmoniously by. But how little do my pupils think that, in all probability, this is the last Session that I shall teach in Rockford.

The next lines in this December 14 entry were struck out, as if later on, Jennie decided it had no bearing on her life.

My thoughts are much upon my California home. I do hope one day to be there. Surely a wise Providence has arranged all. I shall be a happier and more useful woman when I am married than now. My mind more than ever [is] settled upon this matter. If Providence opens the way I shall surely go. It will be painful to part from my home, and go where I can see them no more, but it may be for the best. I believe I can make more out of life, and then I shall have a permanent home. I will trust in my Heavenly Father. He will order all things for his glory.

December 25 - Monday - Christmas - Jennie's Diary
I have taken Christmas dinner with Mother; where I shall be next Christmas is a question. This is a quiet, beautiful day. The sun shines warmly as springtime. I am at home, my own dear home. I have been busy in preparing some outlines of lectures on history for my advanced class, when school opens. We have holiday until Thursday, Jan 4, 1855. My feelings are much enlisted in my school. I would I had the wisdom and means to make it what I want it to be. I do want to do something.

1855

Jennie's first document, a letter to her brother James on the occasion of his twelfth birthday, bluntly states that she might not be around to watch him grow up. She continues to angonize over important decisions in her life. She still has hopes, for example, that she might marry and move to California. Though

Jennie makes very few diary entries during 1855, we do know she was reading The Life of Horace Greeley, *which was published in 1855. Jennie seemed to be able to acquire books as soon as they were published. We know the Greeley book is hers because her name is inscribed on the first page, along with the place, Rockford. She was at Rockford only a short period of time. Her written comments in the margins are in her own hand, and the underlined passages are consistent with her Christian worldview. (Many of the marked paragraphs along with her remarks are mentioned in the introduction of this book.) Ann provides a detailed essay on home and warns us not to trust "reality." Aaron returns home with his wife, America Speer, to recuperate from consumption.*

January 9 - Jennie's Letter to her little brother James, who is twelve years old.

Rockford
Jan 9, 1855

My dear little brother, this your birthday shall not pass away without some token that your absent sister remembers it as a happy day; a day that gave to her a little brother as a blessing and a joy. I am glad on this your birthday and my heart prompts a richer moment than this prosy letter, but alas for the means!

I am glad you have grown up with a body and mind so strong and beautiful, and that wise and affectionate parents are with you to help you cultivate all things which are most lovely and useful. You are a little boy yet, but I will tell you something which may do you good when you are a man. I tell you now, for when a man you may have no sister Jennie. This is a great and beautiful life which God our Heavenly Father has given you, and it is a life which will never end. For when it is done in this world it begins in the Spirit World a life that is still greater, higher and more beautiful. Now, with a mind such as God has given you, you can make this life an honor to yourself, a blessing to your country, and a praise to him who made you.

I expect <u>much</u> of my little brother Jamie when he becomes a man. I do not say this to flatter you, but that during all these boyhood years, and in all your boyish thoughts and actions you may remember you are preparing yourself for that great work of life which is to bless the world. And at the head of all the needful traits of character which you should have, I will place <u>Truth</u> and <u>Honesty</u>. No two things are so indispensable to success and true greatness as these. They were the distinguishing marks in the life of the greatest man our nation has ever seen. "Speak the truth in your heart, and with the love of it."

I do not call your attention to these because I have any reason to think you are wanting in a careful observance of them now, but that they may occupy a special place in your heart. Now, somebody says this is a sober letter to write to a merry hearted school boy of only twelve years. So it is, but I think my little brother will understand it. If not, put it away in some little nook until another birthday comes and then read it again.

May no future birthday have less sunshine and gladness in it than this. May you become a man, wise and good. Be vigorous and healthful to enjoy the happy return of your birthday for fifty years to come.

And whoever rejoices with you on any birthday, [I am] sure no one will more earnestly crave your success, or wish you more hearty good cheer, or love you more devotedly than does

Your sister Jennie

January 11 - Thursday Evening - Jennie's Diary

Too long have I neglected my Journal. Many interesting things have come up since I wrote, but none have given me more comfort than the harmony and good effort which I believe prevail in the school. I do so long to make this school all it should be. I have well nigh concluded to make this place the center of my labors. By remaining here I can be a comfort and pleasure to my mother, and there is no sacrifice which I would not make to give her pleasure. I am influenced in this also by a conviction that my life will not be long, and would it not be better to be content to remain here so that I may be with my parents during my last days? O! That I knew what to do.

January 13 - Saturday Night - Jennie's Diary
Tonight many thoughts come upon me, thoughts sad and oppressive. The Seminary gives me many anxious hours. I long to make it something of real worth. The Examination will soon come. I want it to be an honest and favorable one, but I cannot consent for it to be a humbug. It must be honest if not brilliant. Oh! I will trust in my Heavenly Father. He has always directed me. He still will.

Beginning with "My mind turns . . ." Jennie crossed out the rest of this entry.

January 28 - Sabbath Night - Jennie's Diary
The last Sabbath of the month is now almost gone. It has been snowing all day. The young ladies are singing some beautiful Sabbath hymns. My mind turns to many things tonight, among others, to my home in California. Tomorrow I mail a letter containing my consent to go. This is rather a solemn matter, the step a responsible one. But I believe in it. I am guided by my Heavenly Father. He has opened the way; I follow. I believe his blessings will be upon the course I have taken.

Nearly five months will pass before the next entry in Jennie's diary.

March 9 - Ann's Essay - Untitled

Greensboro Female College
March 9, 1855

Had I chosen a day in the whole year for peculiar efficiency in awakening memories in the soul by its wild gleamings of the past, I could not have been more fortunate in my selection than in this day. It is unclouded and brilliant. The deep blue of the over-arching sky is relieved by a hazy cream tint all around the horizon.

From my window is an extended view of woodlands, interspersed with the somber evergreen pines of North Carolina, and broad intervening fields slightly undulated. The March wind sighs sadly through the grove and taps frantically at the window for entrance.

But my mind is too much occupied to heed its ravings, until rattle, bang, whang! goes some unlucky blind, and down come window panes crashing to the floor. But it is sweet music to me. It heralds the return of spring. What a thrill it sends to my soul! How it reminds me of long ago, when I sought the early spring flowers in my papa's meadows, or culled them from my mother's garden. When I plucked the early violet that nestled so fondly to the cold pulseless bosom of the giant rock. When I watched the birds as they warbled their happy welcome to spring in the budding trees, and chased the butterfly on the green. When I listened to the free happy laugh of my brothers as they exulted in the freshness of youth.

Hark! Why do I start? Was that my papa's footstep on the threshold? Did I hear my mother's voice singing among the shrubbery? Was that my brother's silvery laugh? Did my sister call? Oh! Why does the vision fade? Am I not the same happy careless girl that I may run and fling my arms around my mother's neck? Alas! It is but a dream. I am still in the land of triangles and logarithms. It is over. The vision flies. Imagination, why seek thus to start the tear to my eye? Why gild the veil with such life scenes, that reality starts as it rends the tissue from my mind. Such is life. Reality is ever folding the scroll that fancy paints with such glowing colors, is ever razing the palace [that] imagination so exquisitely adorns.

A little child played on the margin of a lake. She carelessly tossed a diamond in the air, and laughed a merry childish laugh as she saw the fanciful streaks of the sunlight on the gem. An unlucky whirl sent [the precious stone] sinking in the cleaving wavelets, and the waters sunk in many a circle over it. Reality sent a chilling dart to that child's heart.

An invalid, reclining on a couch by the casement, gazed on the glowing sky, and falling leaf, and the breeze that swayed the snowy curtain in many a graceful fold, gently lifted his dark curls from the pallid brow. His widowed mother bent over his pillow to catch the last whisperings of the Spirit Land until she forgot her grief. The lamp of life flamed a moment, and another soul entered the Spirit Land. Think you not that reality lifted the veil from a heart rending scene for that desolate Mother?

A captain slept in chains at midnight. A gleam of gladness darted [across] his brow as he exclaimed "I am free." But he sprang from his pallet of straw to find his fetters binding him more firmly to his dungeon. That delusive dream unnerved the strong man, who had borne his captivity with fortitude. Reality linked him to despair.

A youth framed a tiny vessel, his life boat, and sent it to sail on the ocean of time. Untold treasures were entrusted to its keeping. It was beautiful and its owner danced in the sunlight of gladness. But the storm king sent it whirling down, down with its freight and the waves passed unheeding. The youth saw his loss, and reality sealed him for despair.

A warrior wreathed his brow with laurels plucked from the waysides of life. Ambition moved his proud heart to action. He conquered, and the world heaped [praise] upon his shrine; but in an evil hour he fell. There was more of sad reality in his fall than in all his previous brilliant career.

But if all things beautiful are doomed to wither at the touch of reality, why need we sinfully repine? God and heaven are exalted by reality, and far, far surpass any conception we can form. Eternity alone can unfold the splendors of that Better Land, and it seems almost sacrilege for feeble man to attempt to paint its faintest hues.

June 27 - Jennie's Diary

A long, long time has it been since I took up my pen to write a line here. Could these pages be spread out before the world, wonderful ideas would there be of my stability. Now that I have changed my mind again surely I cannot have much claim to fixedness of purpose. The past five months have been months of intense study and much anxiety. In the time the Session has passed away—the Examination come and gone. All passed off with far more success than I had dared hope. Soon the school opens again. What another year will bring remains to be seen. I go to the work with a braver heart than one year ago. Now I hope to do something for the establishing of a good and permanent school at this place. I will work for it patiently.

August 19 - Sabbath Day - Jennie's Diary

Sometimes I regret that I have an impression of a destiny upon me. I am restless, anxiously reaching towards something future, to a wider place, to a greater work. It does seem to me there is something more than this for me. But maybe I am mistaken. If I could only feel that Rockford is the place for me I could be content. Some things are here which must always work against me I fear.

We know that on September 6, brother Aaron Speer returned home with his wife, America Speer, to recuperate from a severe illness. We do not know why Jennie did not mention this in her next entry.

November 30 - Friday Night - Jennie's Diary

How long since I have written in my Journal. This is the last day of the month. One more week and the school is out. Tomorrow, a protracted meeting begins at this place. How much I have dreaded it. I know my pupils cannot pass thro it and be uninfluenced by it. I have but little hope that it will do them good. Hence my dread. May my Father save them.

CHAPTER FOUR

PROVIDENCE

1856-1858

1856 begins an era of great sorrow for the Speer family. We begin with brother Aaron's death from consumption February 1.

c. September - Newspaper Clipping

Obituary for Aaron Speer

On the 6th of September, 1855, Aaron Speer returned to his home in North Carolina and there amid its sunshine and quitude, blessed with the father of watchful care, and a mother's tenderest love, he hoped soon to be well again. But alas! A few weeks sufficed to show to anxious friends that he had only come home to die. As the cold of autumn and winter came on he sunk rapidly, until one week from his twenty-fifth birthday he ended his mission on earth. He was perfectly conscious during his last hours. About midnight he gathered the family about him, and to each he gave his parting admonition, and taking them in his arms, bade them good-bye. He again and again enjoined upon his brothers to be good men, for now that he could not live, they must do his work as well as their own. He often expressed a wish to live, not that he feared death, but that he might do good in the world. On Saturday, the 21, the funeral services were conducted by Reverends J.M. Gunn, and W.L. Van Eaton in the Methodist Church, after which the remains were conveyed to their quiet resting place in the churchyard.

The inscription on Aaron's gravestone reads:

Let me go, the day breaketh.

*Ann's response to Aaron's death was to think about joining him.
This is not unusual since she and Jennie both had thought
frequently about an early death and what it might be like in the
spirit world.*

Undated - Untitled - Ann's Poem

I would not live, there's nought to charm
The spirit to the earth
And oh! there's nought the soul can harm
After the eternal birth

Why should we live? Disease and pain
Are ever in our frames
And slander's staining hands may touch
The most secure names

But still we'd live, we cling to life
With what a reckless grasp
Uncaring for a future state
As if this were our last

I would not live but one there is
Who tempts my longer stay
But if my Father calls me home
I must His voice obey

I would not crush this earthly love
Too blessed is the dream
It bursts upon the weary soul
As bright as beauty's gleam

But oh there is a higher love
My inmost soul must sway
True as the eternal source of life
That formed my frame of clay

And to this love let every power
Within my bosom bend
And to its source at every hour
A humble prayer ascend

And if from earth I'm called away
Oh Father, with the blest
Love me, and through th' eternal day
I'll with my brother rest.

This letter from Jennie to Ann tells of her bereavement over Aaron.
Jennie's spirit is broken and her health begins to fail.

February 19 - Jennie's Letter to Ann

Rockford, 19 Feb 1856
Night

Dear Sister Ann,

I admire both name and <u>writing</u>. I am glad to hear from you and home. I almost jumped up and down when I heard Brother Vet had come. I have been so lonely in heart. The past comes to me often so vividly as to completely overcome me. I cannot yet be reconciled to this bereavement. It is worse now than at first. I dream so often of watching at that same bed of suffering, and again going through the trials of that last night. But I will try to bear it.

I wish I could have seen you, it will now be <u>so long</u> before I can. What will poor Sister Meck [Aaron's wife, America] do when you are gone? What will Mama and Papa [do]? But I am glad you are going to Dr. Wilson's. I will write you often as I can. I can only say now do your best in everything, especially insist on thoroughness in first principles.

I am glad Mother got my things so nice. I am ever so much obliged. The skirt will be no trouble. I wish I had sent my shawl, but I thought you would have so many things to color.

I have had no news since I came back, one letter from Miss Evans, one from Miss Reamey. And what is that you have to tell? What new things in the land? How could [you] excite my curiosity so? I cannot write much tonight. Bettie sends love to you and to Sister Meck, she is very anxious to have her come over. She will write if she has time.

Love to all at home. I will come soon as I can. I want to come so much, and yet it will be a trial. I shall have much solicitude for your success. Trust in God and do right.

Goodbye, with love
from Jennie

February 21 - Thursday Afternoon - Jennie's Diary

The past few weeks have been to me weeks of great sorrow. I have seen my brother, my darling brother sink under disease and die. And now have followed long and lonely days of bereavement. And what a bereavement it is to me. I cannot reconcile my feelings to it. He was a brother of brothers to me. We had the same tastes, and about the same views of life. We had chosen the same work. How shall I do without his companionship? No more brotherly words. No more mutual plannings. I am bereaved. I am lonely.

Ann continued to soothe her bereavement with poetry. A.C. Speer is her brother Aaron Clinton Speer.

On the Death of Mr. A. C. Speer

Our loved one is gone,
We miss him at home.
So loving and kind were his ways,
Like the young rose bud,
Cut down in full bloom,
Its fragrance and beauty decays.

A dutiful son
A husband so kind

An affectionate brother was he
A dear loving nephew
His examples now shine
Like apples of gold on a tree

May his kind admonitions
With heavenly dew
Be watered and grow in each heart
Till we all meet above
In that glorious pew
Where we never, no never, shall part.

In token of love
We'll embrace in his arms
All the loved ones and kindness did dwell,
Then in a sweet voice
With heavenly charms
He bid an affectionate farewell.

Farewell child of glory
Thou art gone up on high
To rest in thy mansion of love
And while tears of sorrow
Here drop from each eye
Thou art praising thy Savior above

The casket here moulders
But oh! With what lustre
The gem is now shining above
God gave it and took it
High up in bright glory
It blooms a ripe flower of love.

*In this letter we are introduced to a Mr. Hinshaw, Ann's suitor.
Ann will speak of him more in the next year.*

February 28 - Jennie's Letter to Ann

Rockford, February 28, '56

Sister Ann,

Dear child, your letter was handed me today by Dr. W. [Wilson?] but he was in so much hurry I could not write in reply. I did intend to write you by today's mail but I have not been well; I am not well now. My head is a constant trouble to me. I am now taking some medicine.

I am glad to hear from you. I have been anxious to know how you were situated and how you moved off. I wish I could be near you to say a word to you when you need advice, but you will soon learn to rely upon yourself, and then you will be all the stronger. You must be hopeful, and cherish a just degree of confidence in yourself. Be faint-hearted not a bit. You have the resources within yourself, so never fear.

I will write you often as I can, and tell you anything I may think will do you a service. In the meantime you must ask anything you want to know. Heaven alone knows how much I long for your success. You are young, <u>well</u> and <u>strong</u>, and can do much. You may have to finish up your sister's work. I have but little heart or strength for teaching just now, tho I wish more than ever to devote myself to it. Teaching is dearer to me now than ever; it was the chosen work of our sainted brother, and now that he is gone I feel given to it more than at any former time. Sometimes when I am tired and weary, and want rest, I think of what dear brother Aaron would have done if he had had only the strength I have. Then I feel reproved.

You must not be uneasy about me. I shall be better after awhile. I dwell too much upon the past. I know I do, and yet I love to. I can't read anything but that I come across something to remind me of our darling, but lost brother. It is in my waking thoughts, and in my dreams. I have a presentiment, but maybe it is my own fancy.

I will try to be cheerful as I can. I want to go home. I wish I could go and stay with Mother. Poor dear Mother. Was there ever such a Mother? Forgive me dear child, for all this digression. I did not mean to say so much. But there is no one here I can talk to about these things. I always get excited.

You must be cheerful and strong. We owe a duty to the world, and must not let anything unfit us for it.

I shall indeed hope and pray for your success. And any service I can be to you will be gladly given. Let me know [about] your classes and how you have them arranged. I would say this, make no regulation until it is demanded. Govern by principle as far as you can. In the family be kind, polite, and sociable with the children, but never too familiar. But toward Dr. and Mrs. W. be as confiding and frank as is consistent with true politeness. Ask their advice; consult their wishes. Keep to the RIGHT, let who will, oppose. Remember you are seated for a year, begin all things then as you think you will have strength to carry on. I wish your room were more private, but make the best of it. It will soon be warm weather, and then you can go in the woods, or stay at the school house. Will you have to teach on Saturday? Try to have all things commence well, even if it be slow. Insist on thoroughness.

I do not see any impropriety in your corresponding with Mr. Hinshaw, as he asks it probably for his own improvement.

There is nothing new in Rockford. You will accept the love of the family here. The girls are anxious to see you.

Give much love to Julia, Mary, Mrs. W., and the Dr. The Dr. gave me warm invitation to come and make a visit, and I shall be happy to do that thing.

I intended to write more, but I have a headache. You will excuse me. I will write when I can.

In much love,
Your Sister

From the content of this letter, the placement seems appropriate here.

Undated - Jennie's Letter to her Mother, Elizabeth

R. F. Seminary
Friday

My dear Mama,

I must think you are somewhat anxious to hear from me. I am improving slowly. My appetite is not good yet, my head troubles me, and I am yet so weak, but my bowels are better.

I have been to the Seminary every day, but I do but little. I am glad today is Friday; tomorrow and next day I can rest. I am needed in the school, tho I think Sister Ann has managed very well. I want to get stronger soon, for if I do not I can do but little of what I thought to do this Session.

We have no more new scholars. The Wilsons will be over in a few days. Sometimes I get the blues terribly. How I am to hold up while the school is no more profitable I know not. The mere thought takes away much of my strength to teach. But I know I ought to be more cheerful - and I will. I will try very hard to get well, and stay well. I will come home when I can, but it will be a long time I reckon.

I crave fruit so much, but I am afraid to eat. Come over Mama, when you can. My heart clings to you more than ever. Love to all.

Good bye
Your Jennie

Sister Meck, mentioned below, is the daughter of Joshua Kennerly Speer II, and is Aaron's first cousin as well as his wife.

March 3 - Jennie's Diary
This week Sister Meck is with me. So vividly does her presence bring to mind my lost brother. I miss him on every hand. Now when I write home there is no special message to him. When I send a little parcel home there is no little nice bit for Brother Aaron. When I read an article of unusual interest, I think of him. But he is not here to share it with me. And in this it is worst of all. I have no one else to enjoy the same reading. Once he did. He entered into my feeling, and I doubly enjoyed an article because he did relish the same.

March 10 - Jennie's Diary
Night. Yesterday I returned from a visit home, my first visit since Brother Aaron left us. How much sadness was in that visit. The vacant seat, the vacant room were there with all their weight of

associations, and in all their silence, but my brother was not there, as I have always found him. And there was nothing to do for him—no watching—no "<u>sip</u>" of cool water. Oh that stillness, that stillness. Shall I ever get reconciled to this bereavement!? Sometimes I think I shall not be long separated from my brother, but maybe it is fancy. I do not want to live only to finish my work.

March 15 - Saturday Evening - Jennie's Letter to Ann

Rockford March 15/56
Saturday evening

Sister Ann,

This evening while I am sitting here in my room, you are <u>at home</u> enjoying all that home gives. I am indeed sorry that I cannot be there, but so it is. I am not well enough to come. I want to see you so much. It has been so long, and will still be so long. And then you have something to tell me.

I was home last week. I had a pleasant time, but still sorrowful. There was that vacant seat, and no demand for anything I could do. Mama seemed more cheerful than I expected to find, but poor papa, he is so sorrowful, and has fallen off so. His heart is suffering deeply about something. I have never heard him pray so affecting a prayer as he did when I was at home. I went to brother Aaron's grave on Sunday morning. The morning was beautiful, and everything so still, and as I stood there so near his grave I thought surely his spirit might be near me. It gave me comfort to be there and I felt better reconciled afterward. We will plant something nice around that, his last resting place on earth.

March 18 - Tuesday Morning - Jennie's Letter to Ann Continues

Sister Ann, I intended to write you much last night but an evil genius in the shape of sleep cheated me out of it. I do not know why it is but I can do but little at night. And I do want to do so much. Time is so precious, so fleeting and yet I make so little out of it. If I had someone with me who would be a stimulus to me maybe I would do better.

I am afraid you think hard that I did not come home, but Saturday I was not well enough, and Sunday I thought it was best not to go. It was hard to deny myself. If I have an opportunity I am coming to see you. I want to know all about how you succeed in your school. I have so many things to ask you, so many things to talk about.

Evening. What a rainy cloudy day we have had. And it has been about as cloudy in the school as out of doors. "Some days will be dark and dreary," says Longfellow, and I have often found it so. And sometimes when the sun shines brightly without, everything has continued to go wrong indoors. I hope you will not find it so.

We have two new scholars, Caroline Burrus and Mary Hamlin. Mary comes she says because she is tired staying at home!! She comes in the morning and recites chemistry, then draws until recess, then is a young lady for the remainder of the day. Miss Dougherty [colleague] is taking drawing lessons, I cannot yet tell how she will do. Did you want some patterns? Sister Meck said something about it.

And now about the business part of your letter. There is not a pair of shoes you can wear in Rockford except one pair, and I do not know [how] to send them. They are not good and you might not wear them. I will have Mr. Burrus make you a pair if you will wear them. He made me a very nice pair. You ought to have good thick shoes to walk in. I don't know what to do for you. Shall I send No 7 or not?

I do not know yet what I shall do about teaching next summer. I think it is very doubtful about my staying here, tho for Mama's sake I would, and Papa's. I have written to Mr. Jones about a situation. I would like to go to Texas, but I reckon I am not well enough. And Mother wants me near her, and I would now more than ever be near home. I do hope that when my task is done I may spend my last days at home. I sometimes think about going home and resting this summer. If I knew Sister Meck would go home and Mother be alone I think I should. And yet I have lost so much I hardly know how to quit work. Do you know whether Dr. W. has ever said anything about getting us both to take a school in Doweltown?

Did Miss Hamlin make a favorable impression in the Dr.'s family? Miss Dougherty and Miss Hamlin are teaching a Sabbath school in the church. In other respects Rockford is the same. The students were here last Saturday in a wondrous spree. Mr. Lee was extra drunk. Rockford will never be any better. I am out of heart.

To wind up with the usual formalities, Bettie sends love, and so would all the family no doubt if they knew I was writing.

Mr. Cloud is not in town, or Mr. Teller. Write when you can; love to all. Go and see Mrs. Hauser [wife of T.C. Hauser] for me, tell her so, and give love.

Your Sister Jennie

We suspect that this poem was written in the spring, possibly on May Day. Little did Ann know as she wrote the poem to her dead brother that her sister Jennie was seriously ill. But this poem shows us that Ann believed that the disease was in her own body and that she too would succumb to it and "decay" next to her brother.

c. May 1 - Ann's Poem

To My Brother in Heaven

The earth is beautiful my brother
In its bright green vesture clad
There's music steals from every bough
And all the earth is glad

How softly speeds the breeze, Brother
Above the gladsome vale
There's music in our earth, Brother
It laughs on every gale

'Tis nature's May-day now, Brother
And from thy lofty sphere
Thou lookest down on me, Brother
But I would not have thee here

For I know that where thou art, Brother
That beauty there is found
Untouched by sin or blight or death
That here on earth abound

Thou art far happier there, Brother
At home, thy own bright home
Than richest prince in stateliest halls
On earth, or proudest dome.

There naught can mar thy peace, Brother
Thy Savior's ever near
Thy spirit lives in heaven, Brother
And angels watch thy bier
And I shall come to thee, Brother
My spirit can not stay
A blight is in my frame brother
That wears its strength away

And soon beside thy tomb, Brother
My body shall decay
By thee I'll sleep beneath the church
Where oft we knelt to pray

And as my spirit homeward flies
Far to the better land
Oh! I shall meet thee first, Brother
Amid the blood-bought band.
How blessed a thought!

In July Jennie's health worsened to the point that she had to leave Rockford. She gathered her students together and announced that she would have to leave teaching in order to recuperate. We know from two accounts that the students wept when she left, an event that contradicts her own self-evaluations.

Obituary c. December - Reverend William Van Eaton, Principal of Jonesville Methodist Academies

> . . . with great reluctance she called her pupils together, and gave them a farewell talk and left them all bathed in tears; and returned to her father's to recruit her health.

Six months pass before Jennie writes in her diary. This is the last entry she will make before her death.

September 1 - Jennie's Diary

Long, long and weary months have passed away since I wrote in my Journal, and to me have brought many changes. The Spring Session closed the first week in June. The Fall Session opened July 10. My health was very frail, and I taught but a few days when I was compelled to give up the school, and since that time I have been confined to a sick room. Now I am some better, able to sit up and walk about. It was a sad blow to me to have to give up teaching, to see the school in Rockford go down so suddenly. There the Old Seminary stands alone and forsaken. No merry voices are heard among the shady walks. The rooms are all empty, and the desks vacant. The "big bell" is heard no more ringing out its call to "study hours." Thus has passed away another dream of my short life. Once I fondly hoped to build up a school in Rockford; a school which should embody my ideal. But now even that "is no more." I am worn out, completely broken down. I know not that I can ever engage in teaching again. My physician gives me but little hope. But maybe I can turn my life to some account some other way.

The Van Eaton Obituary Continues

But alas! The seeds of death were too deeply sown in her system. She lingered some six months, carefully watched by devoted parents and eminent physicians, but her disease being consumption baffled all skill, and marched on to its final destruction.

In 1853 Ann wrote this poem, which may have been an uncanny prediction of Jennie's last days or her own.

The Dying Maiden
March 19, 1853

The moon shone bright - the night was still
When yonder cot beside the hill -
All decked in flowers fair
And waving trees in silence bowed
And forest songsters warbled loud
The sweetest vespers there -
Was one deep scene of silent grief
For life's bright journey had been brief
And on a couch she lay
A maiden calm with face so fair
With languid eyes and curling hair
But her spirit cannot stay
Consumption dire has marked her his
She slowly sinks - she breathes a prayer
Her spirit takes its flight
Her kindred gathers round the bed
But O! her ransomed soul has fled
To Heaven, the home of light.

The Van Eaton Obituary Continues

I visited her fast passing away a short time before her death. When I addressed her on the subject of religion, I found she had committed all to the Lord. She said she had some desire to live from the fact that she saw so much work to do. She had a desire to help do it, and if the Lord had any more work for her to do, she would get well; but if he had not, she was fully resigned to go. Finally, when the last thread of hope was broke, and friends were convinced she must die, and she felt that her dissolution was near; with a calm and serene countenance, and prospects for heaven bright, she talked to parents, brothers, and sister who stood around her dying pillow, and told them to be cheerful and weep not for her but to try to meet her in heaven.

Jennie gave her father the names of the people she wanted to attend her funeral. She selected a text from the Seventeenth Psalm to be read at the event.

"When I shall awake with thy likeness I shall be satisfied."
Jennie died from consumption on December 22, 1856. She was twenty-eight years old. At her funeral the minister read her own words in order to comfort those present.

I have carefully examined my life since I have been sick, and I have no fears of the future; all is calm and serene. Heaven is a reality. Oh! What would I have done if I had not squared my life with the Bible in health. Our leading motive should be to serve God, because he is good and as such he loves goodness.

The Van Eaton Obituary Continues

Oh what will poor sinners do, and what will become of those who do not serve him? Then let us dry up our tears, and look forward with pleasing anticipations to the time when we shall see her come forth wearing a robe of righteousness whiter than the driven snow, and as she clasps her hands, [cries] out and says, "Oh death, where is thy sting? Oh! Grave where is thy victory?" May the Lord help us all live the life of the Christian that our last end may be like hers.

The inscription on Jennie's gravestone reads:

I have no doubts or fear. All is well.

1857

In Greensboro, the Times *published another obituary for Jennie. Had she been able to read these beautifully crafted words about her life, she might have known just how much she was admired and loved. We suspect that the "Stranger Friend" who wrote this was Dr. Deems, since he was the only person—other than family—Jennie was close to.*

January 14 - *Greensboro Times* - Nancy Jane Speer's Obituary

Many of your readers will be pained to learn that Nancy Jane Speer is no more. She died at the residence of her father in Yadkin County, on the Evening of the 22nd ult. [December 1856].

Death is ever a startling messenger, and though he had been even at the door, for months passed, yet, when the spoiler came, the grief seemed too much for bleeding hearts to bear. It is natural that friends and relatives should weep for the departed. But when one so young, so kind, so intelligent, so useful, and so beloved is thus stricken down in the morning of life, it enshrouds the community in a dark mantle of gloom, and saddens the heart of the thoughtless and gay. It might justly be said of her that "those who knew her best loved her most." The deceased was a graduate of Greensboro Female College where she remained some time as an efficient and acceptable instructress in the literary department of that institution. She was then induced to take up her residence in Rockford, N. C., where she founded the Rockford Female Seminary, and won the commendation of all as an able instructress and Christian woman. But the hand of disease pressed heavily upon her; and during the past summer months, she was compelled to abandon her school. Her parting interview with the weeping pupils of that institution, will not be soon forgotten. Little did the writer think, when he witnessed, two short years ago, the first annual examination of the classes of that Seminary, that it would so soon be his lot to record the death of its gifted and accomplished principal. Truly, "in the midst of life, we are in death."

A ripe scholar—with an earnest, penetrating intellect, united with indomitable energy, the deceased had acquired an amount and variety of knowledge rarely attained by her sex.

The writer is conscious that he expresses but the language of a sorrowing and appreciating community, when he says, we may never look upon her like again. Who shall take her place?

A STRANGER FRIEND
January 14th, 1857

That same winter Ann became ill. She believed, after her brother's death, that her body housed the same disease and that she would soon follow him to the grave. She did not at the time include her sister as another death partner because she did not know the severity of her illness. Ann seemed to deal with her failing health the same way she dealt with her brother's — by writing poetry.

Undated - Untitled - Ann's Poem

I am dying Day by day
Fades my Star of life away
Hurries on each fleeting hour
Firmer grows the Conqueror's power
Earth is beautiful and gay
And I would not haste away
But a Stranger points me on
And ere night I must be gone

Lo my west is growing dim
And the low sweet vesper hymn
Bids me haste ere twilight shades
Into deeper darkness fades

I am going, let sweetest song
Echo all my path along
Let earth's music greet my ear
Till a nobler strain I hear

Let no tear drop dim an eye
When I lay me down to die
Let no sob of anguish heave
Let no heart my going grieve.

For there are beyond the sea
Mansions reared by one for me
And His everlasting arms
Will support me from all harm

The path is dark, the night so drear
But that star shines bright and clear
It glimmers onward through the gloom.
Pointing ever to my home.

I am going, earth I leave thee
Richer joys, I feign would see
Enter I at heaven's portal
To enjoy a life immortal

In this diary entry, Ann laments her ill health and the toll it is taking on the family. She is reading the diaries of her sister Jennie. Jennie's descriptions of her unworthiness add to Ann's despair.

August 25 - Ann's Diary

I am sitting by my mother's bedside. She has suffered much, and I do rejoice that I have been able to wait on her. I know it has wrought sadly on me but I would watch over her did I know it would make me worse. I feel wretchedly worn out, but maybe I will recover strength sometime; but I doubt it. This weakness and pressure in my lungs speaks too plainly of the future for me to misunderstand. I believe if I had followed faithfully the directions of Dr. Fitch I should have recovered, as it is I doubt it. I know I ought to bathe daily, but I do so dislike to trouble the family. I must have a fire in the stove if I bathe, and could I do all myself I would not mind it, but I must bother someone else. Oh this life, pleasant as it is, is full of care and grief. Sometimes I almost long to go to my brother and sisters and be free from sin, free from earth. I know that just now I am going down. I have been falling off the last two weeks. But I do not see any trouble about my disease. I would love to live for my parents and brothers' sake, but if my Father says come, oh let me fly away to Him. I have been reading my poor sister's journal and it makes me sad. Poor child! She led a miserable life, just because she had no self-confidence, and because she thought no one loved her as she wished, but I know she was almost idolized in college. I wish she had possessed a happier disposition. She was rather distant and reserved, for which I could never account, but now I see it was because she thought she was not lovable, but she was and many loved her. As it is I am almost glad she is now free, that she is now where she is understood, and where she is happy. Dear Sister, she was worthy of love.

September 10 - Ann's Diary

The day is cool and bright. I have been not so well. I do wish I could improve rapidly. Winter will soon be here and I shall not be able to contend against it. I often think I shall not live through the winter. I would be glad to live for my parent's sake, but if I must die, I must. I think of it very much, and the idea of leaving those whom I love so dearly and lying away in the dark moldering tomb, while I shall so soon be forgotten, makes the big tears come and I must weep. Oh Earth, earth, has thou not a solace for thy dying children? Shall thy cold arms hug me to thy chill bosom, while those whom I love will forget? Oh to be forgotten! Ah! I said forgotten, but will it be so!? Will my name not still dwell with constancy in the hearts of those who meet daily around our fireside!? Yes, yes! I know they will not forget. But far away o'er the sea of death, far in the eternal land is a home. Oh there are joys purer, greater, and infinitely higher than any of earth. There my brother, my sisters are awaiting me; they are forming a family there where we shall ever live in blessedness. Our family circle is broken here, and the remaining members here are sorrow hearted and weary, but the loved ones gone are calling us away. Shall I not gladly hail the day that gives me immortal life? Oh Immortality! Blessed gift of God to man. Shall I indeed be a child of immortality? Shall I see the Creator infinite in wisdom and goodness, him who breathed into my soul this longing for life eternal, this insatiate thirst for a higher existence? Oh shall that blessed home be reached that the weary heart has pined for, where our Father himself will comfort us.

Oh let us not sorrow tho life's heartstrings wear asunder and the soul's casket crumble to dusk. Life, eternal life is just ahead. Oh blessed Father support me in thy everlasting arms of love.

Mr. Hinshaw, the faithful suitor, is mentioned again in Ann's diary. He fully believed she would get well. She believed she would not and felt it was her obligation to break off the engagement.

September 20 - Ann's Diary

I feel that I am rapidly declining, at least I am worse. It makes my heart ache wildly as I see my parents' anxious eyes bent mournfully upon me, and the big tears start to fill my eyes, ere I can crush them down. Oh how infinitely dear to me are those whom I love. They grow daily nearer my heart, and instead of preparing myself for a separation, I find I hug them closer, more fondly to my heart. This is wrong for it unnerves me for the great final conquest I must gain o'er the world and death. And it is true that after a few weeks, maybe a few months, my footsteps, my voice shall forever be silent in this room. Shall I no more rest my head on my papa's loving bosom, or listen to affectionate words of my mother or feel this warm kiss on my brow!? Shall my brothers' return merry and gladsome from their labor and no sister ever again near to meet and love them!? True, true. Oh my Father, I pray for thy Holy Spirit to hush this anguish in my heart. It is almost unendurable. But I will strive to give up my earthly loves, if thy children will soon unite with me again in thy better home. Oh Holy Spirit, breathe o'er the troubled deep of my heart and call the wild heaving waves to "be still." There is one thing that gives me pain and that is my engagement to Mr. Hinshaw. I thought I should recover soon when I promised to be his, and I loved truly fervently. This love I retain pure still. But I have suffered him to hope too much. He thinks yet that I will soon be well. But never again I fear will we see each other face to face. I proposed to break the engagement last winter when I thought there was no hope for my recovery, but he utterly refused to listen to such a thing, saying he would be untrue to his honor, his love or his word as a man if he consented to abandon me when I was sick. There was however a chance for my getting well and I did not persist. But it might have been best. He would not then have had his hopes flattened so. Oh how deceiving this life. But amid all this affliction and illness the thought that I love and am beloved has been a solace in sorrow, a blessed vision bursting in beauty over my spirit, charming its sadness away. And until death severs the music cords of my heart, will the melody of that love play over them, tho shattered now by disease. I wish I had my daguerreotype for him. I promised him one.

1858

Ann holds on for some time but makes no more entries in her diary. She has been sick for nearly a year. Although she stops writing in her journal, she continues to compose a few poems and essays. This poem, which gives the "rules" for her burial, is neither titled nor dated.

Undated - Untitled - Ann's Poem

Lay me down gently when wild flowers spring up
When the dewdrops are sparkling in each tiny cup
Where the violets nestle and the live myrtle twine
That bows over the spot that our loved ones enshrine.

Lay me down sadly, weep not one tear for me
But weep o'er pale corpse, the spirit is free
List to the low winds, my requiem lying
Breathe forth some soft strains when my spirit is flying

Lay me down softly, for life's hopes have fled
And buried themselves in the home of the Dead
Lay me down gladly, my Savior lay there
Oh send forth a song, a blessing, a prayer

Lay me down prayerfully, for soon you will come
And rest near beside me in my narrow clay home
Lay me down hopefully that your Spirits may rise
To the angels' abode, my home in the Skies.

Ann wanted to die in the spring because of her passionate love of flowers. Annis Melissa Speer followed her sister and brother, dying of consumption April 23, 1858, at age twenty-three. Her parents, Aquilla and Elizabeth Speer, had lost four of their children. Her obituary, from the North Carolina Christian Advocate, *reads,*

DIED - on Friday morning, 23 [April], at the residence of her father, in Yadkin County, Miss ANNIS M. SPEER. Thus has departed, in the morning of life, one that was a bright ornament to society and much loved by her connections and friends. In early youth she united with the Methodist E. [Episcopal] Church, and lived as a Christian should, and died as only a Christian can.

The inscription on Ann's gravestone reads:

> I thank the Lord for sparing my life
> 'til the flowers of spring have come.

It seems fitting to end with Ann's last essay, written one month before her death. This composition is a beautiful depiction of the spirit world where she meets her brother Aaron and her sisters, Jennie and Sylvia.

c. Spring - Ann's Essay - *North Carolina Christian Advocate*

The Dream of Annis M. Speer
One Month before Her Death

On last night, I had a dream, or a vision, which made me forget earth and all its pleasures. I dreamed I was in a strange place, where I saw a narrow passage that shined with exceeding brilliancy, and my brother and sisters came and stood near me. And I saw God, and he blessed me: and I gazed along the shining way, and longed to go up — but God withdrew from my gaze and my sister said, "Come with me." But I lingered; I would feign go up. But they said, "not yet." And we entered a strange doorway— into a wide-open space resembling a meadow. It was perfectly level and completely matted over with the richest green grass. O! It looked like a fairy region. I asked, "Where are we?" They said, "This is Elysian fields," and they led on to a stream of water so clear and sparkling as though ten thousand diamonds were dancing on its surface. And my brother told me to drink — and I drank— and he told me to go in and wash — and I plunged into its shining waves. And a thrill of delight—such as I never experienced in life before possessed my whole frame. And I discovered while I washed, my sister had left me — but my brother sat on the green grass a short distance from me. After a while my sister came with a basket in her hand, and she told me the Great Father had prepared and sent me a new spring garment. And she dressed me. O! It was white and glittering — such as adorned her own saint-like form. And I looked about me — and I saw, at a distance, groups of shining forms, all dressed in purest white. And I asked who those creatures could be. They said, "They are angels—redeemed spirits—who are now triumphing over death and sin." And while we conversed — for we had been long parted, and we were now rejoicing together — I heard a strain of sweet melody. It was the evening hymn of the Redeemed! And they came nearer and nearer — and hailed me into their happy circle! O, joy — joy! I was safe in God's Kingdom! And just then, to my utter sorrow, I awoke!

Epilogue

The deaths of Aaron, Jennie and Ann occurred on the eve of perhaps the greatest crisis the American nation has ever experienced. During the Civil War their older brother Asbury would fight to defend the South, while their Unionist parents pleaded with him to resign from the Confederate army. Asbury repeatedly refused their request, and as the war progressed, he became colonel of the Twenty-Eighth Regiment N.C. Troops in Robert E. Lee's Army of Northern Virginia. In August of 1864 he was mortally wounded at the battle of Reams' Station, only three weeks after he was elected to the North Carolina Senate. His mother, Elizabeth, expresses her grief and sorrow in a letter she wrote in 1867 to her brother Jackson Ashby. This is the only letter we have that Elizabeth wrote.

August 1867- Elizabeth's Letter to Brother A. Jackson Ashby

Ever Dear Brother

In my last letter to you I told you of my bereavement. My oldest son Asbury was killed in the Rebel Army. He was Col. In the 28th North Carolina Regiment. He was killed at Reams' Station. My poor heart bleeds when I think of my poor child being murdered. It was no better than murder to make men go to the army and get killed. He lived four days after he was wounded. A piece of shell struck him in the head and broke his skull. He was in his sense all the time and said to those that stood by, he should soon be where there was no war. That he had given his body to his country and his soul to God. If that be true he is better off than to be here in this troublesome world.

Throughout the course of the war, Asbury tried to protect his youngest brother, James, from the fighting. But even with Asbury's help, James was unable to avoid spending time in prison. Serving in the Home Guard did not protect James from being drafted into the Confederate army. It was only Governor Zeb

Vance's decision to protect members of the state military organization from conscription that saved James. He was allowed to remain in the Home Guard until the end of the war. In the late 1800s and early 1900s, James operated a tobacco factory at Providence, while raising a large family. He died in 1928 at the age of eighty-five.

Brother Vet would become the Civil War sheriff of Yadkin County and was caught in a fierce cross fire of opposing factions as a war within a war was fought on Yadkin soil. On one occasion during his term in office, thirty-three anti-war bushwhackers stormed the jail, released all the prisoners, and then seized the arms and ammunition belonging to the Home Guard. The situation in the Yadkin Valley became so volatile that Robert E. Lee sent General Robert Hoke's command to western North Carolina to quell the unrest and round up deserters. Somehow Vet managed to survive the war and would later serve as clerk of court and county commissioner. He died at the age of fifty-three in 1890, the same year as his mother.

Parents Aquilla and Elizabeth lived to a ripe old age. Aquilla became a staunch Republican after the war and served three terms as county commissioner. He died in 1888 at the age of eighty-four. Elizabeth outlived her husband and all seven children but one, dying at the age of eighty-six in 1890. In the August 1867 letter to her brother, Elizabeth expresses her belief that the tragedy that has befallen her family in the Civil War was a sin of rebellion against God and government.

Elizabeth's Letter Continues

I sit down to answer your kind letter which you wrote July 27. It gave me much satisfaction to hear that you was well and in the land of the living. I feared you was dead; it had been so long since I had got a letter from you. You don't know how glad I was. I can't express my joy and pleasure in reading from my only brother. As you know, Brother John died last July two years ago, as I wrote you in my last letter. Brother James; I know nothing about him. He talked of going to Florida when last heard from. I fear he is dead. I can't get any letter from Brother John's family. It has been a long time since I heard from them. There was two sons dead when last heard from. One died in the war, and one son after the war closed . . . .

I have had seven children. They are all gone but two. One of them lives with us, the other a few hundred yards from us. He has two small little boys, four and two years old. The youngest married last spring a smart little wife.

We are doing as well as we can. We have plenty now but we shall be scarce another season. Crop can't be half crops. Let the season be as it will, there is hundreds that will not make seed, owing to the wet in the spring and the drought in the summer. There was not a good wheat crop. Some made a little while others made some to spare. Corn and wheat is very high but there is not much to sell. Some thinks corn will bring one dollar at the heap. Bacon is scarce, not much to sell. It will not be had at all next summer, I fear at no price. The hog cholera is raging in this country, as a great many have lost all they have got and they can't get any to fatten. There appears to be no cure for it. Poor people is bound to suffer. We could not expect any better. The nation is so sad. It is a wonder that we are spared and have as much as we do. It is better than we deserve. We have rebelled against our Maker and against our Government, and we could not expect nothing but judgement from the Almighty. Our country is in great distraction. I feel awful when I think of the state of things in this country. I wish I was away from this rebel state. I never wanted to leave the old South until they seceded from the old United States. If I was not so old I would try my best to persuade the rest of the family to move. But it looks like folly to break up now. We are so old and settled and have everything around us to render us comfortable, for we can't have many years to spend. I am now in my sixty-fourth year and I shall soon be the way whence I shall not return. I don't feel like I could live many years, although I may live longer than I expect. I am able to do tolerable work, yet can walk two or three miles.

I would like to see you and your family and would be so glad if you could come see us. I seem almost to see your face smiling at me like you used to do when I would come down to Fathers. You would run and say, "Yonder comes Betty," and hold up your little arms to carry me to the house and then you would gabber and tell me something that had taken place since I was there before. You was very good and was counted pretty. You was so much like Mother, more so than any of the children. I am still trying to get to the Good World. May the Good Lord direct you and me and ours that we live so that when we come to die, in peace with God and all Mankind, [we] can say all is well. All is well from your devoted sister.

Elizabeth Speer

For the Speer family, Providence Farm mirrored Inman's dream of Cold Mountain, a place where scattered forces could gather. But it was also where the full weight of sorrow was measured and stored. The afflictions and burdens my family endured, along with harsh storms that assaulted their lives, appear to me to be nearly unbearable. Yet I firmly believe that though their faith was severely tested, it did not falter.

Again and again my wife, Janet, and I visit Cemetery Hill, where my father, aunts, uncles, cousins, and generations of grandparents going back to the 1700s are buried. We walk from stone to stone, read the inscriptions and remember the passion and pain associated with this place. Yet there is something redemptive here that transcends anguish. I believe it is, in Ann's words, the "thought that I love and am beloved." And because of this love I do not dwell on grief; I only remember the faith that sustained my family for nearly a century.

When I see the words inscribed on Ann's grave—"I thank the Lord for sparing my life 'til the flowers of spring have come" —I am overwhelmed with gratitude. The epitaph on Aaron's headstone—"Let me go - the day breaketh"—is an epiphany of expectation and hope. The inscription on Asbury's grave marker —"After life's fitful fever, he sleeps well"—is a haunting reminder of the hellish world he inhabited during the Civil War, yet it also evokes an image of peace and repose. When I come to Jennie's grave, I grieve for her troubled soul, and recall the windy night in the 1960s when a tornado uprooted an oak tree, causing it to fall and crush her tombstone. For some reason, probably an oversight by one of the parties involved, Jennie's original epitaph was not transferred to the stone that now serves as a replacement. There is no room on the new marker for an inscription. Even so, the words engraved on the original monument—"I have no doubts or fear, all is well"—are, I believe, Jennie's true legacy. These were the same words used by Blind Aunt Nancy to finish her songs and recitations, and by Jennie's mother, Elizabeth, in the last sentence of the letter written to her brother Jackson Ashby. And by saying "all is well" I also believe that Jennie's dream of sharing her words with the world, a dream deferred for one hundred and fifty years, will now finally be fulfilled.

Still, Jennie is a mystery to me as she was to herself and to sister Ann. Ann could never understand why Jennie was so distant and reserved. If it was pride that was the source of Jennie's despair, and I suspect it was, then it was also pride that was the essence of her genius. Along with the many natural gifts she possessed, Jennie's pride fueled her desire to become a perfect Christian, yet it was her awareness of this pride which caused feelings of unworthiness to arise. So from the depths of her soul she cried out to God, and the result of this summons was a gut-wrenching search for redemption and grace. The soulful yearning for something more and the deep terrible longing for God are Jennie's and Ann's remarkable gifts to us.

Just last year—1999—my Great-Uncle James Speer died. He was, as I mentioned in the introduction, the grandson of Jennie and Ann's youngest brother, James. Uncle James was a modest, hardworking man, the last living link to the Civil War generation. But it wasn't until after his death that we discovered the many medals he received during World War II. Not even his family was aware of all the decorations and commendations he was awarded. He told no one. I often wonder whether Uncle

James' childhood memories of his grandfather's expectations, either conscious or unconscious, were the source of his reticence. Did he, and do <u>we</u>, wrestle with the same demons our ancestors did? Was Jennie's quest for perfection, as well as her pride, passed on to us? Was the simple reticence that Uncle James possessed a response to what he perceived to be excessive family pride?

As a child, when I compared myself with my aunts, uncles and older cousins, I did not believe that I would ever measure up to their standards. Yet I idolized them, and was embarrassed for not being as smart as they were. Did Uncle James feel the same way when his grandfather told him, in so many words, that he would have to justify his existence? And did Jennie somehow receive the same message when she was a child? Perhaps pride and guilt are part of the same package, the price paid for being human. We reach for the sky, long for the sun and stars, and are ashamed of ourselves for wanting so much; I do believe this was true for my family. The <u>extremely</u> high expectations passed from generation to generation carried with them, in the minds of some family members, the unwanted afflictions of unworthiness and shame. I know this was true for me, and I suspect it was true for Jennie and Uncle James. James chose to share his accomplishments with no one, and Jennie's only confidant was her journal.

In any case Jennie and Ann, as well as my Great-Uncle James, who is buried close to them, played the hands they were dealt. And they did it well. They worked hard to justify their existence. It was justified.

I miss my Uncle James. I remember him. I remember them all.

Acknowledgements

I would especially like to thank my friends who read the drafts of *Sisters of Providence* and offered many excellent suggestions: Hazel Barton, Sheila Phipps, Alison Gulley, Wayne Morris, Michael Joslin, Bill Watterson and Fred Hobson.

Thanks are also due to Pam McKirdy, Judy Cheatam and Lindsey Lambert (Greensboro College) and to Helen Snow (Greensboro Public Library) for their help with the research. I am also indebted to Patricia Albright and Peter Carini at Mount Holyoke College Archives for their assistance with the materials in the special collections section of that institution.

I express gratitude to Julie Shissler and my wife, Janet, for typing the diaries, letters, essays and poems of Jennie and Ann, and thanks to Julie for doing the book layout and design.

Financial support for *Sisters of Providence* was made possible by a John Stephenson fellowship awarded through the Appalachian College Association with funding provided by the Andrew Mellon Foundation.

I also thank Lees-McRae College for allowing me the time and support to complete this book.

I acknowledge my mentor for the project, Fred Hobson, and my mentor institution, the University of North Carolina at Chapel Hill.

My main source of encouragement for this book came from my co-editor and wife, Janet Barton Speer, whose editorial suggestions were invaluable.